Also by Curt Sampson

HOGAN

TEXAS GOLF LEGENDS

THE ETERNAL SUMMER: PALMER, NICKLAUS,
AND HOGAN IN 1960, GOLF'S GOLDEN YEAR

FULL COURT PRESSURE

THE MASTERS:
GOLF, MONEY, AND POWER IN AUGUSTA, GEORGIA

FIVE FUNDAMENTALS
(WITH STEVE ELKINGTON)

Royal and Ancient

VILLARD

NEW YORK

Royal and Ancient

BLOOD, SWEAT,

AND FEAR AT THE

BRITISH OPEN

———

Curt Sampson

All rights reserved under International and Pan-American
Copyright Conventions. Published in the United States by Villard
Books, a division of Random House, Inc., New York, and
simultaneously in Canada by Random House of Canada Limited,
Toronto.

VILLARD BOOKS and colophon are registered trademarks of
Random House, Inc.

Grateful acknowledgment is made to the following for
permission to reprint previously published material:
The (Palm Springs) *Desert Sun:* Excerpt from
"Golf, Arnold Palmer & L. W. Dennis," an article that appeared
on the front page of the Sports section on February 2, 1962.
Used by permission of *The* (Palm Springs) *Desert Sun.*
John Murray (Publishers) Ltd.: Six lines from "Seaside Golf,"
from *Collected Poems* by John Betjeman. Reprinted by
permission of John Murray (Publishers) Ltd.

Library of Congress Cataloging-in-Publication Data

Sampson, Curt.
Royal and ancient : blood, sweat, and fear at the British Open /
Curt Sampson.
p.   cm.
ISBN 0-375-50278-5 (alk. paper)
1. British Open (Golf tournament)—History.   I. Title.

GV970.3.B75 S26 2000
796.352'66—dc21   99-087568

Villard Books website: www.villard.com
Printed in the United States of America on acid-free paper
24689753
FIRST EDITION

To Mac, Jack, and Jean

THE BEST LAID SCHEMES O' MICE AN' MEN
GANG AFT A-GLEY
AN' LEA'E US NOUGHT BUT GRIEF AN' PAIN
FOR PROMIS'D JOY!

—*from "To a Mouse," by Robert Burns*

The bartender at Dunvegan's in St. Andrews watches the clock on the wall, his left hand resting on a green beer tap, his right hand gripping a half-empty bottle of dark rum. At forty seconds before eleven A.M., the left hand pulls the handle that activates the flow of McEwan's bitter into a half-pint glass, while the right simultaneously pours a couple of ounces of darkness into another, smaller glass. While the head on the beer settles, the barman briefly places the glass of rum under a stream of water running from a spigot in the sub-bar sink. At precisely eleven someone whisks the now-legal drinks from the bar top and delivers them to the greatest caddie in Scotland.

James "Tip" Anderson nods in thanks. "Cheers," he says.

In the peculiar calculus of caddies, Anderson "won" the Open three times and finished second once during a six-year stretch in the sixties, although Arnold Palmer and Tony Lema actually swung the clubs. "Wish my horses did as well," he says, a line he didn't just think of.

He's a tall, dignified man despite clothing that's between very casual and somewhat dressy, with gray, once-white jogging shoes battling a plaid sports coat. In his lapel and on his white golf cap he's stuck a half dozen pins—South Carolina, Juventus, Alaska—and someone suggests to him that he looks like the rear bumper on a tourist's station wagon.

Windblown November rain splashes the windows and drums the roof. But it's cozy in here, and Tip Anderson has stories to tell and time to kill. How Arnold's shots flew like a jet off an aircraft carrier. What Lema said during his one and only practice round at the Old Course.

What about this year's Open, a bar patron asks. Ever see anything like what happened at Carnoustie in 1999?

A sip, a pause. "Never," Tip Anderson says. "Never ever."

Contents

Prologue

Two sets of footfalls pounded the weathered wooden planks of the North Berwick dock. The son first, a young man in a tam, whose untamed brown mustache matched the ruddy weave of his tweed jacket. A heavier, slower tread followed, the sturdy boots of the father. Golfers. Their loose clubs clattered onto the deck of a waiting fishing boat; golf bags weren't much used in 1875. They climbed aboard, and someone untied the mooring rope and threw it over the gunwales. Sun shot through the clouds of the short, early September afternoon, summer's end in Scotland, and the water sparkled on the Firth of Forth.

In legend, the son rowed alone across the wide bay in a tiny skiff. In truth, with a word and a look the older man procured the fastest sailing vessel in port for the hasty voyage north to St. Andrews. Old Tom Morris had clout. And he had a secret.

Earlier that day, a messenger had worked his way through the spectators at North Berwick links and solemnly handed a telegram to Mr. Morris, Sr. A big match was on: the Morrises versus Willie Park and his brother Mungo. Should Old Tom interrupt the competition to tell Tommy, his son and partner, the awful news? No. Tom Morris let the match play out; better to maintain the happy illusion for a few minutes more. Better to pretend that he and Tommy, the best golfer in the world, would still take on any comer for all the pounds and pence in Scotland. To pretend that shops would close when they played, wagers would be laid, and drink poured afterward in celebration or commiseration. That proud rivals like the Parks boys would always appear, each opponent an inspiration.

The Morrises beat Willie and Mungo, one-up. Then the father said, "We must go, Tommy. Your wife. We've no time for the train."

The ship slipped across the firth on its hasty voyage, and still Tom Morris did not reveal the telegram's contents. Perhaps he perceived a hidden brittleness in his son's strength, and suspected that the news would ruin him. Perhaps at that moment he himself felt the stinging remembrance of Tommy's older brother—also named Thomas—who had died at age four.

So Old Tom waited a while longer, playing away from trouble as usual. His calculating style had won him a life of employment in the game he loved, and four of the first seven Open championships. The limber shaft on his driver bent like a willow switch, providing snap to his cautious swing. He smoked a pipe. As he aged, short putts began to bother him mightily, and Tommy teased him about it: "If only the hole was always a yard closer, Da," Tommy said, "ye'd be a good putter."

The son followed him into the family business, but plainly he was not his father. He was even better. Eighteen-year-old Tommy entered the Open as a professional in 1868, looking like a boy-soldier from the just-completed American Civil War, unshaven, roughly dressed, and unimpressed. A tough customer was Tommy, always on the attack. He played chicken with bunkers and burns, the flamboyant, never-in-trouble style of the brilliant putter. "Dook!" Tommy would command as his ball rolled near the hole, and usually it dooked right in. And Lord, was he strong. As his contemporary Horace Hutchinson wrote, "Young Tommy Morris used to waggle his driver with such power and vehemence in his young wrists as often to snap off the shaft of the club close under his hand before he even began the swing proper at all."

Tommy won the Open in 1868, and the next year, and the next. In an odd compliment to his dominance, no tournament was held in 1871. Mr. Fairlie, the one-man band who ran the event, had died. No one burned with sufficient curiosity to reidentify the champion golfer of Scotland and the world—obviously, it was Tommy—so the Open took the year off. Besides, Fairlie had retired the victor's prize—a red leather belt with a big buckle, like a rodeo cowboy's. By prior agreement, anyone winning the event three times in a row got to keep it. Embossed on the silver clasp of Tommy's new belt were two bagless caddies, their gentlemen's clubs clamped beneath the armpit.

The Open resumed in 1873, with a cup for a prize this time, and Tommy won for the fourth consecutive time. The early Opens descended from the archery tournaments that had been held in Scotland and England for centuries, and the Morris men were Robin Hood and Robin Hood, Jr. Young Tommy and Old Tom even finished one-two in the race for the belt in 1868 and 1869. Glory days.

Now, abruptly, about to vanish.

"Tom did not tell his son that all was over till they were walking up from the harbour," recalled his pastor. "I [will] never forget the young man's stony look . . . and how, all of a sudden, Tommy started up and cried, 'It's not true!' I have seen many sorrowful things, but not like that Saturday night."

Margaret, Tommy's young wife of less than a year—"a remarkably handsome and healthy young woman, most lovable in every way"— had died that afternoon giving birth to a boy. Another Tom Morris. The infant had also died.

Tommy never recovered. For the next few months he wandered the echoing stone streets of St. Andrews in a depressed trance. Golf held no allure. He'd never been a drinker, but now he drank. Induced to play with his father in a match against two aspirants at the end of October, Tommy fell apart. Four-up with five to play on their home links, the Morrises lost the last five holes, and the match.

Tommy played again in foul November weather, giving shots to a Mr. Molesworth. Rain and cold descended on them, and the champion built a big lead. But Molesworth would not quit the scheduled marathon until the last putt was holed, and Tommy lacked the assertiveness to say "To hell with this." He caught a cold.

A week before Christmas he took the train to visit friends and pubs in Edinburgh, returning to St. Andrews after dark on Christmas Eve. Tommy scuffed the few blocks from the train station to his parents' narrow two-story stone house overlooking the green at the home hole. His invalid mother, Nancy Bayne Morris, was still up; they chatted for a few minutes. Then he called good night to his father and retired. At ten o'clock on Christmas morning Tom went to wake his son. But Tommy never woke.

Due to the suddenness of his death, the pathologist at the Cottage Hospital in St. Andrews performed an autopsy. "Burst artery in the right lung," he announced, but probably it wasn't that simple. Modern physicians surmise that depression and whisky had compromised Tommy's immune system. The air cells in his lungs, the alveoli, had likely become hard and inflamed. He had pneumonia, in short, and couldn't breathe. Depression reduced his body's ability to fight the infection.

Yet none of the arid medical explanations contradicts the myth of Young Tom's passing: he died of a broken heart.

YOU FEEL A little shiver about the shoulders as Peter Crabtree hands over the old leather-gripped stick. A cold mist pries at the third-floor window of this choir loft of a room, and the host's cool blue eyes ask if you have the faintest clue about what you now hold in your hands. "This is one of Young Tom's play clubs," he says. "One of his favorites, I think. Obviously a club for a gutta ball. And here is Bob Ferguson's cleek."

The least romantic soul can feel the tug of the past in Mr. Crabtree's private museum. Crabtree and his wife, Peggy, live in Keighley, west of Leeds, England, a ruggedly beautiful outpost in West Yorkshire. Their house on a hill looks north, toward Scotland, just eighty miles distant. Rounded hills, hedgerows, and sheep recede in the rainwashed distance. The mind, enhanced by a glass or two of lunchtime Merlot, can see history in the drizzle: Romans in dazzling metal helmets lead a hurried parade, their flight from this wild island hastened by the tall, red-haired natives, who after four hundred years would tolerate them no more. Twice the legions built gigantic coast-to-coast walls to cover their retreat. Is that the sound of first-century war you hear, or a neighbor dropping a wrench on his concrete driveway? Calgacus the Swordsman would be the first Scot to make the history books, the leader of a band of warriors who painted their faces blue. "They make a desert, and call it peace!" he said of the invaders. The legions replied to his eloquence with a permanent gag order—delivered by sword—as Calgacus scrabbled over a foothill of the Grampian mountains. With that, writes John Prebble in *The Lion in the North,* "the long brawl of Scottish history begins."

After the Romans left, England alternately became Scotland's bitterest enemy and its uneasy ally—uneasy for both sides. In 1297, a guerrilla fighter named William Wallace (he of the movie *Braveheart*) defeated the English spectacularly near the mouth of the Firth of Forth. Then, in retaliation for past offenses, the charismatic Wallace and his men walked and rode south across the fluid border, igniting the flammable parts of England's northern counties, "wasting all the land, committing arson, pillage, and murder," according to *The Lanercost Chronicle,* an English history. Wallace and his peasant warriors lived on oats and beans carried in bags tied behind them, wore rough leather tunics, and continued the tradition of sky-blue war paint. They made their own weapons. They were not much for archery; they preferred to deliver death more intimately, with spears and swords. And they were not invincible. A year after Wallace's raid, King Edward I of England, his gray, once-yellow-blond hair hanging down to his shoulders, ground the Scottish freedom fighters into the dirt at Falkirk. But Wallace escaped. Furious, the king rode on to the town of St. Andrews and burned it to the ground. The Scots detested King Edward.

Wallace disappeared for a while, probably into the Highlands, possibly for a time to France, Scotland's traditional ally. But at a pub in Glasgow, in August 1305, a fellow Scot betrayed him, and English soldiers spirited him away. After a mock trial at Westminster Abbey, custom dictated a humiliating four-mile ride for the condemned man atop a horse-drawn crate to the Tower of London. Wallace's captors hung him by the neck from an elm tree at nearby Smithfield Market. They cut off his privates, slashed open his torso, and burned his intestines before his dying eyes. But the tortured man refused to declare allegiance to King Edward or to England.

Within a hundred years, possibly far less, the not-so-distant ancestors of the martyr and his army began to play golf. It's not hard to imagine young men resembling Tommy Morris, their faces painted, their dirty hair braided and hanging down their necks. On a break from killing English, they put down their spears and hit a ball with a stick at a rabbit hole.

In and out of the irresistible past you go. You stare without focus out Peter Crabtree's window and smell wet wool. Something in the mist whispers history's secret: it has all happened before.

"More wine?" asks pretty Peggy Crabtree.

Months later, on a chilly Sunday night in November, a Vauxhall veers off the main highway toward a sign reading FORFAR. The lights are out in this little Scottish village, except, inevitably, for the hundred-watt bulb illuminating the door of a tiny whitewashed pub. Clean smells, no music, and a reproduction of a winning £67,000 lottery ticket framed and hung in a place of honor. The barmaid swishes a rag over the dark wood and politely plunks a pint of bitter on a paper coaster. "Excuse me, gents," the visitor says into the quiet. The three men at the bar stop pretending not to notice the stranger on their turf. One of them looks like slapstick actor Curly Joe, the last third of the Three Stooges, a successor to Shemp. But this Curly Joe has no funny lines and no pratfalls, and watches the unfolding tableau in silence. "I wonder if you can help me. My great-grandfather came from here in 1840. He was less than a year old when he and his family sailed to the U.S., and went on to Chicago. His first name was Robert. . . ." And the visitor immediately feels foolish. How many times have they seen this scene, some half-assed American genealogist searching for his family's Kunta Kinte? But the question is taken seriously. Brows furrow. Murmurs are murmured, the phone book is consulted, drinks are bought, and bought again. Your ancestors, it appears, may have included Ian the postie and his son David, the owner of a toy store. Postie? "Mailman," says Bill, the youngest of the three, and the spokesman. "David had the twin girls, Irene and Ona. I went to school with them. Aye, certainly, they were lovely girls."

And what, Bill asks, brings you here? He's noticed the American's windshirt and his windburn: is it the golf, this time of year?

"I'm researching a book on the '99 Open championship," answers the stranger. "Not the whole tournament—I'll just follow three or four players." But the words feel like a lie as they come out of the traveler's mouth. What he's really doing is chasing ghosts.

Or is it the other way around? Maybe the ghosts chase you. The pilgrim golfer in Scotland often feels something supernatural merely by observing the day's field of play. The links look like the bordering sea, or the land you imagine under the sea, and induce the same hypnosis available at an oceanfront bar with a picture window. And the country's violent and vivid past makes a mere round of golf feel like a reenactment of a battle fought with spears and mace. Certainly history and the supernatural converged on the Bishop of Galloway one sad day in 1619. While playing at Leith links, according to *Historie of the Kirk of Scotland,* two phantoms came upon the bishop with drawn swords. The trembling cleric, in an "afrighted and commosed way, cast away his play instruments," walked home, and crawled into bed. And died.

Other responsible men of that time saw beyond the veil. In 1603, the kingdoms of Scotland and England united; the first monarch of the United Kingdom believed in witches, and executed them when he could find them. Nothing unusual in that; Cotton Mather and friends would still be dunking and hanging covensfull in colonial Salem a full century later. No, the amazing thing about King James was that he was a Scot, and the son of Mary Stuart, the tragic Mary Queen of Scots. London buzzed with the novelty of a Scottish king, and everything related to the strange, savage relation to the north suddenly became fascinating.

James I was known to love the theater, so a local playwright with a bit of marketing sense studied Raphael Holinshed's history of eleventh-century Scotland to look for some grist for his mill. And in his studies, William Shakespeare discovered a banquet of assassination and betrayal, with side dishes of superstition and apparition. Inspired, Shakespeare produced one of his greatest plays, *The Tragedy of Macbeth*, in which a Scottish noble becomes king the old-fashioned way, by killing the king, the successors to the king, and the witnesses to the murders. Quoth Macbeth to the night:

Stars, hide your fires;
Let not light see my black and deep desires

The Weird Sisters, a trio of witches, aided Macbeth in his evil schemes. Appropriately for a man from a nation that produced a number of great moral philosophers, Macbeth eventually felt bad about the whole thing.

The king gave the play two very enthusiastic thumbs-up, and Shakespeare's company, under James's patronage, became the King's Men. But James had other passions besides the theater. He had the

Bible rewritten, as is well known. And though he railed against the game back in Scotland—it interfered with the practice of archery and thus the national defense—like his mother before him, he himself played golf, a leisure pursuit never before seen in England. London had no course, of course, so the king and his Scottish cronies, like the earl of Mar and the earl of Panmure, played a makeshift version on local fields. Shakespeare did not seem to notice, however, and no one in his plays played the already ancient and now royal game.

Golf spread without the Bard's help. It didn't need it. In Britain's ensuing age of empire, you could get a game in Bangor, Bangalore, or Brisbane, on a good course, often with a Scottish instructor. But the heart of the sport still beat in its birthplace. All its champions lived within a few miles of one another, and there was only the one championship. The Open.

The Open is the tasseled scarlet bookmark in golf history, the jumping-off place. Virtually everything else in the modern game—the ascent of rules and administrators, for example, or the deification of the top performers—grew as the Open grew. As the United States emerged from the world wars as the most powerful nation on earth, three of its major golf tournaments became, by acclamation, majors. But the Open, held since 1860, was the only world championship. Seventy-two years passed before the first Masters, the favorite event of most of today's top players. But, as they say in Georgia, that don't mean squat. Parochialism and too little prize money often obscured the Open's importance. "Why would you wanna go three thousand miles for a short bed and bad food?" asked American pros, counting their change.

But the American majors and that country's great early golf heroes would have been burgers without the bun if not for the Open. Before Bobby Jones founded Augusta National and the Masters, he made his reputation by winning the British Open three times, including in 1930, his best year. When he helped Alister MacKenzie design Augusta National in 1931, both men frankly prayed they could duplicate the allure of the most frequent Open venue—their dearly beloved Old Course at St. Andrews—with pine trees, of course, and without salt water.

Ben Hogan played in just one Open, in 1953, *his* best year. Mighty were his preparations, mythic was his striking, and breathtaking was his execution. Frank Sinatra, cigarette-thin and nightclub-pale, rode in from Dundee with his publicist and his manager to join the throng (he had a gig that week at Caird Hall). Frankie, his career in a slump, was not mobbed; instead the crowds hung on every shot and gesture from the other American. This was something big, and everyone there knew it. Hogan versus Carnoustie mimicked Sir Edmund Hillary versus Mount Everest, a win-or-die sportsman against a natural enemy that could just about kill you. Hogan conquered Carnoustie, because it was there. The swelling crowds and the British press loved everything about him, from his impeccable wool and cashmere clothing to the fire beneath the ice of his personality. Hogan further endeared himself by slipping on a gray tweed jacket—and removing his hat—to accept the Claret Jug. But the Hawk did not avail himself of the chance to play St. Andrews's nearby Old Course during his fortnight in country, a shocking oversight. Why would he choose to be the only major champion in golf history never to tee it up on his sport's most hallowed ground?

Two reasons: missions defined and missions accomplished pushed Hogan's buttons, and the Old Course was not on his to-do list. He and Mrs. Hogan were going to France for a week's vacation before sailing for home. And second, though he'd won, the effort to conquer Carnoustie had worn Mr. Hogan to a nub. He never returned.

JAMIE ANDERSON, the son of Da, Old Tom's caddie, succeeded Tommy Morris as the keenest golfer in the land. Robert Ferguson—whose club Peter Crabtree cherishes—followed Jamie. A stoic, powerful, and now totally forgotten figure, Bob Ferguson played a cleek like Segovia played the guitar. His low-ball striking—and putting—with the equivalent of a modern two- or three-iron was so impressive that a group of sportsmen arranged a one-club match in the late 1860s between him and Tommy Morris at Prestwick. After fifteen holes of playing cleek-to-cleek, Ferguson led by four holes and won the match.

Over the years he also beat Old Tom six times, about the best record anyone had against the original Open champion. But Ferguson did not linger long for the postmatch toasts. As he told *Golf Illustrated* in 1906, "I cannot say that I was ever particularly fond of company."

Neither was he especially curious about the world outside his little town east of Edinburgh. Born poor less than one hundred yards from the eight-hole Musselburgh links, Ferguson lived there, died there, and rarely left unless a money match called him away. He started in golf in the traditional way, as a caddie. Economics then dictated a two-tiered system: "carrying caddies" toted the clubs under their arms like so many pool cues, and conferred with their employers regarding strategy and club selection, while forecaddies—usually newcomers like Wee Robbie Ferguson—ran up ahead to mark the final resting point of the very expensive leather-and-feather golf ball. Then the forecaddie would scoot ahead again to indicate the line to the hole; Musselburgh had no flagsticks.

"We had to use a few simple signals to make the golfers acquainted with the kind of lie their shot had secured," recalled Ferguson. "If the ball landed in decent country the forecaddie had to face about toward the players and stroke his breast downward with his right hand. If the ball fell into whin or bunker the mishap was telegraphed by a downward stroke of the right fist held out from the body. Two downward strokes indicated that the lie was very bad indeed. A downward stroke and a gentle motion of the hand from right to left indicated that the ball was in the hazard but lying hopefully on a smooth surface." After delivering this semaphore, the forecaddie marked the ball's location with a scrap of paper, then advanced to the next hill for more reconnaissance.

Young Mr. Ferguson earned two shillings for forecaddying, and about the same for sweeping the snow off the greens when winter golfers approached the links. On summer nights he watched, transfixed, as gentlemen held putting matches, often for large sums, often by candlelight. He found a crusty but durable leather ball hidden in the whins, and began to play a bit himself, using a hockey stick for a club. Then one day, the gods came to town: "When I saw old Willie Park beat Tom Morris in one of their big matches at Musselburgh when I was a boy running about the links, I determined to do all I could to come to the front, and was very constant at practice." He quit school, and gave himself up to golf. He was eleven.

Ferguson won his first tournament at age eighteen, at Leith, using mostly borrowed golf clubs; he owned only one or two himself. But in what he called "the great annual contest," he never placed higher than fourth. Then Tommy Morris died, and Jamie Anderson faded a bit, and the dour ace from the moody dunes of Musselburgh took his place at the top of the game. In fact, he came within a hair of equaling the late Tommy's feat of taking the Open championship four years running. Though his scores were not as gaudy as the martyr's had been, Ferguson won in 1880 at his home links, won again at Prestwick in '81, and again at St. Andrews in '82. The primary benefit of being the Open champion, Ferguson found, was in the improvement in the quality and quantity of the golf bags he got to carry back at Musselburgh. Lord This and Lord That now asked for him by name. "My cup was full," he recalled, "and I was very much taken out."

The Open returned to Musselburgh, and Ferguson finished with three 3's to tie Willie Fernie for first. In the eighteen-hole play-off, the defending champion led by a shot with the tiny clubhouse in sight. But he could only make four on the short final hole, while Fernie drove the green and holed a long putt to win.

Ferguson fell into disrepair after that. After his failure to take his fourth straight Open, he survived a bout of typhoid fever, but he lost his golf game. Some say he picked a fight with demon rum, and lost that, too. Yet his reminiscences for *Golf Illustrated* are lucid and orderly, and his photograph seems to reveal a bright-eyed man of fifty-eight, not a drunk. His heavy eyebrows raised halfway up his forehead and the tidy gray beard covering his chin elongated his face, giving him a quizzical look. Ferguson peered into the camera lens as if he could see through it.

He died nine years after sitting for his magazine portrait, exiting golf's stage the same way he'd come in, as a caddie and greenkeeper on Musselburgh links. But Ferguson did other things with golf, the same things done more famously by Old Tom Morris. He learned to make clubs and gutta-percha balls, and for six years sold what he made in a little shop in Musselburgh. He laid out a handful of golf courses, too. One survives: Braids Hills, in Edinburgh.

And like Morris, Musselburgh's caddie emeritus and former Open champion spent many of his final days as an instructor. He often punctuated his tips to his students by whacking the backs of their legs with the grip end of a club.

"Nerve, enthusiasm, and practice are the three essentials to success in golf," Ferguson observed. "But to be great requires the gift."

Royal and Ancient

CHAPTER ONE

The Pretenders

———

Steve Elkington: Career prize money on PGA Tour: $7,023,912;
victories on PGA Tour: 11; majors won: 1995 PGA;
international victories: 3; world ranking: 13

Andrew Magee: Career prize money on PGA Tour: $4,883,387;
victories on PGA Tour: 4; majors won: none; world ranking: 40

Clark Dennis: Career prize money on PGA Tour: $1,148,075;
victories on PGA Tour: none; majors won: none;
world ranking: 192

IN THE WEEK before the Open, the golf professionals arrived, each checking into hotels according to his station. Steve Elkington ensconced himself, his wife, and their two young children in the luxurious Old Course Hotel in St. Andrews. Andrew Magee acclimated to warm beer and cold July with a week of golf in Ireland; then he, too, checked in to the Old Course Hotel with his wife. Clark Dennis prepared for the Open by playing in the European Tour event at Loch Lomond, near Glasgow. He missed the cut. Counting pennies, Dennis took one room for himself and his caddie, Kevin Hughett, at the £35-a-night Staki's Hotel in Dundee, and made the grim discovery that Hughett snores like a drunken buffalo.

Another dozen well-known professionals who might have enriched or been enriched by the proceedings passed on the chance. They recited white lies—sore wrists or elbows or spines needed a rest, psyches or family units had to be attended to. But truer excuses lay in what the cautious sportsmen had heard about Carnoustie. When they contemplated Carnoustie, they heard the bass fiddle soundtrack music from *Jaws.*

Elkington, Magee, and Dennis stood on different rungs of the same ladder. Superficially similar, each is married, in his thirties, with a beautiful, dark-haired wife and two or three children. Each lives in the humid or arid heat of the American Southwest. All three attended college, but none graduated. But while they travel to the same places, they move in different circles. They are nodding acquaintances, polite fellow competitors going after the same prizes, not really friends. Elkington plays for glory, Magee for fun. All three want the money, but Dennis needs it most.

That they do not dine and drink together après-golf is no surprise; it would only be surprising if they did. On the stratified and status-conscious professional golf tours, everyone seems to follow Confucius's advice: have no friends not equal to yourself. Even the lowliest minitour develops a caste system, and the boundaries only get more rigid in the big leagues. Elkington resides at the top, with others who have won a British or U.S. Open, the Masters, or the PGA. The members of this little club are often paired in the same threesomes in the first two rounds of any PGA Tour event; players are matched up according to their scores after that. Add the big Cups—Ryder, Presidents, World, Dunhill—and Elkington, Nick Price, Hal Sutton, and two dozen other Group A men repeatedly find themselves in one another's company.

Magee's coworkers live in the slightly more numerous and less exalted world of Group B; winners with no majors. Dennis's deep and wide peer group forms the bottom of the pyramid. They are a breed apart compared to even the best amateur golfers, but, as Magee says, "there are seventy-five Clark Dennises on our tour."

Of the three, only Elkington could be expected to challenge at bloodcurdling Carnoustie. He'd won a major, the 1995 PGA at the Riviera Country Club in Los Angeles, and finished just two shots out of the John Daly–Costantino Rocca play-off in 1995 at St. Andrews. The PGA Tour considers the six biggest tournaments in professional golf to be the four majors plus its own Tour and Players' championships, and in these events, Elkington had three wins among ten top tens. Elkington came to Carnoustie to win.

Magee came to play. First would be a traveling golf party in Ireland, then what looked to be a difficult week at Carnoustie, followed by an intriguing couple of days of exhibitions in Norway and Denmark. For such a steadily successful player, his record in the big ones was surprisingly dismal. In eight U.S. Opens, for example, he'd made just one cut. Magee's lone shining major moment had come in 1992, a fifth when the Open was played at Muirfield. His attitude toward the majors is sacrilege to some: he feels sure he'll live if he never wins one. "After thirteen years, I've become numb to all this, traveling to a different golf tournament week after week. To my kids, gone is gone. They don't care if it's the British Open."

Dennis presented an entirely different picture. He'd yo-yoed on and off the tour throughout his career, and had never had two good years in a row. Elkington and Magee owned exemptions into the Open, but Dennis would not get to participate unless he finished very well in a thirty-six-hole qualifying tournament. As an experiment, he'd tried this the year before, playing the European Tour event at Loch Lomond, which he loved, and attempting—and failing—to qualify for the Open, which he hated. But Scotland enchanted him. Like a tennis player who has played on cracked concrete all his life, then serves a few balls at Wimbledon, Dennis felt he'd discovered the purist's game.

A tie for sixth in the 1994 U.S. Open proved he could handle the big time, but because of his up-and-down career and the mildness of his personality, better players underestimated him. For example, at the Colonial Tournament in Fort Worth, his hometown, Dennis once drew

Hale Irwin as a playing partner for the first two rounds. It seemed like a mistake. "I belong in an A group," Irwin, a past winner of two U.S. Opens, complained on the first tee, within earshot of Dennis and part of his large gallery of family and friends. "What am I doing with *this* guy?" Irwin bitched and moaned throughout the front nine, shuffled about, or took practice swings when Dennis was hitting, making his indignation plain at every moment. Observers wished that Irwin's uppance would come, and it did, though in truth it had nothing to do with his bad behavior. During the first nine, the now ex-wife of one of Dennis's friends, a playful woman, repeatedly asked Irwin for two of his golf balls. On the tenth tee, the unhappy golfer finally relented. He reached into his bag and handed the pretty blonde two Titleists. "Look, you guys!" the woman called out. "I've got Hale Irwin's balls!" Chortles filled the air, and Hale's ears glowed.

A couple of years later, again at Colonial, Dennis shot 64-74-76, Elkington scored 68-68-77, and the two were paired for the final round. "Elk had been close to the lead until the back nine on Saturday, when I guess he played pretty badly," Dennis recalls. "He still seemed to be mad the next day. He didn't say a word to me or to his caddie the whole round, and I don't think he cleaned his golf ball, or looked at a yardage." So what did he shoot? 80? 82? "No," Dennis says, with wonder and a touch of something else in his voice. "He shot 66."

ELKINGTON REMAINED a hard guy to figure. Most obvious, there was the physical thing. A strapping six feet two and 190 pounds, and with abs so strong you'd hurt your hand if you punched him in the gut, he was also surprisingly fragile. The 1999 PGA Tour media guide stated the case succinctly: Elkington "was unable to defend Players Championship title in March due to sinus surgery . . . was diagnosed with viral meningitis the Wednesday before the GTE Byron Nelson Classic [in May], his second [*sic*] bout with that disease . . . over ten-month stretch prior to his meningitis diagnosis, suffered strained rota-

tor cuff, strained hip and strained foot along with seven sinus infec-
tions . . . also withdrew morning of second round of British Open with
pinched nerve in his neck."

The viral meningitis symptoms—an inflammation of the lining of
the brain, accompanied by a headache so severe it causes nausea—had
occurred twice before, not just once. Elkington endured spinal taps
each time, and a week or so of bed rest in a dark, quiet room, because
with his brain on fire, the beating of a butterfly's wings sounded like
a helicopter taking off. Before that he'd suffered through a Roto-
Rootering of his sinus cavity, a particularly unpleasant day surgery.
Postoperation brought more misery, because they unload the surgical
cotton in the canyons behind the nose a little at a time, at doctor's visits held weeks apart. But Elkington endured and never complained.
His physical strengths—some a gift from above, others developed in
the gym—complemented obvious mental gifts. His thirty-nine-inch-
long arms helped produce the kinetic art of his swing—a swing that
looked utterly logical, like the spokes in a rolling wheel. And his liga-
ments were so loose he could point his toe and make a straight line
with his leg, or throw a foot up on the roof of a golf cart, knees straight,
as part of his usual preround stretching.

He grew up on the wrong side of the mountains. The coastal side
of the spinelike Great Dividing Mountain Range in eastern Australia is
green, prosperous, and populous. Elkington started life on the dry,
endless inland side, West Texas Down Under. Surfers, resorts, and big
cities doing big business line up on the right; sheep stations and mo-
notonous agriculture scatter on the left.

His father's job as a branch bank manager kept his family in motion between various aboriginal Hootervilles and Mayberrys. From
Penrith to Goulburn to Narrabrai to Wollongong to Wagga Wagga they
journeyed, the last holding the most importance in Steve's life. In
Wagga Wagga—the name means "the Murrumbidgee River forks here,
and again over there"—farmers tilled the rust-red dirt and borrowed
money from Ross Elkington's bank. Milk bars, the social hub, all

seemed to be owned by Greek or Italian families. They were cool and dark inside, and the aroma of burgers on the barbie overpowered the stale body odor wafting off the farmers. A bloke could take a date there. The couple would dine on fish and chips with vinegar and salt, or adorn their burgers with egg, tomato, and beetroot. To wash it down, a milk shake for him and bodgie's blood—a Coke float with sweet red syrup—for the Sheila. The couple could sit in a booth and listen to the jukebox, or they might spread out a picnic by the muddy Murrumbidgee.

The Wagga Wagga golf course lay flat as Vegemite on toast, just a couple of miles from the Elkington's front door. One of the outbuild- ings of the Murrumbidgee Turf Club served as the golf clubhouse, and every summer the browned-out fairways looked like so much unappe- tizing pasture for the racehorses. Steve put down his cricket bat and picked up the Kel Nagle model irons his father bought him, the three, five, seven, and nine. He improved with startling speed. Within a few years the teenage Elkington brothers made the finals of the club cham- pionship. Both were likable kids, but Rob, the older boy, had the bigger smile and the easier way with people. The coltishly long-limbed little brother owned the superior golf game, however, and an almost fright- ening competitiveness. With a hole in one on the seventeenth hole— with a three-iron—Stephen beat Robert.

By age eighteen, Steve had won the New South Wales Junior, the Australasian Amateur, the Doug Sanders World Junior, and a scholar- ship to the University of Houston. As part of the national junior team, he'd been to Scotland, and had fallen hard for the smell and feel of the place. Like young golfers the world over—except in the United States—his favorite sports fantasy involved winning the British Open. Brother Rob settled for the good life of amateur golf, a family of four, and a career in golf equipment sales.

"Steve was also a very good soccer player and cricketer, an excellent batsman," comments Ross Elkington, pausing by a melaleuca bush on the seventh hole at the Australian Club in Sydney, during the 1998

Greg Norman Holden Classic. Ross Elkington is tall and straight, and he wears shorts on this hot February day, revealing long, muscular sprinter's legs, the same well-shaped stems his son has. "He played mid-on or silly mid-on. Me? Back in my day, I often played the slips." In baseball terms, father and son were infielders, playing in for the bunt.

Here comes Rob; he's got something for you. "Have a hat, mate," he says. "Have two hats." Big grin, light-brown steel-wool hair, he's his brother's slightly older, slightly shorter twin. Script TITLEIST adorns the crown of the lids in white on black and black on white. Up ahead walks Margaret, Steve's mother, from whom he got his broad nose and his ability to charm. With Margaret is Steve's wife, the former Lisa DiStefano. The youngest of the nine children of a television repairman and a secretary, Lisa grew up in a two-bedroom, one-bath house in south Houston. She first met the young and ebullient Elkington at a fraternity house mixer at the University of Houston. They drew close when they found themselves in the same geography class, and within a few months she invited her beau to meet the folks. "At first, it was very intimidating," Elkington told an interviewer in 1996. "There were forty-seven people in the family. There'd always be fifteen hanging around. Her family didn't have anything, and yet they had everything because they had themselves."

Lisa taught first grade in a poor Houston school district early in their marriage, then adapted to two profound changes: motherhood (a girl and a boy, Annie and Sam) and money (Steve banked about $3 million in 1997). Hers is a soothing, low-key presence, the counterpoint to her restless, driven husband.

A stocky man in a big straw hat and tinted prescription lenses lags behind the others in the gallery. But Alex Mercer, Steve Elkington's first instructor, never misses a shot. They've been together since 1976, when Steve and Rob made the New South Wales junior golf team, the Colts. Mercer, the pro at the Royal Sydney Golf Club, imposed a kind of martial law on the squad. No shave, no shoe shine, dirty clubs, no crease in your trousers? No lesson for you. For his best prospects, like the Elkington boys, he ratcheted up the discipline still further, withholding approval, using silence as a spur to greater effort. It worked, but for a long time Steve thought the coach didn't like him.

"Golf's not a game for a nonconfrontational person," Mercer says softly but sincerely, raising binoculars to his eyes. He resembles jowly Broderick Crawford, the star of the 1950s TV cop show *Highway Patrol.* "If you back off, you're gone. Steve wouldn't back off to anybody. When he was fourteen, he and Rob used to get on a train on Fridays and ride all night to come see me for lessons. Then back on that train on Sunday night, ten hours each way. For three years they made that trip. How keen can you get? He—" The conversation abruptly stops; Elkington is about to play from the tee. Hundreds of Australian heads swivel. Mercer mutters an evaluation of the shot, then folds his dark green walking stick/chair and trudges along. "Every time he tries to fiddle or get too technical I tell him to go back to the basics, to trust his swing," says Mercer. "We communicated by fax back in his days at university, and I'd underline the phrase *trust your swing* about six times."

Mercer watches, marches; then: "You asked if we talk about visualization. Well, visualization is just fairy-tale stuff unless you are already capable. You hear that sort of thing from the announcers on television all the time. They tell all these half-truths, like 'Smith missed that putt because he didn't accelerate the club.' But you don't accelerate on putts! You just don't decelerate. A good putter goes back and through at the same speed."

Another hundred yards. "Rhythm and tempo? Yes, I taught that at every lesson. 'Ticktock' . . ." The old pro's soft voice trails off as his student prepares to hit again.

Elkington swings, a two-iron from the tee of a tight par four. The ball concusses off the forged iron club with the brief, hissing music of a solid hit. He follows through in perfect balance, and holds the magazine cover pose for a second, his posture belying the violence he's just done to the golf ball. The gallery says "Ooh," and a father whispers loudly to his son, "How'd ya like to have that swing, eh?" After a few holes of this, Elkington's signature is plain. The rhythmic, hypnotic beauty of his striking, the somewhat formal golf clothing he prefers, and his hauteur blend into a kind of elegance. Where others grunt and flail, he's a six-foot-two-inch Fred Astaire, making a difficult task look easy. His reactions to the vicissitudes are carefully muted, as if his emotions are a thousand miles away. He acknowledges friends and family out in the open briefly after a round, never during one, and autograph hounds get what they deserve, which is nothing, unless it's a practice round. Before the first round of the Masters, he walked a gauntlet of outstretched pens between the locker room and the practice tee at Augusta National, the only place on the grounds autographs are allowed. "I'll sign after I hit," he said. But after unlimbering his full swing, Elkington slipped across Magnolia Lane to the practice bunker, and then to the putting green, and then to the first tee. He had avoided the signature seekers entirely.

As much as possible, he also determines the time and place of his interaction with the media. "Recently some writer comes up to Gypsy, my caddie, while I'm hitting balls, and asks if he can talk to me. Gypsy says, 'Not if you want to keep feeling the way you do now.' " Elkington smiles, obviously pleased with the clever way Joe "Gypsy" Grillo told the guy to get lost.

How about the equipment vans? Does he mind if someone approaches him there? Manufacturers park semitrailers full of clubs, components, and repair machinery near the practice tees at most big pro tournaments. Players, technicians, and writers mingle informally: "Can you bend this one more degree upright? Have you tried that new driver? How do you like these greens?"

"I don't go in the equipment vans," Elkington says. "I work on my clubs myself. What you do with those guys in the media is *you* pick *them*. When you decide it's time, you talk to them. Like Venturi, I give him respect every time, and he gives it back to me. But it's got to be a two-way street." Whenever Elkington appears on his monitor during a telecast and the producer says "Say something, Ken," the CBS TV golf analyst Ken Venturi never fails to observe that the tall Aussie owns the best swing in golf. And he never fails to say the efficiency of Steve's swing reminds him of a machine "stamping out bottle caps," a now very tired allusion first conjured by Herbert Warren Wind forty years ago, referring to Ben Hogan.

His ambivalence toward the press revealed itself again at what might have been a love-in after the final round of that tournament in Sydney in 1998. In his one annual appearance in his home country, he followed three workmanlike rounds with a 64, which almost drew him even with the eventual winner, Greg Norman. He walked his graceful duck-foot walk into the interview room in the press tent, sat on a platform behind a white-paper-covered table on a bright green carpet of faux grass, adjusted the microphone, and cleared his throat. "It was a great round," he said into a microphone. Twenty pens hovered above twenty notebooks. Writers called out questions regarding clubs hit and length of putts made, the standard postmortem. Elkington answered briefly, his face and eyes inflamed by summer heat and allergies. Usually he handles this chore with aplomb, but this time he suddenly had no patience for it. "I'm not gonna go into every detail," he said. "It's too bad you guys didn't get out of the shade in here to watch. You might have seen something."

Elkington spritzed again in early March 1999, when once more he shot a godlike 64, in the final round to win at Doral. But he double-bogeyed the very difficult final hole, and savagely kicked the metal siding of the scorer's trailer before he signed his card. Made a hell of a dent. "What size is your shoe?" asked a writer. "Turn around and I'll show you," Elkington replied.

Stephen John Elkington is a thoroughly modern golf professional with endorsement deals, appearance fees, and a rental jet, yet at the same time he recalls an earlier generation. He's proud of his self-containment, and of his ability to fix a club or a swing, or to make a tournament volunteer's day with a breezy comment. "Great day, mate," he'll say, in his up-talking Australian accent, sounding like the smoothest country club pro greeting a member. "Your course is in fantastic shape." But when expressing his thoughts on the inferiority of "golf pros nowadays" or "golf equipment nowadays," he sounds world-weary and grizzled, more seventy-six than his actual thirty-six. "A lot of these guys don't know how to talk," he says. "They don't even know how to tip."

Spreading the wealth and seeing people get paid for their work is a special issue for Elkington. Perhaps because he did hard physical labor as a kid—wielding a cleaver in an abattoir, for example, or caddying, or pushing a greens mower—he can't abide a cheapskate. As Sam McKinlay wrote in the Glasgow *Herald* in 1956, "golf professionals make a great parade of their parsimony," and that is still true. But Elkington loves to tip, and enjoys defending tipees. He stood up in a meeting of PGA Tour professionals to lobby for instituting a twenty-dollar fee to be paid to locker-room personnel at each tournament. "And who do you think was against it? The leading money winner of all time, Tom Kite."

After Jesper Parnevik won $140,000 for his tie for sixth place in the 1997 PGA Tour Championship at Elkington's home course, Champions, the intense Swede left town forgetting to leave the traditional emolument for the locker-room staff. "Hey, Jesper," Elkington said the next time he saw him. "I know some guys in Houston who are sticking pins in a little Jesper doll." Parnevik, a superstitious man, quickly forked over four hundred dollars to get the voodoo called off.

"I'm a blue-collar guy," Elkington says. If he is, he's a Joe Lunchbucket who knows the Latin name for almost every flower, shrub, and tree he sees, who elbowed his agent aside to negotiate his own $1 million contract with Titleist, and whose talent with a brush yielded a scholarship to the Sydney College of the Arts—an opportunity he passed up in favor of golf at the University of Houston. And if Elkington is a blue-collar guy, he's the rare one who is anti-union, specifically the PGA Tour's nascent Tournament Players Association.

"The union is a piece of shit," he says. "They want what everyone in the history of the Tour has wanted, a check when you miss a cut, because that's when you're most vulnerable. Because none of [the union's leaders] can play a lick. 'What about the NFL?' they say. 'They make more than us on average.' But football players have to wear a uniform and do what they're told. And at the end of the year they can cut your ass. But on the Tour you can do anything—[wear endorsement logos on] your hat or your shirt, or take a week off whenever you want, and we play for a hundred twenty million dollars. I'm with Finchem."

While the PGA Tour commissioner, Tim Finchem, surely appreciates the support, Elkington's expressive style and regal manner have made enemies. "He thinks he shits vanilla ice cream," says one rival. But such carping is not a concern. Jack Burke, Jr., the whirring dynamo who owns and operates Champions Golf Club in Houston, Elkington's home course, is his principal instructor now, and he has addressed the subject with him many times. "The Tour is kind of like combat," says the ex-marine, and PGA and Masters champion. "You might have one or two friends, but you don't get too close to people in competition, because someone's gonna get hurt. You have a lot of regard for the other players, but you're not quite aware of them, or concerned with them."

B URKE'S BLUNT AND PROVOCATIVE ADVICE on a hundred subjects seeped into Elkington's psyche. But instead of changing him, the old pro's counsel made his student more what he already was. Though he remained in Houston after college, Elkington became more the prototypical Australian sportsman. You can't look at him without seeing the shadows and auras of forebears who combined technical brilliance and inspiring competitiveness with an absolute refusal to put up with any bullshit. Are these traits due to the testosterone-rich patriarchy of Australian culture, or to convicts' blood, or to mere coincidence? While sweethearts like Kelvin Nagle and Bruce Devlin do not fit the mold, others in the pantheon seemed to run their lives in distinct imitation of the father of Australian golf, that feisty son of a bitch from Melbourne, Norman Von Nida.

He's eighty-five now, and legally blind, but Von Nida (nye-da) still plays golf near his home in Brisbane, with fluorescent yellow paint dabbed on his golf ball and on the heels and toes of his clubs. Like one of those Carnoustie pioneers, Von Nida was the first from his country to pursue golf around the world as a tournament player, and he won dozens of tournaments in Australia, Asia, and Great Britain. Several times, though he never won, British bookies installed him as the favorite in the Open. "Von started it all," says Jack Newton, also an Australian, and the runner-up in the 1975 Open at Carnoustie. "He's the grandfather of Australian golf, the shepherd. When the best players in the world came here to play exhibitions after World War Two, Von took Peter Thomson into the group. Gary Player could do nothing but hit hooks until Von taught him. Gary became the best bunker player in the world because of Von Nida." "A giant among sportsmen," wrote Peter Thomson in the foreword to his mentor's autobiography. "A credit to his profession and a great Australian."

A giant? No, at least not physically; the jockeylike Von Nida weighed about 125 pounds. And his regular dustups with writers, caddies, golf bureaucrats, and other players (especially American players) may put the rest of Thomson's encomium in some doubt. The worst of his public relations missteps occurred in front of the scoreboard at the Lower Rio Grande Open in Harlingen, Texas, in 1948. Perhaps it was the incongruity of the thing—a fistfight at a golf tournament!—that would make that day live in infamy. The other guy swung first, according to Von Nida, the other guy being Henry Ransom, a man possessed of an odd set of superlatives: he was the cheapest (he once celebrated a tournament win by sleeping under his car, because he judged the local hotels to be too dear), fastest (he played at a racewalker's pace, and barely slowed down to hit a shot), and, probably, the best part-time player on the American tour. And, at the moment that Von Nida confronted him, he was certainly the angriest man in golf.

Ransom had whiffed a three-inch putt on the first hole, but didn't want to own up to it. Von Nida, who'd been in Ransom's threesome, was not a man to put up with such nonsense. With scant diplomacy, he reminded Ransom he had to count 'em all. "You must be seeing things," Ransom said. He towered over the little Australian, who wore, as usual, a black beret.

"I've got eyes in my head," replied Von Nida. "You made a five at the first."

Bitter words were exchanged through clenched teeth, and spectators looked on in embarrassed fascination as Ransom's fist contacted Von Nida's noggin. But the little man grabbed the offending arm and pulled it and his opponent to the ground. Characteristically, Von Nida landed on top. "And stayed there," he recalled, "until a sheriff pulled me off." Von Nida's version of the incident was verified as fact, and the Texan was disqualified from tournaments for two months for altering his score. But, because the incident confirmed or added to his reputation, the Aussie got the worst of the publicity fallout. He seemed drawn to trouble, or it to him, and he always spoke his mind. Among other things, he complained bitterly that his Teutonic surname caused his mind-numbing World War II posting guarding the Outback on foot—instead of attacking the enemy from his preferred seat in a fighter plane. He quarreled openly with other players, especially if they were American. Comportment issues, usually. At an exhibition match in Sydney in 1954, Von Nida instructed Tommy Bolt to "behave like an adult. I told him his behavior both on and off the golf course was rude and people were sick of it. . . . My advice was not well received, to put it mildly." Many of his problems, wrote Von in his autobiography, were the result of the sensation-seeking press. "Quite a few [newspaper writers] are dishonest," he said.

Perceiving a responsibility to pass the torch, Von Nida took a curly-haired nineteen-year-old amateur from Victoria under his wing in 1949, proclaiming him "a future champion of the world." And he was. In fact, Peter Thomson was a golfer so good he would win the

British Open five times, and a man so annoying even Arnold Palmer didn't like him. "How I hated to play golf with Peter Thomson!" recalls Alex Mercer, Elkington's first instructor. Mercer won twenty-three important tournaments in Australia, but it would have been much more if not for the brilliant and occasionally infuriating Thomson. "If you missed a short putt, he'd give you this little grin. Then you could hole three one-woods in a row, and he wouldn't say 'Nice shot.' Oh, he knew the mind game, all right."

Thomson delivered a famous zinger in 1972, when he arrived fashionably late for his eighteen-hole play-off with David Graham for the Australian Open at Kooyonga in Adelaide. "Hi, David," said Thomson breezily, making the first two syllables of his greeting rhyme, a big smile on his face, his hand extended in greeting. Graham, then twenty-six, and shaking like a Cuban shortstop, had quite understandably placed his ball on a tee while waiting for Himself. But Thomson suggested they toss for the honor. The five-time British Open champion correctly called heads, and coolly drove down the middle. The callow youth quick-hooked out-of-bounds. Thomson made four, Graham seven, and the rout was on.

His business partner, Mike Wolveridge, delivered a curiously damning defense in Thomson's biography, *The Complete Golfer*: "A player might have just hooked his driver out of bounds and Thomson might say 'Crikey, you almost hooked it that time!' Or if they came to a tee with a lake on the left, he would say 'Well, you won't want to hook it again at this hole!' and invariably the other fellow would. Players would immediately think he was trying to put them off. But Thomson interpreted golf as fun . . . it's a game, for goodness sake."

Though his gamesmanship offended Palmer deeply, it represented only a thread in the Thomson tapestry. The more important parts of the weave were his absolute competence on the golf course, the artistry of his swing, and the amused-with-it-all look on his face. Often he strolled between shots with lips pursed as if whistling, like Fuzzy Zoeller. But while you'd be loath to let Frank U. Zoeller take the SATs for you, Thomson backed up his haughtiness with a first-class mind. Though his formal education ended the day he received a high school diploma, he always seems smarter than anyone else in his orbit. "Exactly what he wants you to think," says Mercer. But Thomson proved his intellect in the column he wrote for Melbourne's *The Age,* in which he lucidly and regularly announced himself to be against things: appearance fees, yardage books, the big ball, videotape, golf academies, pretty much anything new. He also expressed lukewarm feelings about Greg Norman, his successor as Australia's greatest sportsman. Regarding the culture, cuisine, golf tour, and influence of the United States, he made his disdain plain.

The up-front payment of large sums to get the world's best golfers to perform Down Under drove him to particular eloquence: "Appearance money, like bribery, corrupts those who give it as well as those who take it," he wrote. "[It] is demeaning to the other players in the field, and it destroys the whole credibility of a championship."

The big ball debate lit another fire in his typewriter. Golfers in the United States had used an easy-to-chip 1.68-inch-diameter golf ball since the early 1930s, while the rest of the world hit the wind-cutting 1.62-inch ball. When the Royal and Ancient Golf Club of St. Andrews made the big ball compulsory for the 1974 Open, Thomson wrote, "The decision must now call into question the R and A's role as custodian of the rules of golf.... The British Open is now hooked on the appeasement of the U.S. professionals because the outsize prize money depends largely on the U.S. television fee.... The British Open is now sadly an appendage of the U.S. programme.... The R and A has forfeited all credibility.... As in so many other fields at this point in history, I believe the tired British elite would be pleased to be rid of the responsibility."

Such a man was born to lead. Thomson served as president of the Australian PGA for thirty-two years, and he ran for Parliament in 1982. Some Aussies chuckle at the memory of the campaigning Thomson uncomfortably glad-handing strangers, kissing babies, and walking about with his pockets stuffed with licorice for the children of potential voters. The Labour Party won big in Australia in 1982, and Thomson, a conservative, was not given a chance. But he almost won.

Thomson led again in 1996, when Elkington and others overthrew David Graham, their assigned captain for the first biannual Presidents Cup, in favor of Thomson. The banquet on the eve of the match was a glittering affair, held at the State Dining Room in the White House. The 110 distinguished guests hushed as Thomson rose to speak. He smoothly introduced each member of his International team, along with flattering and amusing biographical snippets. He also recognized various multisyllabic dignitaries in the room, such as the ambassador from Fiji, Vijay Singh's home country. In closing, he posited that being asked to lead this team was the greatest honor of his life. The opposing captain couldn't believe his ears. "Jesus, does this guy have amnesia?" whispered Arnold Palmer. "Did he forget about winning the British Open five times?" Palmer spoke next. A veteran after-dinner speaker and a very good one, Arnie, as usual, used no notes. But it had been a long evening, and he stumbled on Jim Furyk's name and Justin Leonard's hometown. Elkington, Norman, and the other Internationals felt themselves to be one-up before the first ball had been struck.

"Thomo drowned 'em. He was unbelievable," Elkington recalls. "He writes, writes, writes his speeches, then he delivers them with no notes. He's not one to go by the seat of his pants. And his control of the English language is complete."

No points were awarded for best introductory remarks, however, and the United States team won the Cup.

WHILE WORKING ON an instruction book in early 1998, Elkington reached into a tall, narrow glass case behind his desk from time to time and removed a heavy bronze life cast of Harry Vardon's hands on a golf club. He'd sit there for a minute, examining Vardon's huge paws to confirm or clarify something about the perfect way to hold a club, looking like Rembrandt's famous painting *Aristotle with a Bust of Homer*. "See, just like they say, his hands looked like two bunches of bananas," Elkington would say, or "See, the right pinkie does go on top of the left index finger." Elkington won the Vardon Trophy for having the lowest stroke average on the PGA Tour, 69.62, in 1995. That same year he won the PGA championship, his only major title.

His office window looks out to a porch the width and twice the length of a three-lane bowling alley and beyond it to an immaculately shaved putting green of a lawn. The outstretched arms of huge trees shade a Zen-like perfection of raised flower beds, a butterfly garden, a guest house, and the big house itself. Spanish moss sways softly in a whispering breeze from the Gulf of Mexico. His adorable young children, Annie and Sam, play quietly in the hall. All looks perfect. But all is not perfect. The book. Elkington rants a little bit, but cannily, without real anger, and you suspect he's actually enjoying making order from the chaos of the book that is not yet a book. "Tell the publisher I'm not satisfied with their effort," he tells his collaborator. "The cover is shite. The title is shite. The colors are horrid. And what are these little circles, these little balloons, on the back cover? I'll walk away if things don't improve.

"We need to go up to New York and straighten their asses out," he concludes. "We're gonna get this book *done*." So he flew to Manhattan on what he calls "Air Elk," a Citation CJ2 jet with two pilots, eight seats, a dozen bagels, fruit, juice, and coffee, a cramped but effective loo in the back, and only two passengers. At seven A.M., as the flying limousine reaches 50,000 feet and 500 miles per hour—both almost double the numbers for a lumbering passenger plane—Elkington explains the economics of jet leasing. For about $1 million in advance and a fairly substantial per-use charge, he can pretty much go anywhere, any time. The benefit being? "Twenty-nine extra days at home last year."

As the jet engines drone, Elkington recalls his first trip to Scotland, a favorite story. He and his mates on the Australian national junior golf team were billeted in dorm rooms at St. Andrews University. Someone suggested sausage for breakfast the next morning; Elkington volunteered to get it. Hearing his accent, the butcher asked why the wire-haired young man was in town; a minute later the two were comparing grips. Elkington cannot forget the immediate sense of community he felt with the meat cutter, or the sight of the man's bloody hands surrounding a handy golf club. "It was classic," Elkington says.

A SILVER PORSCHE BOXSTER streaks through the desert night. Top down, two red leather seats, a single widemouthed exhaust pipe, eight cylinders g-r-r-r-rowling, Brooks & Dunn warbling on the CD. The driver actually knows the musicians he's listening to, has played golf with them, slugged Coors Lights with them, and he doesn't consider that to be a big deal. As Andrew Magee turns into the restaurant parking lot, his sandy-brown, almost blond, hair waves in the chilly wind. Unless it gets really cold, he keeps the top down.

He's just won half a million dollars. In the first event of the new four-per-year, $5 million World Golf Championships, the Andersen Consulting Match Play, Magee made the finals, and made friends and influenced people all week. "This guy's different!" chirped ABC TV anchorman Mike Tirico. "This guy's a card!" They ran the tape of Magee's interview after he'd defeated John Huston in the semifinals. "I'm sure at some point I'll stop and think . . . this putt's for *one million dollars*," Magee said, putting his left hand by his mouth, palm out, pinkie extended, the trademark gesture of Dr. Evil in the Austin Powers movies. Not everyone got the reference, but anyone could see that Magee was chocolate fudge almond swirl compared to the plain vanilla of his finals opponent, Jeff Maggert. But plain beat fancy with a heart-stopping chip-in on the second hole of sudden death, and Magee was stuck with the runner-up prize of $500,000.

He parks in a good spot in front of Los Dos Molinos, purveyor of the hottest Mexican food in Phoenix. It has been a fairly standard day at home: errands, an hour of physical therapy on his sore left shoulder, and fourteen holes of golf at The Raven, his home course, with a couple of old friends. The golf was cut short to ensure a timely rendezvous with his wife, Susan, and two of their three kids, and David and Gena Stoll and their two kids, at Los Dos. (Gena Stoll is Magee's travel agent.) "Chile relleno, right?" the waitress says to Magee. "And a margarita." As beads of jalapeño-pepper-induced sweat form under the host's eyes like dew on a windshield, an air of excitement builds at the big table in the corner, because it's hockey night in Phoenix, and the Magees have season tickets.

"Hey, Billy." In America West Arena, Magee mouths a greeting and raises a paper cup to Billy Mayfair, sitting sixty yards away behind the west goal. With his unruly albino's hair and his Phoenix Coyotes jersey, Mayfair looks like a big kid. "When Billy takes a week off from the Tour, he gets up Monday morning and hits five hundred balls," says Magee. "I just can't do that. I like to play golf with guys you met today, like Gary Hewson. Gary McCord and Phil Mickelson [who also live in the Phoenix area] call me when we're all home and they want to play hundred-dollar one-downs. I always say no."

TV time-outs and period breaks give professional hockey a lot of downtime, which provides Magee opportunities to chat. Professional golf encourages almost toxic levels of self-involvement, but Magee thrives on give-and-take. And it's not all sports talk. He offers startling gems in the course of an evening, like a few bits of mock Shakespeare and his thoughts on the space-time continuum. He's prounion. "[PGA Tour commissioner Tim] Finchem asks me why, and I tell him, I think you need something to do. He says, 'You think I need watching?' I think he secretly loves the challenge. He worked in the Carter White House and as a lobbyist and he's a lawyer. Those guys can hide anything. Do you think Finchem will have any trouble with a bunch of golf pros? But I support the union because I know there's plenty the Tour isn't telling us."

As the Zamboni wipes a new sheet of ice over the old, Magee recalls his college days at the University of Oklahoma. "Our coach was pretty good friends with Paul Runyan [the PGA champion in 1934 and 1938], and he got him to come out from California to spend a day or two with us. Great short-game instructor—he talked about the elbows making a forty-five-degree angle when you chip, and keeping the arms and hands in opposition. At the end of the thing, we're all gathered together in the cafeteria, and he says, 'Boys, do you know what's the most important thing in tournament golf?' And we all draw in closer to hear the secret. And Runyan says, 'Regular bowel movements.' Do you think there's a book in that? We could call it *The Magic Move to Better Golf.*"

Magee was born in Paris in 1962 and grew up in London. He remembers family vacations in Scotland, when his father would have the family Volkswagen put on a train, and the Magees would chug north from Victoria Station to Gleneagles or Inverness, stay awhile, then drive slowly back to Hampstead Heath. Mobil Oil transferred his father, a geologist, to the home office in Dallas when Andrew was nine. "I came home from school one day and my mother told me we were moving to Texas. I pictured *Gunsmoke,* and swinging saloon doors, and riding a horse to school. Then we got to Dallas and I saw asphalt. My whole world was turned upside down."

Oklahoma, North Dakota, Venezuela, Portugal, Algeria, France, England, and Farmers Branch, Texas . . . The final leg in the Magee family's global wandering began around Christmas in 1971. Jane Magee stayed behind so that Mary Margaret could finish her senior year at the American School in London. John Magee took the other three kids, Jonathon, Matthew, and Andrew, to Texas. The Magee men house-hunted by locating their potential new golf course first, then casting their net about two hundred yards from the first tee.

MAGEE INTRODUCED SPIKED hair to the plaid pants Republican world of the PGA Tour. He lists his hobbies in the PGA

Tour media guide as "travel, swimming, fishing, whistling." During his high school years, he hosted a weekly, invariably rowdy Monty Python–watching soiree at his parent's house. He competes ferociously on the golf course, but several times a round he'll chat up friends and strangers as if he's the host of a walking garden party. Though golfers are the best pro athletes to interview by far, still most of them keep ready a list of prefabricated and sanitized responses to a writer's questions. But the computer in Magee's brain does not automatically scroll through the Cliché File when a question is in the air. Instead, he is refreshingly and dangerously honest. "I'm scared shitless about what you're going to write about me," he said. "But at the same time, I'm secure enough that nothing you say could really bother me."

Another dividing line between Magee and his peers is his attitude toward the weekly Wednesday tournament prelude, that tedious throat-clearing before the tenor sings, the bane of Lanny Wadkins's existence, the pro-am. Magee loves the ritual of adoration, jangled nerves, and marketing; most pros' feelings about playing golf with four wealthy strangers hover between toleration and loathing. He repeats the possibly apocryphal first tee greeting of Wadkins to his pro-am partners: "How do you do, I'm Lanny Wadkins. I'm not looking for your ball in the rough." But Magee's wide-ranging intellect and gregarious nature cause him to regularly hit it off with a new set of pals every week. "If I wrote my autobiography," says Magee, thirty-seven, "I'd call it *My Life Is a Pro-Am.*"

This ability to bond got him an endorsement deal made in heaven, a contract to promote a beverage he already drank. "We looked at everybody," Carl Barnhill says a few months later. Barnhill is the senior vice president of sales for Coors Light beer. "When I met him I said, 'This is our guy.' He's articulate, he's bright, and he'll slam a few Coors Lights during a round of golf with a big retail account. They always like Andrew. He's got charisma."

The whistle blows—icing the puck—which gives Magee a moment

to consider the Masters, the first major of the year. He describes his tournament preparation. "The first thing I do when I get to Augusta is to go to Target and buy two kiddie pools, and put them in the backyard of the house we're renting. One we fill up with ice and beer. The second we fill with water, and spread pine needles on top." Pool two is the target for a nightly lob wedge contest, which begins after Magee and his housemates have made repeated visits to pool one. The pine needles break the surface tension of the water, so fewer shots hit and skip. Wagering is permitted.

The hockey game is over and the paper cups are empty. The Coyotes have lost. The somber crowd shuffles to the exits.

WHEN THE MAGEE MEN hunted houses in Texas, they looked at suburbs north of Dallas and selected Brookhaven, getting in near the ground floor of the Levittown of golf. An idea as much as it was a golf course and housing development, Brookhaven pioneered the affordable country club, and was the seed from which grew Club Corporation of America, the largest golf course owner-operator in the world. CCA would be criticized for homogenizing American golf, and for removing the pride of member ownership at hundreds of golf clubs. But Brookhaven and CCA undoubtedly did some things right.

"Jonathon and I had played a little bit at Hendon in northwest London," recalls John Magee. "But the English really discriminated against kids on their golf courses. They were seldom allowed to play, never during prime time." No such problem at family-oriented Brookhaven, where upper-middle-class salary men in insurance or oil or electronics plunked down their families before Exxon or EDS transferred them again. Dues were low, turnover was high, and kids were kings at the forty tennis courts, three golf courses, and five swimming pools. The Magees easily won father-son swimming contests, but the junior golf competition was surprisingly tough. Incredibly, two other neighborhood kids Andrew's age would also advance to the top of the game, and join Magee as competitors in the Open at Carnoustie. They are Brian Watts and Scott Verplank.

John Magee takes you to Brookhaven's charmless practice range, which his youngest child started using in earnest at age twelve. He points to a plaque by a live oak tree at the far left, a memorial to a man named Orville Stump. "Stump had no official capacity, but for years he enjoyed being helpful to the juniors here, Andrew included," said John Magee. "Then a mother who had an embryonic good golfer complained about Orville injecting strange thoughts in her son's head. Orville was dismissed, which broke his heart."

ANDREW REMEMBERS STUMP and the tree, but the pro at the club made a bigger impression. "Joe Black would put signs up around the club saying something like, 'I will be hitting practice balls today from three-thirty to four-thirty.' I always watched. He wasn't a great player, and he wouldn't talk to you while he hit, and looking back I'm amazed at the arrogance of those signs. But I'd never seen golf balls hit right before, with that ski-jump flight. It fascinated me."

Fascination inspired dedication, dedication led to success. "It was pretty late before Jane and I realized Andrew was not just another boy golfer," recalls John Magee. The lights came on one summer afternoon when John watched a junior tournament in Wichita Falls. "I saw some kids hit their second shots on eighteen, and I noticed a swing absolutely like the pros on TV on Sunday, and the ball rolled right up by the pin. That was Andrew.

"His crowning achievement was the Doug Sanders World Junior. He went all the way through that thing, then he had to go to England for the finals, by himself. He changed planes and didn't lose anything, and he won the tournament. He was seventeen. In fact, he went to all those junior tournaments by himself."

John Magee might have seen more of his teenage son's golf if he weren't himself hitting the road for Mobil Oil, evaluating formations and negotiating leases in Somalia, Cameroon, and a dozen other countries. "The Africans were so *venal*," he recalls. "I found I was working for the personal enrichment of corrupt government officials. They were always requesting status meetings at four-star hotels in Rome." He'd return to Texas from Tripoli or wherever with pictures and slides and artifacts geological or archaeological. And each time he came home, he'd remake the same discovery: like four colliding marbles, each of his four kids was moving to his own point on the compass.

"They're all so doggone different," he says.

Mary Margaret earned a Ph.D. in English literature and became the head of the upper school—the principal of grades nine through twelve—at Hockaday, the best private girls' school in Dallas. "As an informal guide, yes, I believe birth order may be significant," says Dr. Magee. "Andrew was the most daredevilish of any of us, always getting in trouble, always doing crazy risky things. Maybe that has something to do with being the youngest, maybe not.

"My father always used to say, 'He's the smartest of all of you.' Andrew is very bright, but he never cared that much about school. As a school person, I perceive that as a waste."

The military life appealed to Jonathon, the oldest brother, and physical fitness became a second religion. He's a lieutenant colonel in the Army Reserves now, and sells commercial real estate in Dallas. Andrew had golf, and girls, and another party. Matthew, the closest to Andrew in looks, and in age—he's thirteen months older—looked at life and its meaning and found absolutely no answers in sports. His search led him to art and then to art school, and an ascetic life on Manhattan's Lower East Side. He works for Robert Rauschenberg, whose "combines" of crumpled newspaper and bicycle seats sell for millions of dollars. Matthew's own paintings arguably require more craft, but they're less accessible, more abstract. You can buy one for three thousand dollars. His brother cannot understand him or his art.

"Andrew even has a LeRoy Neiman in his house," laughs Matthew, but he's not a big laugher like his younger brother. The street where he lives—with fire escapes clinging to old brick buildings—looks like the set of a turn-of-the-century movie. He eats a bowl of granola at the restaurant on the corner and articulates thoughtfully, and softly. "Golf took over when Andrew was a freshman in high school, and I was a sophomore. Our friends just never meshed. We went our separate ways.

"Dad might spend six months in Mogadishu, but he'd bring back slides and interesting rocks. That definitely fed me as an artist, and helped us realize there was a world outside." John also took Matthew on fifteen to twenty camping trips in the wastelands of the desert Southwest to look for archaeological fascinoma, like cave paintings and fossils. "This was Dad's way of telling me he approved of me, I think," he says. "Andrew never went." The hieroglyphs and pictographs he saw on those trips echo in many of his symmetrical, geometrical paintings. Often one side mirrors the other, like the two halves of a scorecard. Matthew Magee paints a secret language of repeating circles and squares on canvas or maple boards, and he had a tattoo artist etch those same images onto his feet and ankles.

"I'm very obsessive-compulsive, just the opposite of Andrew. Yet he has to make a score in golf by himself, just as I have to work by myself. We both have to be focused. You can see his work just as you can see mine. So the same things are required of him and me. We're very different and a lot alike."

M AGEE FINISHED HIS tour of duty at OU without a degree but without a doubt about what he wanted to do. He turned pro in 1984 and played and practiced at Oak Tree Golf Club in Edmond, Oklahoma, and there he fell in love. A beer-bellied go-between told Magee about the exceptionally attractive new receptionist at the country club. Magee talked his way into a date. She thought he looked a little like Tom Hanks, the actor.

The former Susan Ellenberg tells the courtship story herself, embellishing the tale with details such as what she wore on their first date—a white halter top—and the fact that prior to their introduction, she had already seen young Mr. Magee in the bar at Cleopatra's Barge, a casino in Las Vegas. "Someone pointed out this table of golf pros and said the one with light-brown hair is from Oklahoma, so I pretended I had to go to the bathroom and I gave him a look. When I saw what a good time he was having at two in the morning, I said, 'Well, he's not a very *serious* golfer.' "

Susan Magee dipped luckily into the gene pools of the Campbells in Scotland and the Creek Indians in Oklahoma. She combines exotic good looks with the same disarming honesty as her husband. They have a great time, their friends are not confined to other professional golfers, and their conversation is not confined to golf. As a result, the Magees are not the most popular couple on tour. Not that they're unpopular; they just look like they're having too damn much fun. It's a mixture of envy and awe at their ability to deal with an unforgiving business in a very open and friendly way.

Their house in the Phoenix suburb of Paradise Valley is a Spanish-style square, wrapped around a courtyard filled with the water music from a gently dripping fountain. A walk around the grounds with Andrew and Oliver, age seven, and Campbell, ten, reveals another fountain in the pavestoned driveway, and a series of little flags stuck in the ground here and there, which you assume incorrectly are for target practice for the master's wedge. They are instead feng shui banners, something to do with the Chinese art of keeping the house spirits happy. "I told a writer that my wife just feng-shuied our house," says Magee. "His eyes go like this"—and Magee bulges his eyes like he's just seen a ghost. He leads you through a maze of lemon, orange, tangelo, and tangerine trees. "I called home and Susan asked if she could plant a citrus tree," he says. "I said sure. When I came home, there was this *orchard.* That's exactly her style."

In the spring of '99, Magee read *King of the World,* David Rem-

nick's biography of Muhammad Ali. He reviewed it in a note to a
friend:

*Mixed emotions about Ali. Great focus toward a goal. I guess it would
be fun to taunt other golfers before a round, but I'm not sure I could take it.
I've been thinking about asking you to write a page about me for me.
Who am I?*

O_N A SURFACE LEVEL, Magee tells the world who he is
every time he steps inside the ropes: he is Cleveland Golf. The company gets its investment back (he declines to say how much) through
the script CLEVELAND GOLF embroidered in black on white on his hat
and bag. TV's the key. If Magee does well, he and his logos (the Lacoste
crocodile suns itself above his heart, and he wears COORS LIGHT on his
left sleeve) get air. TV ads during a PGA Tour event cost about
$100,000 per half minute, so when the endorser can win or come close,
the manufacturer quickly recoups its cash. Good finishes also inevitably result in full-page ads in golf magazines. In one such, Magee is
quoted as saying "I won $500,000 the first time I put a QUADPRO dri-
ver in my bag and hit the ball further than ever before." The word
"Cleveland" appears nine times in the spot, "Quadpro" six. To the marketers, repetition is key.

In the midst of these bloodless transactions, love blooms. Though
the basic assumption of golf club sales and marketing is that you can
play the exact same clubs as your professional hero, Magee adored this
particular set of sticks. He had the twelve Clevelands, a Never Compromise putter, and a ten-year-old oddball of a three-wood, a J's Professional Weapon. Keeping his basic fourteen company in his roomy
bag were two or three rain jackets, two pairs of shoes, a laser yardage
reader, and several extra putters and drivers.

So when his favorite luggage failed to appear on the baggage
carousel at the Atlanta airport in early June, Magee felt momentarily

morose. "We had a nice little thing going," he said of his stolen loves. He played poorly with replacement clubs at the U.S. Open and missed the cut. In the final two rounds of the Western Open, his next tournament, he three-putted a maddening seven times.

Magee knew he'd need every advantage to make a dent at Carnoustie; now he'd lost his favorite arrows, and his quiver. He usually placed a £10 bet on himself in the Open, but this time he didn't bother.

CHAPTER TWO

The Hogan Card

———

We are inclined to go back to where we were.

—*Ben Hogan, giving a lesson to John Derr*

CLARK DENNIS LEFT the loch at half nine on Saturday, driving east from Glazgo toward Enbra for a few kilometres. Turnbree, the site for the 2004 Open, lay to the south, but Dennis veered north, toward Stirling Costle, then east toward Sin Tandrews. He drove the Cortina on the left side of the dual carriageway, of course, breaking the habit of a lifetime. But he drove fast.

After four days of his second-ever visit to the birthplace of golf, Dennis had learned a little of the local lingo, including that "cheers" is Scottish for "good day to you," ice cubes are doled out reluctantly, if at all, "bitter" means a kind of beer, and "steak-and-kidney pie" means botulism. Being a foreigner invigorated him. The shortness of his bed and the eight ounces of tepid cola in his glass when he was used to twelve on the rocks led to philosophizing, not complaining. "They seem to have a problem here with *scale*," he observed. "But I didn't come here for the food. Or for the beds."

He ran his life with the fearlessness gained from having four brothers, three of them older. Certainly the Open qualifier held no terrors. Ten times he'd run through a more punishing gauntlet, the PGA Tour's brutal qualifying school, and three times he'd survived. In 1996 he was one shot out and charging when the Tour—inexcusably lacking a backup plan in case of foul weather—canceled the final round. Twice his preliminary scores for the U.S. Open had been the lowest in the entire country. That he'd had to qualify at all spoke to certain problems with his game, but grace under pressure was not one of them. Dennis was thirty-three, and had been a pro for thirteen years.

To make it into the Open, he would have to be one of the low twelve finishers of the 112 players assigned to Downfield, a spiffy inland course in an iffy neighborhood on the north side of Dundee. Dennis played his Saturday practice round alone until the fifteenth hole, when a wide-eyed, wiry kid from London asked if he could play in. "Zane," he said, extending his hand, sounding like Mick Jagger. "How'd ya do? Nice to meet ya. Yeah." Zane politely asked the American if he should look into getting new model Mizuno irons, the brand both golfers played. No, Dennis said, you seem to be hitting the ones you've got just fine. It came up during their four holes together that Zane's last name was Scotland. Whoa, Dennis said to himself, what a handle. Then the young man with Davis Love's swing and Tiger Woods's body said no, he did not work in a club or play on a tour or even go to college; he's only sixteen years old, yeah. *Whoa.*

Dennis decided the par 73 course suited him, with its five par fives, all of which he could reach in two. But another scale problem bothered him. Flagsticks in the United States are seven feet tall, usually; Scottish poles are two feet shorter, and thus look farther away to an untrained eye.

After dinner Dennis cased Dundee. The ancient seaport looked to him like Amarillo by the sea, which is to say, not much. He and caddie Kevin Hughett wandered the old stone city in the Ford with the air conditioner on and the passenger window half open to vent the smoke from Hughett's Marlboros. They came to a casino by the waterfront but bet not a pound, due to a requirement that first-time visitors endure a twenty-four-hour waiting period. They filled out forms and left. On the way back to their single hotel room, they passed a nightclub by the Tay Bridge called Sinatra's. The martini glasses with toothpick-speared olives depicted on its marquee needed a wash. Dennis and Hughett drove on by.

SUNDAY: THE RAT-A-TAT-TAT of dysentery sufferers echoed off the hard white walls of the men's locker room. An apparent victim of a sleepless night lay motionless on his side on a bench, with a rolled up towel for a pillow and his black-and-white golf shoes on the floor. Toilets flushed. Stern signage warned against washing your shoes here or leaving a towel there, and players came and went with their heads down and their eyes focused on the air two feet in front of their noses. When they emerged from the dimly lit recesses of the necessary room, they squinted in the brilliant sunlight like afternoon drinkers stepping out of a pub. To Dennis the aroma of fear and anxiety in the air confirmed what he'd suspected, that a lot of these guys were in way over their heads.

He walked down a short steep hill to Downfield's practice field, where golfers could aim at whitewashed truck tires embedded in the spongy turf at fifty-yard intervals. The club did not supply practice balls, however, so Hughett would have to be a human target. He'd done this the previous day, before the practice round, and he didn't like it. His body language spoke loud and clear: this shit *never* happens on our tour. The caddie emptied a plastic garbage bag of about forty used Titleists at Dennis's feet and strolled wordlessly onto the firing range, immediately turning his head to watch for mishits from the seven other players who were also warming up. Heat poured down from the cloudless sky. Scotland's two-day summer had begun.

Dennis felt loose enough to talk before teeing off. "Did you hear that Vicki is pregnant?" Um, no. Planned? "Um, no. But welcome."

He unzipped a side pouch on his blue-and-white golf bag, took out a black marking pen, and began ritually customizing two sleeves of golf balls. First his sons' initials, CWD (age three) and TAD (age one). A line through TITLEIST. And three dots around the number on the ball. "Did you hear about all the guys who withdrew?" Dennis said. "I can't believe you could be exempt [from qualifying] for a major and not play. Those guys are wimps." Then he took off his shoes and socks, stood on a towel, and clipped his toenails.

A blue blazer standing by the first tee looked down at a clipboard. "Match number six," he said in a conversational tone. "Clark Dennis, United States . . ."

ARNOLD PALMER LIKED to fly his plane in the crystal-blue air above Palm Springs, and he liked to take Dub and Daisy Dennis with him. Clark's parents were a fun couple, and they were PGA Tour insiders. A photograph of Dub pretending to help Daisy with her swing—and two pictures of Arnie—graced the front sports page of the Palm Springs *Desert Sun* on February 2, 1962. The accompanying story read:

> L. W. Dennis, Jr., prominent Houston, Tex., oilman, who is a member of the board of directors of the Houston Golf Association, is in Palm Springs with his wife, Daisy, and family to take in the Golf Classic.
>
> The Houston Golf Association, of which Dennis is a board director, sponsors the $50,000 Annual Houston Golf Classic . . .
>
> His wife, the former Daisy Dean, was in the entertainment field for many years before becoming Mrs. Dennis. She sang the lead in the big Broadway musical "Finian's Rainbow." In recent years she has appeared on radio and TV with Jack Carson and Jack Haley in New York.
>
> "But being a mother to three handsome youngsters, Dubby, 9, Eben, 8, and Auburn, 7—all boys—is a full-time job now," stated the very attractive and charming Mrs. Dennis.

His father, a wildcatter, rolled the dice in the oil patch and usually won. His mother had the poise and talent to perform on the biggest stages in the world. So much for nature; the nurture part of the Clark Dennis equation is equally straightforward. The family lived at Champions, the golf oasis in north Houston famous for attracting low-handicap members. A U.S. Open and a Ryder Cup had been staged there, and a never-ending parade of touring pros came through to absorb wisdom from the owner-operators, Jack Burke, Jr., and Jimmy Demaret. The Dennises moved to Fort Worth when Clark was a teenager, and joined another great golf club, Colonial, and a mediocre one, Woodhaven.

As his ambition grew, Clark began to eschew the "don't do this" instruction of his brother Eben in favor of the more cerebral approach of the Woodhaven pro, Dan Strimple. "Clark already had a great game when he first came to me," recalls Strimple. "He told me, 'I don't care if I know a lot about the golf swing,' so I tried to give him a minimum of technical information. The remarkable thing about him was that he had no bottom number—he played with no fear. He shot a 62 at Woodhaven, a course record, when he was sixteen."

"I'd have never made the tour if not for Dan," Dennis says.

The stubbornness that kept him on the practice tee revealed itself in other ways. Dennis's wife, the former Vickie Vargas, hails from Ozona, a tiny outpost in the west Texas outback where time stopped at the last century. Dennis always brought his clubs on Thanksgiving or Christmas trips the couple made to her hometown, and the denizens of the local country club let it be known they'd be thrilled to have Clark play or practice on their grounds. But he discovered that his own in-laws were not welcome there. No Spanish surnames allowed. So Dennis told OCC to go piss up a rope. He hit balls in better company—at the Ozona graveyard.

He'd do anything to improve. He tried the Triangulator and researched the Rhythmiser; he tae-kwan-doed, step aerobicized, and hired a Marine Corps drill instructor of a personal trainer. Now he boxes, in a real gym with a mouthpiece and headgear and a sparring partner. He cut out fat, sugar, red meat, and egg yolks. He cut in oatmeal, fish, and audiotapes from the motivational pooh-bahs Zig Ziglar and Tony Robbins. And in 1995 he switched to an even more Socratic instructor, Dana Bellenger. A typical exchange:

DENNIS: My left hand feels stronger with this stance.
BELLENGER: And is that a good thing or a bad thing?

Or:

DENNIS (after hitting a slice): What'd I do?
BELLENGER: You hung back, dropped inside, and blocked it with your hands. Why do you think you did that?

Bellenger modulates patiently, soothingly, supportively. "No touring pro ever hit a bad shot," he says to a bystander. "It's always the club's fault, or the turf, or the instructor. That attitude is what makes them great." During a walk in Dennis's gallery at the GTE Byron Nelson Classic, Bellenger revealed that although he is only in his forties and looks reasonably healthy, he's already selected the music for his funeral: the second half of "Layla" by Derek and the Dominos, and "Happy Trails," as performed by Roy Rogers.

Dennis qualified for the tour in 1989 with tears in his eyes, two weeks after his father's death. Told that he needed to par the 108th and final hole to make the big leagues, his body suddenly went numb as Novocained gums. He chopped his drive into the woods, chipped out, chopped on. But he recovered his spark in time to make a twenty-foot putt for par. That one hole would be a template for his career so far: bad followed by good, a year on the perk-laden Big Tour followed by a dry white season on the minor-league Nike Tour. He almost starved in 1996, winning just $20,003. But in 1998 he had by far his best year, earning $401,440 in official cash. He bought two treeless lots by the fourteenth tee at his home course, Mira Vista in south Fort Worth, and a medium-sized black Mercedes-Benz, used.

Now it's nervous time again. Only the top 125 money winners stay qualified for the PGA Tour, and Dennis is 129th. Something is missing, something is wrong. But the gambler's son antes up again.

On the first hole at Downfield, a narrow 410-yard par four, Dennis blistered his big-headed Ping driver about three hundred yards down the middle. Then he spun a pitching wedge to within ten feet of the hole. But his putt described an L, spinning sideways off the lip. On the second tee, he hit what he thought was a perfect three-wood, only to find the ball was buried in the face of a bathtub-sized bunker. Double bogey.

Four hours later he three-putted the eighteenth green for a bogey and a two over par 75. "Just . . . nothing happened," Dennis said, scanning the scoreboard in the twilight. "I'll have to shoot 66 tomorrow." That night Hughett returned to the casino and lost £40 playing blackjack. Dennis stayed in and watched a BBC2 documentary on defensive techniques in cricket. He slept soundly.

MONDAY: DURING A ONE-HOUR fog delay Dennis sat in the mist on a bench in front of the pro shop. He mused about the high cost of this trip, which seemed about to end with no offsetting revenue. He analyzed the motives of the exempt players who stayed home. He concluded that a "Danger: High Rough" posting on the super-efficient professional golf grapevine was mainly to blame. "Kite, Crenshaw, Couples, Daly, Jones, Hoch . . . Maybe one of them is really injured. But Hoch hates it over here, so he's no surprise. Crenshaw has the Ryder Cup. And John [Daly] doesn't practice anymore. I doubt he could find the fairways at Carnoustie."

Hughett's mood had brightened. He did not have to shag this morning; Dennis swatted out the garbage sack of balls, and left them.

Both men wondered aloud about early flights back to the States. The caddie, a former minor-league baseball player and for a year a member of the Hilton Head, South Carolina, police department, missed his girl back in Connecticut.

"Hey, how you doing, Zane?" Scotland stopped by Dennis's bench on his way to the practice range, his manner the same as before: polite but relaxed. A skinny kid, 160 pounds on a six-foot frame, big dark eyes, wispy sideburns down to the earlobes.

"Six undah. How'd you do, Clock?"

"Not so good. Two over."

"You'll shoot six undah today."

He didn't. Dennis chipped in for par at the first, and birdied the 240-yard par-three third with a gorgeous three-wood and a twelve-foot putt. But when he lipped out a five-foot putt for birdie on the par-five fifth, he realized he wasn't going to make it. The music for Dennis's plod around the remaining holes was written 150 years ago by a depressed Russian: "The Song of the Volga Boatmen." After signing his card, Dennis walked to his car, fished his cell phone out of the trunk, and tapped buttons. His Atlanta-based travel agent confirmed that his heavily discounted plane ticket allowed little flexibility for changing his flight; he had twenty hours to kill. What to do? Dennis didn't want a pub crawl and he didn't want to see Carnoustie as a mere spectator. Someone noted that another Fort Worth golfer had been to this area just once in his life but had failed to visit golf's shrine. Did Dennis wish to repeat Ben Hogan's mistake? He did not.

An hour later, Dennis stood in brilliant sunshine in the green grass of the St. Andrews graveyard, contemplating the mottled headstones of the two Toms.

NEAR MIDNIGHT, the superintendent of the links stalked fogged-in Carnoustie. On the wild terrain of his golf course, grandstands and scoreboards formed giant shapes more sensed than seen, and light from the town and the new hotel refracted into dim halos. No-nonsense men from Group 4 Security patrolled every green, wearing black raincoats with traffic-cop-fluorescent yellow-green stripes on the front, the black as shiny as a seal's back. They'd walk around a bit pointing useless flashlights, then sit on stools in tiny tents in the lonely night and try not to doze. But staying awake presented no problem for John Philp.

"Look at that! That's Lyme grass. That's *powerful,*" he said, and here he balled his fist and shook it. "I love it!" Fog clung like a cloud to Philp's curly hair, and coalesced into droplets, which dripped to the shoulders of his dark sweater when the superintendent of the links bent to point out something in the lush terrarium of Carnoustie rough. He did not have to bend far. "This rye grass is like *wire.* This is going to be a real problem, a real problem." He walked a few more steps into the knee- and thigh-high vegetation between the fifth and sixth holes. His Toyota truck idled inaudibly on a crushed seashell service road fifty yards away, its headlights illuminating nothing but themselves.

"This is bent grass, fine as silk and purple-brown. Lovely. See, see how soft the stem is? Here's some fescue. Tan on the top. See how it's dropping its seeds? Here's some red sorrel. . . . That's Yorkshire fog grass.

"The color green is god on American courses. Not here. Green means soft and sappy. We're after a harder grass."

In the truck again, the tires crackling over the seashells. Gesticulating like a TV preacher, Philp pointed out the "silly Corsican pines" on the ninth hole, "straight as soldiers, completely unnatural on a links." Despite howls from some Carnoustie regulars, he'd already removed hundreds of the evergreens from the fifteenth and sixteenth holes. "They aren't even Scotch pines! They'd imported them from Italy!" He hopped out of the truck again near the fourteenth fairway to show you the thirty-degree slope in the grass faces of the Spectacles bunkers, and the tiny sprinkler nozzles embedded therein. When you squat to feel the firmness of the double green that serves the fourth and fourteenth holes, he squats with you, still talking, still keeping eye contact. You see blond eyebrows above lively brown eyes, and a seamed, tanned face; Philp looks ten years younger than his fifty-one years. "Must be the salt air," he says.

Maybe it's his zest for his job. His alarm—a harsh electronic beep-beep, not music from a clock radio—had gone off at three-fifteen that morning. After a shave, a bowl of Weetabix, and a cup of tea, he drove to the concrete and corrugated steel maintenance building nestled behind the trees to the golfer's left of the eleventh green. In addition to his usual greenkeeperly duties this extraordinary week, he'd spoken with dozens of newspaper chaps, all asking the same things: What about the length? What about the rough? Is Carnoustie unfair? Then he'd go to the practice range and meet a handful of the world's best golfers. They had questions, too. Philp parried and thrusted like he'd been waiting to do this all his life.

"Ernie Els says he reckons this is the toughest course he's ever played. And Elkington says the condition is 'immaculate' and that four or five over will win. But Seve Ballesteros was crying in his soup. 'Evil,' he says to me, 'this "evil" rough. Not true links,' he said, 'to have rough this high. You must have watered this rough.' I said, 'That may have been true in the past, but for three years the only water this rough has seen fell from the sky. But if you really want to object,' I told him, 'you better speak to Mr. Hugh Campbell of the R and A.' Seve says, 'I don't think I'll bother.'

"Sandy Lyle said that we'd fertilized the rough. Rubbish. We don't tamper with roughs, we just apply seaweed and wetting agent to strengthen the leaf in the weak areas. The wet winter made the roughs grow here and on every course in Scotland. Just ask them at Turnberry or Muirfield about their roughs."

Philp drives through hollows between shaggy-topped sand dunes, and the golf course disappears. "The journalists do not want to talk about the romance of this course. Or to try to understand the subtleties of bunker placement, or how the new mounds blend in. They want to demonize this thing. This tournament is going to be topical, I know it is. What would Hogan have said about all this complaining? He'd have said 'What the shit.' " That phrase would become Philp's refrain: what would Hogan have said?

Through thickening fog Philp finally begins the five-minute drive to his home. He flicks on the windshield wipers. "I often think about Armour or Cotton when I'm out here at night," he says, and the wipers squeak. "But especially *Hogan*. What would happen if his ghost came out on that practice tee? Would these players stop and watch? Would they even recognize him?"

TOMMY ARMOUR, HENRY COTTON, Gary Player, and Tom Watson possessed vivid personalities and superlative golf games, and each won an Open here, but only the 1953 champion haunts Carnoustie. "Ben Hogan is without a doubt our greatest asset, and you can quote me," says Martin Roy, the Carnoustie caddie master. That's the Hogan House Hotel across the street from the course, and the brochure a multipierced teenager hands you in the street proclaims that it houses HOGAN'S ALLEY: THE BEST GOLF LOUNGE BAR IN CARNOUSTIE. The Hogan Suite in the new Carnoustie Hotel costs £850 per night during Open week. That's the Hogan Bunker in the center of the sixth fairway, and Hogan's (other) Alley to the left of that sandpit, and the little plateau from which the contestants drove on the sixth in '53 is called, what else, the Hogan Tee. And what's that ugly industrial building across the railway opposite the tenth fairway? "The Hogan Fertilizer Company," quips Brian Watts, and a couple of his fellow pros on the practice tee give his line a little laugh. Tired of hearing what a paragon Ben Hogan was, some pros felt over-Hoganed at Carnoustie. For others, there is no such thing.

The Hawk's greatest champion sits in a strategic spot in the press tent, sipping decaffeinated coffee and dreaming of the cigarettes his doctors won't allow him to smoke. Strategic sitting has been Dan Jenkins's stock-in-trade for forty years. With scarcely a discernable move from his cushioned lawn chair on the veranda at Augusta National or from the coffee urn at Pebble Beach, Jenkins somehow always sussed out the essence of a tournament and got the best quote and the most telling detail, for the *Fort Worth Press, Sports Illustrated,* and now *Golf Digest.* Jenkins had read James Thurber and S. J. Perelman and P. G. Wodehouse, and he'd been first man on his college golf team. The combination gave his reporting insight and structure, with accents of wordplay and biting humor. Why the bite? Because although Palmer and Nicklaus came close, no one measured up to Hogan.

That the dour Hawk liked the smart but smart-alecky kid from the local paper may surprise, until you realize that Hogan enjoyed a joke; he just couldn't tell one. And Hogan's hard-ass dignity and his artistry with a golf club were irresistible to Jenkins. In his fiction, Jenkins used a phrase—"logo clod"—that referred to almost all modern golf professionals. To his disgust, Jenkins could not look at Andrew Magee— he'd call him *an* Andrew Magee—without being overwhelmed by commercials for beer, golf clubs, and clothes. Clark Dennis's hat is a display ad for computer disc drives. Elkington's lid sells Buicks. But logo-free Hogan sold nothing but himself.

"In the fourth round in '53," he says, "Hogan chipped in on five and birdied six. Where did he make his birdies on the back nine?" Hell if I know, Dan, you say. I'd have to look it up. Jenkins's look tells you that you have failed the test. You do not measure up either.

Jenkins had only been Hogan's *second* greatest champion until two months earlier. That's when Mrs. Hogan died, in June 1999. The waning days must have been sad but sweet for the angelic Valerie Fox Hogan, the golfer's wife of forty-two years. As a couple they were famously reticent, but starting about a year before her husband's death at age eighty-four, in July 1997, she began to talk to the press. She told a throwaway golf real-estate magazine that "Ben got depressed so easily," a revealing comment. It was satisfying to defend her husband against perceived inaccuracies—such as that he swore—and bittersweet to be reminded that he was gone. When she visited the new Ben Hogan Room at the USGA museum, she said, "I would give anything if he could be here, even if I were not here."

Dave Anderson of *The New York Times* walked with her between the exhibits and asked about her husband's greatest year as a golfer, 1953. "He didn't want to go to the British Open," she said. "He kept saying, 'I just think you want me to go over there to see me get beat.' "

Hogan was not getting beat very often in the early fifties, but each of the few tournaments he played cost him a piece of his constitution. He turned forty in August 1952, but admitted he felt like sixty, the inevitable result of his near-fatal collision with a Greyhound bus on Groundhog Day in 1949. Soon after his dramatic comeback to the top of his sport, Hogan realized the chronic pain in his aging body wouldn't allow him to continue as a professional athlete for long. So he started his preparations for life after golf: he would manufacture golf clubs. Typically, he didn't tell anyone about his plan.

In addition to physical and business worries, Hogan had a score of other reasons not to go to Scotland. The former World War II (stateside) flier no longer liked to get on a plane, because sitting aggravated his arthritis, so he'd want to make at least the return half of the trip via ocean liner. It would be cold by the North Sea, and his recently crushed and compressed body felt extra sore in chilly weather. Acclimating to the low shots and bump-and-run of links golf presented the least of his problems, since he'd grown up on a burnt-out, land-it-short golf course, Glen Garden in Fort Worth. But with the smaller golf ball used Over There, Hogan would be like a violinist with a new bow.

Finally, expectations would be an intangible but powerful obstacle. Hogan had entered five tournaments that spring and summer, and won four of them, including the Masters and the U.S. Open. Everyone including himself would expect another victory at Carnoustie. The pressure would be stifling.

No evidence has surfaced that Hogan cared a fig about the money that week, but as his rival and sort-of friend Sam Snead had told the world, the British Open was a loser for an American pro. Snead's appearance at St. Andrews in 1947 was a command performance, and the command was given by the president of Wilson Sporting Goods. Wilson supplied his clubs and balls, and provided his largest endorsement deal. Snead went, reluctantly. He won, but made no friends. He dissed the Old Course, a faux pas of epic proportions. "Snead, a rural American type, would undoubtedly think the Leaning Tower of Pisa a structure about to totter and crash at his feet," sniffed the London *Times*. Hillbilly Sam, who brought a new dimension to thriftiness, endured a four-hundred-dollar net loss on the trip. He never went back.

Despite everything, Hogan got on the boat. His announced motive for entering the Open was that people he respected, such as Tommy Armour, Walter Hagen, Bobby Cruickshank, and Claude Harmon, had been urging him to go for years, and now the time was right. But Hogan seldom if ever shared all his thoughts with the intrusive press. Posterity actually meant little to him. Probably his unspoken motivation was the same prosaic push that got Snead to St. Andrews. If he made a good impression, it would be good for trade; he could open up the European market for the as yet unbuilt Hogan golf clubs.

Why did Scotland love him so? The obvious explanation may be the best one: golf was the national game, Hogan was the best player in the world, and they'd never seen him. But the depth of feeling of the Scots toward the wee mon hints at other factors. Like other European countries and unlike the United States, Scotland in 1953 was still paying for World War II. It had enjoyed no baby boom, and none of the robustness a swelling population implies. About 5 million people resided in Scotland, only a small increase from the 1931 census. The home of golf was down-at-the-heels, left at the gate in the economic race, and ready for a hero.

Hero-worship requires emotional sacrifice and a willing vulnerability, traits often seen in golfers. While the Scots accepted and even savored the game's psychic punishments, they cannot be described as followers. When they did elevate a hero, however, they did it with all that they had. The deeds and words of William Wallace, King Robert the Bruce, and Robert Burns burn in the Scottish soul. Hogan is in that league too, at least in Carnoustie.

"Scotland really didn't have its own golf hero," says Jack Burke, Jr. "And don't forget that they got something out of it, too. By adopting Hogan, they could say, 'Our country made him. We gave him the stage for his biggest win.' "

Simply put, they liked his style. A Carnoustie schoolteacher named Robert Blyth remembers being transfixed by the silent little man. "You can't believe what an athlete this is! I'd never seen anything like him. The sound he got from that club on the ball . . . After I watched one of his practice rounds, someone asked me, 'What about his short game?' I said, 'He doesn't need a short game!'

"Hogan was very good-looking, extremely well-dressed, and so mannerly. Just the way he carried himself. Did the women fancy him too? Oh, yes!"

Love takes time, and Hogan arrived in Carnoustie on June 23 for a tournament that would begin on July 8. He seemed like a savior. A combination of things, including the Depression, World War II, and Snead, had shrunk the Open from the world championship it had been. According to the papers, three Americans were supposedly the equals to the greatest players in history, but in their lives Snead and Byron Nelson would play in only two British Opens each. Nelson made a favorable but muted impression, finishing third in a downpour at Carnoustie in '37, and didn't play again until 1955, well after his retirement as an active player. And Snead, well . . .

"Just a handful of us watched Hogan during his practice rounds, but then there was just an explosion," recalls Blyth. "Women with prams and everything." In the second round, in the desperate rush of spectators on the sixteenth hole trying to get to the seventeenth tee, Blyth almost knocked someone into the Barry Burn. "Pardon me," he said. He immediately recognized the face, though up close it was disturbingly pale and pockmarked. The skinny white man wore a tweed sports coat over a dark sweater, a white shirt buttoned to the neck, dark trousers, and brown leather golf shoes. In one of those deliciously unlikely intersections of famous people, such as when Charles Lindbergh conferred with Winston Churchill or when Elvis exchanged chitchat in the Oval Office with Richard Nixon, Frank Sinatra had come out to watch Ben Hogan play golf.

Hogan was Sinatra's pro; that is, Ben worked at the club where Frank was a member. The previous winter, Hogan had begun his very light, very part-time duties at Tamarisk in the Southern California desert. They met then, because the crooner had plenty of time for golf.

The two Americans were, as they say, a study in contrasts. At the very moment Hogan peaked, Sinatra's career and personal life were circling the drain. After his overused vocal cords hemorrhaged at a nightclub in 1950, and after a sloppy divorce from his first wife, Nancy, Sinatra's hysterical popularity with young women vanished. MGM canceled his movie contract. Talent agency MCA dropped him as a client. He was broke, and his second wife, actress Ava Gardner, was already rattling divorce papers. That he'd been booked for two shows in gritty Dundee indicated his sorry state; that Caird Hall echoed with empty seats was worse. At the start of the first performance, Sinatra surveyed the half-empty theater and invited those seated in economy to move up to the fifteen-shilling seats in first class. Fifteen shillings was about a buck.

Redemption was just a month away. With the release of the film version of *From Here to Eternity* in August 1953, Sinatra's career rebounded. Why had he been so low in the first place? "It happened because I paid no attention to how I was singing," he said. "Instead I wanted to sit back and enjoy my success and sign autographs and bank the heavy cash." Hogan at Carnoustie may have given young Blue Eyes some hints regarding self-control and dedication to craft. He might also have taught him something about golf.

"I shall never forget the first morning of the championship and the sight of his opening strokes piercing the cold, gray wind," wrote Pat Ward-Thomas, the golf correspondent for the Manchester *Guardian.* "His scores—73-71-70-68—made a ruthless downward progression." Every Hoganophile knows a few other details of his ruthless downward progression: the Open then was contested in three days, Wednesday through Friday, and the Little Man got sick with flu in the middle of it, and played the double round on Friday on almost no sleep. He lost fourteen pounds during his stay. There were no gallery ropes, so six Scottish policemen encircled him as he walked around the course. The weather was alternately tolerable and atrocious; on the sixth hole in the final round, it *sleeted,* for godsakes. The final-round 68 was a course record. As he limped to the final green—remember his injuries from his car crash—the players on the seventeenth hole gave Hogan a rare salute: they stopped their own games and watched his. He won by four. During the entire tournament, he never knew a yardage. He never missed a fairway.

And his birdies on the back nine came at 13 and 18.

But with the Open's return to Carnoustie in 1999, new light fell on the Hogan legend.

For many years, visitors to Carnoustie Golf Links who did not have the time or the game to play the course have asked merely to be shown the sixth hole. According to a lot of people who were not there and a few who were, Hogan drove his ball on this long par five into a frighteningly narrow passageway between a nasty pot bunker on the right and white out-of-bounds stakes on the left. Taking this direct, daring line to the hole symbolized both the great man's fearlessness and his control. Carnoustieites encouraged the story. Philp and others tried to get the hole renamed from Long to Hogan's Alley.

But was Hogan's Alley, the linchpin of Carnoustie's self-promotion, a sham? In early 1999, a St. Andrews golf professional came forward to debunk. "Hogan was paired with Hector Thomson for the last two rounds, and Hector was one of my best friends," recalls Elliot Rowan, a well-regarded instructor. "I watched every shot. So I had to smile when Peter Alliss said on the television that Hogan drove it in the corridor all four days, because he definitely played out to the right the last two. Then a four-wood [actually a two-wood] and a pitch onto the green. It would have been out of character, wouldn't it, for him to challenge two severe hazards when a safe path was available to him on the right. And he still made birdies."

Rowan went public with his corrections in a letter to *Golf Monthly*. But no one in Carnoustie in July 1999 wanted to believe it, least of all the television commentators. Then you meet Dr. Nigel Gracey of Stratford-upon-Avon in the rare-books booth inside the billowing retail tent. Here is a man to settle the issue.

"I just came up on the train from Cambridge and presented myself," Gracey says. " 'Does any match need a marshal?' 'Yes,' they said, 'Hogan's.' I walked with him all four rounds. I was off scratch at the time, but watching Hogan made me want to give up golf. I didn't know the game could be played that well."

Gracey would go on to achieve such eminence in his field, psychology, that he lectures annually on the subject to newly qualified professionals on the European PGA Tour. But in 1953, armed only with a little flag and an armband on the coat of his gray wool suit, the young physician-in-training attempted to keep enough order for Hogan to play his shots. And did his shots include fence-hugging drives at the Long hole? No, Gracey says, they did not. Drives out to the right, followed by brassies on or close to the green. He also remembers this from the sixth: "In the third round Hogan was about to play his pitch to the green, and he threw his cigarette to the ground as he always did. He hit and the crowd engulfed him. Then for some reason I went through all those people and picked up his cigarette butt and put it in a matchbox, which I kept for a very long time."

John Derr dissents. "It's quite clear in my mind that he drove to the *left* of the bunker," states the longtime CBS radio and TV announcer. He, too, walked every step with Hogan that week. "What is annoying," added Derr, "is that so many experts regarding Hogan have come out of the woodwork in the last few years. I read so many things that I sometimes wonder if I was there."

While Hogan's Alley remains in fog, another part of the honeyed legend finally stood in sunlight. Hogan at Carnoustie would be remembered as a circumspect ambassador of golf and of himself, but he wasn't. Early in his fortnight in-country and before reverting to form as a perfect gentleman, Hogan snidely offered to lend the Carnoustie greenkeeper his lawn mower, so unkempt was the course in his eyes. He spoke of his dislike of the fairways, which he thought were too hard and too scarred by divots. The brownstone Bruce Hotel did not suit him; he checked out before the ink on the register dried, in favor of a house in Dundee.

Three weeks later, on the day the USS *United States* docked in New York and Ben and Valerie disembarked for a tickertape parade, reporters asked him about the difference between golf here and there.

First of all, Hogan noted that Carnoustie was "the hardest course I've ever played." But he didn't like it. "In Britain it seems they just throw up greens and tees and cut out a narrow fairway. They do nothing to the rest of the course. The fairways are just pieces of ground. They cut a swath through the grass, put a tee in, and let it go at that. You never have a level stance . . . and the countryside all blends into one, leaving you nothing to aim at."

Had David Duval or Tiger Woods bitched so systematically about their Carnoustie experience in 1999, their heads would have been on a pike on the Tay Bridge, and the media would have had bloody knives. But Hogan got a free pass. British golf writer Harry Chapman replied to the criticism with more civility than the critic. "Ben forgets golf originated in Scotland, and Scotsmen taught the Americans how to play the game. The 'plumb velvet' courses over there are artificial, man-made constructions and the fact that they bear no relationship to our courses is the Americans' fault—not the fault of the Scots."

One last Hogan mystery took forty-six years to solve. As a child cried in the background and movie cameras whirred, the new champion golfer two-putted for a birdie on the final hole, then a par five. He removed his flat tweed cap and shook Hector Thomson's hand, and the crowd saluted him with a deep-chested roar. Then Hogan vanished for a while.

We know that he walked out of the drizzle and into the tiny starter's box to do a CBS radio interview, because his interviewer, John Derr, is still around to tell about it. We also know that he did not have a jacket and would not appear for the cup presentation without one. He sent his caddie, Cecil Timms, to the car to fetch the light-gray single-breasted to complement the pale yellow of the two sweaters he was wearing.

"Within eight minutes of holing out, Ben was on the air with me," says Derr. "That's not much time to gather your thoughts, but I asked if his chip-in on the fifth wasn't the key to his round. Fortunately, Hogan thought it was, and he went into ecstasy describing it."

Derr stepped out of the hut to invite Valerie in out of the rain, but she declined. Hogan kept talking into the CBS microphone. Like the old pro that he was, he continued to address the absent Derr by name.

Despite the "ecstasy" Derr recalls, not much emotion infected Hogan's uninflected delivery. "And we come to the ninth hole, that's 483 yards," said the CBS radio sports director. The ninth looked a mile long and played into the wind. "And how many yards do you actually believe that hole is?"

"Well, it's about 483," Hogan said.

Meanwhile, the various actors in the final ceremony seated themselves on a platform on the first tee. The provost of Carnoustie, the four runners-up—Frank Stranahan, Peter Thomson, Antonio Cerda, and Dai Rees—and a score of Royal and Ancient officials talked among themselves, and looked at their watches, and waited. The appointed time for the speeches came and went. After another ten minutes, many of the fifteen thousand spectators began to chant "Why are we waiting? Why are we waiting?" Hogan finally appeared, jacketed and combing his hair. The crowd roared again, but they must have wondered, what had the wee mon been doing?

As Elliot Rowan recalls, Hogan did what anyone should do after playing thirty-six at Carnoustie. He drank a big glass of whisky.

STEVE ELKINGTON, WHO yields to no man in his love for Scotland, arrived a week early and brought his wife and kids. At the Glasgow airport he piled golf clubs and luggage in a rented red Jeep Grand Cherokee and proceeded to the Old Course Hotel, a two-hour drive. About twenty miles outside St. Andrews, where the motorway passes around Kinross and Ladybank, the landscape changes from attractive to dramatic. Motorists driving past the rounded, treeless hills wish they had a picnic lunch, or their easel, canvas, and paints, and they envy the cows and sheep that stand like statues in the green. But Elkington couldn't appreciate the scenery as he normally did.

Professional golfers don't travel with their families routinely, because of the expense and the disruption of home life. But the pro is never alone, because golf is the only game in which each contestant is attended by his own servant. Elkington's bearer, Joe "Gypsy" Grillo, was a bouncy little man with a closely trimmed gray mustache, a filter cigarette, and a gold elk medallion around his neck. Helluva hand on the basics of show up, keep up, shut up, and he comported himself with just the right amount of cool enthusiasm. Gypsy baby-sat Annie and Sam from time to time, and cooked expertly for the entourage at Augusta. After ten years on the Elkington bag, he'd become part of the family. Thus his boss could not help feeling some apprehension as he drove across Scotland, because Gypsy was back in San Antonio with the bête noire of sports injuries, the pulled groin.

"Who's your best caddie?" Elkington had asked on a phone call to the Carnoustie caddie master, Martin Roy. Roy's glasses magnify his brown eyes and often slip down his nose.

"I am," Roy replied, pushing up his specs.

Anxious to see the course and to meet his potential bagman, Elkington left for Carnoustie early Friday morning. Roy waited nervously by the front entrance to the new hotel, watching for a red Jeep. Was he really the best caddie? True, he'd been carrying clubs at Carnoustie links since 1967, when he was eleven, when he and his pals made fifty pence for eighteen holes and prayed for a tip. Now the fee was twenty-six pounds, a pound more than at Turnberry, a pound less than the Old Course. Roy had been dragging the caddie master's cut of 12.5 percent since 1983.

But he hadn't actually caddied at all this year. No, wait—he had once, in May, for some Charleston Whitfield III from Chicago. "Charleston Whitfield III" was the Carnoustie caddies' code name for their bread and butter, the prototypical American guest with a 22 handicap and a wallet.

"Visitors play about one third the rounds at Carnoustie but provide about two thirds the income," Roy explained. "The members rarely take a caddie." Annual membership was £215, payable to Angus County, which owns the three Carnoustie golf courses. Local players invariably join one of the seven clubs that play Carnoustie, which costs another £70 per year. The clubhouses for the Dalhousie, the Carnoustie, the Ladies, the Caledonia, and the others sit modestly across the street from the course. The new four-story hotel, white stone with redbrick accents, overpowers them and blocks their view.

Elkington arrived, and Roy toted and recited every yardage by heart during the practice round. Elkington played superbly, his long arms folding and unfolding like accordions. But the tall Australian did not commit to the shortish Scotsman. He wanted a little more time with him to see if they'd jell. "I'll see you again after my pro-am round tomorrow," Elkington said.

MEANWHILE, THE MAGEE party of eight played for the last few days across the Irish Sea. They also managed to get in some golf.

When planning his second annual pre–British Open trip to Ireland, Magee had noted that almost all Americans stayed in the south. The food was better there, thanks to the presence of many French chefs, and plenty of good golf courses dotted the land. He further observed the continuing factional violence in northern Ireland. "Let's go north," the contrarian suggested to his friends, and it came to pass.

The two foursomes of golfers and several of their wives convened at Dublin airport, a van and driver were hired, and the fun began. The parade route went up and down the island's east coast, and included stops at Royal Dublin, The K Club, and Royal County Down. An atmosphere of hilarity prevailed. "Last night my wife says to me, 'Let's go upstairs and have sex,' " related one of the older golfers. "I said, 'Honey, I can't do both.' "

Late in the week Magee put thirty beers in the van to sustain the troops for the hour-and-a-half drive between one golf course and that night's hotel. But the resultant nature calls were answered in pubs along the way, where more drinks were consumed, and the trip took six and a half hours. "A couple of us walked into one of the pubs with beers in our hands," Magee recalled. Coals to Newcastle: "We were asked to leave. Can you think of anything more ridiculous than bringing beer into a pub?"

Everyone involved considered the trip a success, thanks in large part to Magee's attitude. "I wouldn't give a damn if Andrew sold cars for a living, I'd still want to play golf with him," said David Glenn, a real-estate developer from Charlotte, who would go on to watch his friend in the Open. "He and Jay Haas are the two best guys on tour. They don't take themselves as seriously as a lot of guys on the Tour do."

Andrew and Susan Magee flew on to Scotland on Friday. Magee played in the Bruce Rappaport Pro-Am at the Dukes course at St. Andrews over the weekend, as did Elkington and a few dozen of the other top players. On Monday, the Magees checked into the Carnoustie

Hotel. The Elkingtons moved into a private home a five-minute drive from the golf course.

O N T U E S D A Y, A L L the cast and crew assembled for the first Open at Carnoustie in twenty-four years. Down the promenade between the hotel and the eighteenth green and first tee walked Bob Charles, the 1963 champion; Gary Player, who won here in 1969; and Tom Watson, the last Carnoustie champion. Up on the veranda above the walkway strode smiling Jack Newton, who lost by one in a play-off to Watson in that 1975 Open. From time to time you'd see Tony Jacklin (1969) and Peter Thomson, who like Watson won the Open five times.

But as the click and scratch of their spikes on the brick and concrete reminded you, Charles, Jacklin, Player, and Watson are still hale and would be actual competitors this week. Former Open champions are invited to try their luck until age sixty-five, if they are "still competitive." But Newton had not won and would not be playing. His plane ticket from Sydney had been paid for by Channel 4 in Australia. He was working.

Nostalgia did not fill the air. Perhaps nostalgia requires continuity, and two score is too long. Maybe nostalgia needs more visual landmarks than Carnoustie could provide. The drought-stricken course of 1975 certainly looked different from the lush 1999 version; now the shiny new hotel dominates the golf course's start and its finish. Furthermore, a warm look back undoubtedly requires warmth. "The ugliest surroundings in the universe," says BBC commentator Alistair Cooke, recalling the 1975 Open. "A hideous town. Those factories . . . [Writer Pat] Ward-Thomas and I stayed at the Old Course Hotel, and commuted to Carnoustie on the Hovercraft. We were the first, or among the first, to do so. And the tournament was held in the midst of the most appalling drought since the eighteenth century. There was not a blade of grass in Hyde Park that summer."

Cooke's review reflected a general disappointment in the last Open at Carnoustie. Not for nothing did the R and A stay away for almost a quarter of a century. Even the winner was a letdown. Armour, Cotton, Hogan, Player—the past champions were the best or nearly the best players of their eras, but this Watson was a cipher. He'd won two generic tournaments on the U.S. Tour, but if he was known at all in Europe, it was for losing the big ones when he might have won. But things changed for young Tom, of course, and he quickly climbed to his place in the pantheon with the other Carnoustie champs.

Jack Newton's life turned even more dramatically. In 1983, he stumbled while boarding a light airplane, at night, at the Sydney airport. The plane's propellers sliced off his right arm, carved out his right eye, and tore into his torso. Just months after the accident, with a black patch over his empty eye socket and his armless right sleeve pinned to his chest, Newton began his new career as a television golf analyst. "It was the New South Wales Open," recalls Ben Wright, who gave Newton his big break by inviting him into the TV booth. "Earthy people, those Australians. Jack described one putt as a 'knee-trembler,' which in British parlance means making love against a wall. He also said a certain putt by Graham Marsh was 'shit.' Neither comment caused the least notice."

The return of Watson and Newton to Carnoustie provided the natural hook for the nostalgia angle. Yes, they told the writers and the TV cameras, their hair was longer and their pants were plaider then, and it certainly was wonderful to be back. But if anyone hoped for tears or epiphany they were disappointed again. Watson is honest but guarded, Newton is honest but totally disinclined to self-pity; neither man is sentimental.

"A lot of whingers here this week," Newton observed. He'd paused for a moment in the doorway of the hotel restaurant. "And on top of it a lot of the American pros not showing up." Whingers? Is that like wankers? No, explained Newton, smiling behind orange-tinted glasses.

"Whingeing"—rhymes with singeing—"is complaining. But a wanker is a dickhead.

"And this superintendent is quite an outspoken man. I don't think he'd mind a fucking winning score of 300!"

Newton had identified the early mood of the 1999 Open: resentment. The players resented the course setup and the man they perceived to be responsible for it. John Philp resented the players for their lack of preparation. "They all say they love links golf," he said, "but few of them came here prepared to play it." The local newspapers amplified any complaints by the "millionaire golf pros." Several of the elites—including Tiger Woods, defending champion Mark O'Meara, and Greg Norman—commuted to Carnoustie by helicopter from the Old Course Hotel in St. Andrews, and this conspicuous consumption of jet fuel insulted some fans who'd arrived by overstuffed bus or train.

Those players who chose not to attend received particular scorn. Jeff Rude, a columnist for *Golfweek,* and Dave Seanor, his editor, met Clark Dennis as he was hanging around the first tee and eighteenth green at the Old Course. They'd just finished playing.

"I was talking with Tommy Armour [III] on the practice green at the Western Open," said Rude, whose beard and delivery remind you of an Old Testament prophet. "He says, 'So where should I go, Milwaukee or the British Open?' I say, 'Tommy, with who you are, the grandson of the 1931 champion, who won at Carnoustie, you've got to go. Sure, you'll have to qualify, but you could catch lightning in a bottle and it could make your life. You've *got* to go. Feed your *soul.'*" But Armour played in the Greater Milwaukee Open instead. He usually plays well there, he explained. Later, he said he regretted his decision.

"If players can't be bothered to participate in golf's majors, so be it," editorialized Seanor in his magazine's next issue. "That leaves more room for players such as Dennis, who appreciate golf's traditions and are hungry to compete."

And when Dennis didn't qualify, and thirteen Americans didn't show, that cleared space for qualifiers Jean Van de Velde of France; Paul Lawrie, a Scottish lad from Aberdeen; and the second-youngest Open qualifier in the twentieth century, Zane Scotland, from England. Van de Velde rested for a day, but the others got their first look at Carnoustie on Tuesday.

Scotland walked onto the overcrowded practice tee, his body language betraying nothing. But his hat, jacket, glove, golf bag, and shoes clearly showed he'd run into the Titleist and Footjoy representatives; accepting this booty did no harm to his status as an amateur, since both sides described it as a loan. He found a slot next to Greg Norman, who did not turn from his work to exchange pleasantries. In a minute, they were hitting simultaneously, Scotland's big, unhurried swing a counterpoint to Norman's fast slash. Both men attracted little knots of spectators, insiders who stood close and blocked the view of the people in the practice tee grandstand. Watching Scotland were his caddie, Ron Cuthbert; Scott Cranfield, his knit-browed instructor; four or five representatives of the media, including a TV talker and his cameraman; and Zane's father, Bernie.

Most of this troop followed Scotland out onto the golf course a few minutes later, and scurried up the first fairway in his wake. *USA Today* reporter Christine Brennan, arriving late for the party, cleared her throat and apologized for butting in. "This may be a stupid question," she said to Bernie, "but is Zane adopted?"

He paused for a long moment. "You're right," he said finally into the awkward silence. "That is a stupid question." But a logical one: Bernie Scotland is about five feet seven, and Zane stands around six feet. Moreover, Bernie is a black man, and his son does not appear to be.

Bernie obviously feels Zane's heritage is an irrelevancy, as though these writers want to talk about the size of his son's shoes. His people are from the Caribbean islands of Dominica and Antigua, he explained, and his wife, Zane's mother, is Irish. Bernie mentions that one of his great-great-grandfathers was a Scottish judge. Although he offers no speculation on the matter, a considerable number of Scots in the eighteenth and nineteenth centuries ran slaves from Africa to the sugar and cotton plantations in the islands. This could account for the slightly unusual surname.

"Is it safe to say Zane is the best black golfer in Great Britain?" asks another writer. Bernie Scotland smiles at this. He does not want the racial issue to get off the ground; these American journalists seem obsessed by it, and anxious to write about "the European Tiger Woods."

" 'Safe'? " he repeats. "I don't know if it's safe."

Most of his son's whistling tee shots hit and stay in the thin ribbons of Carnoustie fairway, but every third or fourth one burrows in the carefully cultivated jungle. As the round wears on, writers drop in and out of formation behind Bernie like a chevron of geese on a long flight. Without ever losing track of his son's shots, he speaks happily about his family.

Zane Scotland was born in London on July 17, 1982, the second and last child of Bernie and Ann. His older sister and only sibling is Gina, age twenty-six. Bernie is in sales for an energy company, Ann works for a mortgage company. Their home course is Woodcote Park Golf Club in Coulsdon, where the Scotlands live. His slope-shouldered son first picked up a golf club at age eleven. "Within six weeks," says Bernie, "I knew he could be a good golfer." Zane has won several important tournaments, set the course record at Woodcote Park despite a bogey-bogey start, and represented England in the Young Masters tournament.

"I've been telling Zane all week, whatever happens, whether you're in bunkers all day long, just enjoy it," says Bernie. "Say to yourself, 'I'm in a bunker at Carnoustie, in the biggest tournament in the world.' "

Unlike some parents of golf or tennis prodigies, he does not hover, or call attention to himself. He never banged garbage-can lids while his kid hit practice putts, as Earl Woods did. He feels his twelve handicap disqualifies him from giving swing or strategic advice to his son, so Bernie confines himself to bankrolling Zane's tournament expenses and offering such nuggets as "Golf is life explained in a sport."

You wrestle with the wisdom or the folly of that statement and trudge along. During a lull while his young boss hits chip shots to the ninth green, you chat up Scotland's caddie. He hands you his card. "Ron Cuthbert," it says, "remedial therapist, sports fitness consultant." Cuthbert has the approachable manner for the one and the muscles for the other. In addition to carrying the bag in big competitions, he works with Zane on his mental approach to golf, and his nutrition.

"Zane has got a great head for this game," Cuthbert says, touching his graying temple. "We're together up here." He adds that the gallery at Zane's qualifying round had been "marvelous, bloody marvelous. I said I was thirsty and thirty water bottles appeared."

Cuthbert, who has never caddied in a tour event or seen Carnoustie before today, wants the kid to keep it light, have a laugh. But Scott Cranfield wants Zane to bear down. On the practice tee and while walking from here to there on the grounds, Scotland's instructor stays near his ear, a protective, bodyguardlike posture. Not all of the monologue is "keep that left arm straight" stuff; he's mostly concerned that Zane will be overwhelmed by all this: the media, the gallery, and the discouragingly long and trouble-filled golf course.

Instructor Cranfield is thirty-two, blond, handsome, and wound tighter than a hundred-compression Titleist. When he's not on the European tour, you can usually find him at the Fairways Golf Center on Southend Road in London. An up-and-comer, he has two other clients in the competition, Philip Price, from Pontypridd, Wales, and Swedish star Per-Ulrik Johansson. "I was obsessed with golf at age sixteen, like Zane is," he says. "I made a lot of mistakes." He lists the biggest possible pitfalls: that Zane will think more about how he looks and how his shots look than about his score; that he becomes influenced by the not-always-well-meaning people around him, hangers-on Cranfield calls SNIOPs—Susceptible to the Negative Influence of Other People; and that Zane might stop looking out for himself, in terms of diet, exercise, and mental discipline.

After the round, someone notices that Scotland has drawn the same first-round starting time, 4:05, as Justin Rose had a year before at Royal Birkdale. Rose, from Hampshire, England, and then just seventeen, had shocked the golf establishment by finishing fourth. He holed a forty-five-yard wedge on the final hole, his last shot as an amateur. He turned pro and lost his game, an unfortunate and not uncommon occurrence. Rose missed the cut in his first twenty professional tournaments. Would Zane turn pro? Was there a plan?

"Everyone keeps asking about Justin and Zane," says Bernie Scotland. "But they're completely different players from very different situations. Maybe if Zane were older and the sponsorships were there, the management was there, and he finishes fourth here, maybe then it would be a lot tougher to resist turning pro."

Cranfield agrees. "Every coach of a junior golfer learned a lesson after that," he says. "You've got to come into the game in a quieter way. I don't want him to burn out too quickly."

If his instructor has his way, Zane will resist the college golf scholarships offered by Kent State, Purdue, and Tennessee. He'd like him to stay in Europe and play amateur tournaments after he finishes high school in four weeks. Lead a balanced life, and get a part-time job. "In a petrol station, perhaps."

MAGEE PLAYED A PRACTICE ROUND at nine-thirty with Justin Leonard and Mark Brooks, friends who also have ties to Dallas/Fort Worth. Scotland teed off forty minutes later. Elkington, Hal Sutton, Nick Price, and Frank Nobilo rode in golf carts from the distant practice fairway to the putting green and then strolled to the first tee at ten past one. For all but about fifty yards of their journey, fences shielded them from close contact with paying customers. "Frank and I, ten-pound Nassau," said Elkington, orchestrating the bet. The others nodded.

Civilians with some close connection to the players—family, friends, agents, manufacturers—were allowed to follow the practice rounds from inside the ropes. For Elkington that meant Deddick Cah—spelled Derek Carr—a chap from Ayr he'd befriended five years before at the Dunhill Cup in St. Andrews. Carr splits his time between the hairdresser's shop he runs with his wife, and the Turnberry golf course, where he owns a useful five handicap. He greets long-lost friends with "You bostid!" and a jack-o'-lantern grin. A part-time professional musician, he keeps his best set of bagpipes and a kilt in the trunk of his old Mercedes, in case a serenade is suddenly needed. Elkington has been calling him "Wayne" lately, as in wayne-cah (wanker). When Carr prepared to return to Scotland after watching Elkington at the 1999 Masters, the Aussie hid a pine log in the bottom of his friend's carry-on luggage. Carr carried the timber all the way back to Ayrshire. He's been thinking about payback ever since.

"He's hitting it beautifully," Carr observed as Elkington striped another three-wood into an impossibly narrow Carnoustie fairway. "I'll take a gross of those," Elkington said. "Christ, Elk!" said Price. "Can't you save that till Thursday?" Although Nobilo was hitting it sideways, and shooting something in the mid- to upper eighties, Sutton and Price quickly fell two down.

A walk with four of the best golfers in the world might have yielded insight into grip or tempo or attitude or what they say to their caddies, or to one another. But other thoughts intruded. The bubbling controversy regarding the height and ubiquity of the rough had to be considered, as well as the related question of fairness. "Carnoustie is not a Mickey Mouse course with the same hazard repeated eighteen times," Alistair Cooke said. "It has every kind of trouble you can imagine." But one thing Cooke had said about Carnoustie crowded out everything else. "The ugliest surroundings in the universe," he'd stated, while standing before the living room window of his Manhattan apartment. Two hundred feet below and across Fifth Avenue, Central Park stretched out like a mural, and beyond that the Hudson River shimmered in the late afternoon sun.

Central Park, the masterwork of Frederick Law Olmsted, saved

New York City from urban ugliness. Its careful landscaping incidentally provided a model—or, at least, inspiration—for Augusta National. Almost everyone copied Augusta National, the prototypically "beautiful" golf course, which was isolated from Augusta, Georgia, by pine trees and hedges. But Carnoustie bears no resemblance to the original gated golf course community. It is just *there,* in the town, as are St. Andrews and Prestwick and Musselburgh. And what borders Carnoustie golf links? Well, it doesn't have the ocean; the North Sea is visible from only a few spots on a few holes, such as at the top of the Spectacles bunkers near the green on the fourteenth. In fact, much of Carnoustie links is below sea level. Gary Player once called the course "a good swamp spoiled." What it does have is a railway, the town itself, and what Cooke called "those factories."

The factories squat in all their galvanized steel glory along the eastern edge of the burgh, just across the railroad tracks from the course. You can't miss 'em. For about one hundred years the one with the shiny storage silos manufactured vitriol—aromatic sulfuric acid. They also blended ground phosphate rock from North Africa with their acid to make a superphosphate of lime fertilizer. As you'd suspect, the vitriol works stunk. The basic process of roasting iron pyrite to make sulfur provided a steady stench; and from time to time a poisonous brown gas called nitrogen dioxide spewed out of the plant, gagging golfers and playing havoc with gardens and grass. Now Paul's Maltings blends malt for whisky and beer at the site, and you hope to hell they replaced those tanks.

The Panmure Works, the Smeaton family's redbrick jute-spinning operation, sits next door to the stink factory. It began in 1855 and ceased operations in the 1960s. It has been converted into an attractive "multiuse facility." Also in industrial row is the Anderson-Grice engineering company, makers of the world's largest stonecutting saws. A cloth banner stretched on the golf course side of Anderson-Grice's neighbor informed Open Championship guests that DICK PRE-CAST CONCRETE LTD. now resides therein. Perhaps it is no coincidence that most of residential Carnoustie is constructed of precast concrete; some of it must be Dick.

The other building dominating the golf course perimeter is one Cooke would not have seen in 1975: the hotel. Architectural critics gave the building mixed reviews after its opening in the spring of 1999. Some objected to its frank imitation of the Old Course Hotel; others, mostly Carnoustieites, disliked its sheer size. Turned the town into a bloody destination resort. "It's pretty bland and boring, kind of the no-frills Scottish style," said an American woman. "You certainly don't think you're in Italy." But the comfortable, carpeted changing rooms on the ground floor unquestionably improve the golfer's lot. And the nine-feet-two-inch-diameter clock embedded high in the wall facing the eighteenth green of the championship course was a brilliant touch. The world's largest Rolex comforts and unifies those who can see it, like a clock tower on a village green.

Does the perceived homeliness on its perimeter extend to the golf course? Well, yes and no. Although its setting is not inspiring, Carnoustie scores high on the aesthetic elements golf course architects like to talk about. Its proportions are pleasing, that is, its tees, bunkers, fairways, and especially its greens relate well to the ground they are built on. The full palette of colors and contrasts assert themselves in Philp's rough, presenting a far more pleasing aspect than the unbroken green of an American course. And Carnoustie fits in, rather than look-ing placed on. In other words, the details of the golf course echo the larger geography. When Walt Whitman wrote of "the beautiful uncut hair of graves" of Civil War dead, he could have been referring to the mounds and dunes on and near Carnoustie links.

But beauty is a feeling, not a formula, and it rarely coexists with anxiety. And anxiety was all that Carnoustie gave its contestants and sympathetic fans. The colors and shapes in the rioting rough pleased the eye but ruined the perspective. Since a ball in the rough amounted to a one-shot penalty, it was as if every narrow fairway was bordered by a water hazard. Even in their practice rounds, Elkington and his friends hit two-irons and fairway woods from the tees, rarely drivers.

Hogan's Alley told the tale. Given the myth surrounding it, and the fact that it's a par five with one of the few elevated tees on the course, the sixth should have provided a few volts of electricity a third of the way onto the course. The organizers fully expected this to happen; they erected a grandstand by the tee. They also built a new fairway bunker, despite such fierce local opposition that the consortium of Carnoustie clubs at first refused to allow it. The R and A was nonplussed; no host club had ever turned it down before, a fact the championship secretary, Sir Michael Bonallack, mentioned in a sternly worded letter to the local committee.

"In the Scottish Open here in 1996, Tiger Woods carried the Hogan bunker with such ease he only had a nine-iron to the green," recalls Philp. "Several others hit midirons. But when we [Philp and the R and A's architect, Donald Steel] suggested a look at more central bunkering on number six, the members said, 'We're not having that! It's historical!' By the gods! You should be able to adjust to the modern players by adjusting the course. All we wanted was to recover Carnoustie's reputation—tough but fair—*and not dependent on the weather.*"

They went back and forth for a while, with the Carnoustie jury voting seven-to-five against. Finally, after an exchange of letters in November 1998, the R and A prevailed, and Philp and his men dug the new sandpit in the center of the fairway. But the locals successfully stipulated that the new bunker would be filled in within two weeks of the conclusion of the Open, and that the Royal and Ancient Golf Club of St. Andrews would pay for both the digging and the filling.

Who would dare take the direct Hogan line to the sixth green? Who might hit into the Hogan bunker, and recover miraculously or fail to disastrously? From the way Elkington and his group played it on Tuesday, the answer was nobody. For not only did the new bunker dampen the gambling impulse, so too did the incredibly vigorous rough, the out-of-bounds left, and a new back tee. The hole now measured 578 yards. The distance from new tee to new bunker: 315 yards, a carry that would require the kind of fast-twitch swing no one wanted to use on a tight hole. Unless the R and A moved the tee markers forward, the sixth threatened to be a drive from Dallas to El Paso in third gear. Which is to say, boring, unprofitable—and unfair.

Every contestant at Carnoustie talked about it, every writer wrote about it. Not since O. J. Simpson's acquittal had fairness received such a public debate. Golf justice is as hard to get as the legal kind, and it's just as tricky to define. But at its heart, a fair test communicates what is required, while an unfair golf course contradicts itself. Don't give me both a forced carry and a green that won't hold a well-struck shot. If you present me with a 470-yard par four, at least give me space to hit my driver off the tee. Fast greens are okay if you don't cut the cup on a slope. Blind shots offend some, but tiny hidden hazards are an abomination. High rough may be a necessary evil at a championship venue, but the penalty for straying into the hay should be no more than one shot. If I hit the ball five yards off the fairway and you hit it thirty yards crooked but get a better lie, that may not be fair, but it is golf. A certain randomness is perfectly all right. When I want uniformity, I'll play indoor tennis.

On the other hand, I do want uniformly level tees, eighteen greens that roll at similar speeds, and hot dog stands and sanitary facilities at regular intervals. Carnoustie had these last four items, but was it fair?

No, said David Duval. "You can't judge your golf game on this course," he said. "Good shots end up in the hay, bad shots end up on the green." No, said Phil Mickelson. "I don't think there's an individual in the R and A who could break 100 on this course." No, said Nick Price. "If I were a spectator, I'd ask for my money back." No, Alister Mackenzie and Donald Ross would have said. Both of the twentieth century's greatest golf architects abhorred high rough, even for major championships. They put the trouble near their greens, not off their tees. "Narrow fairways bordered by long grass make bad golfers," wrote Mackenzie. "They do so by destroying the harmony and continuity of the game, and in causing a stilted and cramped style . . . of play."

But architects fade in importance with each year of a golf course's life, and the superintendent's influence rises as the architect loses sway. Carnoustie's original designer was long gone. Allan Robertson, a short, swarthy golf pro and ball maker from St. Andrews, had formalized the routing of Carnoustie in 1850.

Fair? Of course Carnoustie is fair, said John Philp. Introduced to Susan Magee and Linda Sluman (wife of Jeff) on Tuesday afternoon, Philp may have wondered what their husbands had been saying about him. He didn't give them an opening to kvetch. "Did you hear what Colin Montgomerie said on the radio this morning?" asked the superintendent. "He said we should stop complaining. Said Carnoustie is real golf. 'Real golf.' That's refreshing." Mrs. Magee and Mrs. Sluman smiled and excused themselves to go buy some cashmere sweaters in the tented village.

In May, two months before the battle, Philp had stated the case quite clearly. "The R and A thinks par should mean something again, and I agree. If a player shoots two-under a day in the championship, okay. The best players in the world, in competition, should be able to break par. But if scores reach fifteen to twenty under par, there's something wrong with the test." Later, R and A officials would claim not to have given the matter a thought. It's all relative, they said.

"The trouble is, there's no Bobby Jones around today to explain to the R and A and the USGA why what they're doing is stupid," asserts Geoff Shackelford, a well-known golf historian and author. "The old saying is that on a championship course, you should be able to show up two days before the tournament and have it ready to go. There's a lot of truth to that. So why do they go to a place with great architecture—like Carnoustie or Pebble Beach—and try to obscure the architecture?

"We don't want to watch pro basketball played with a medicine ball. But people who can't play the game run the tournaments. They've made course setup a control issue, an ego contest. . . . I don't think they have any idea how good the players are today."

Fair? Unfair? The whole question doesn't get off the ground for those who point out that everyone has to play the same golf course. "It's a matter of complete indifference to me whether the professional shoots 60 or 80," says golf critic and author John Strawn. "Therefore the idea of 'defending the course' against low scores is a waste of time. We want each course to have its own identity and flavor, but then we force them to have the same par of 70 or 71 or 72. We should get used to the idea of a flexible par."

Par wasn't always such a hard-and-fast thing, or such a preoccupation. On the eve of the 1953 Open, an American radio interviewer asked the London *Daily Telegraph* golf writer Leonard Crawley an innocent question: what is par at Carnoustie?

"I'll have to avoid answering that question," replied Crawley. "The wind is such at Carnoustie that you never could set par. Some days it might be 69. Usually, it's about 73, 74, or 75."

Par or no par, golf grades the golfer every time he plays. This has led to a form of mental illness peculiar to ardent golfers whose lone, terrifying symptom is the delusion that you are what you shoot. Who are those two guys at the bar? That's a 79 and an 81. Who's that self-crucifying pro hitting another hundred practice balls? That's Mr. 78 with a double bogey on eighteen. With his self-esteem tied to specific numbers between 59 and 72, how could the world-class golf professional shoot 85 without wanting to kill someone?

P UNTERS BET ON the usual suspects to win. Woods, Duval, Montgomerie, Davis Love III, and Spanish phenom Sergio Garcia attracted the most money in Great Britain's legal betting parlors. But this looked like the time to ignore the world rankings for a week. The winner would have to endure many insults to his sense of what constitutes a good score and thus to his definition of himself. He'd need the emotional resilience of a telemarketer, and a chameleon's adaptability. In tennis, a baseliner; in boxing, a counterpuncher; in baseball, a gamer; some little guy who was used to being knocked down but was too smart or too stupid to ever give up.

"I would be very surprised if Tiger Woods does well," said Alistair Cooke, who finds the world's top-ranked player to be too emotional for the horrors at Carnoustie. "When he makes a putt, he's won the Battle of Britain," Cooke said. "When he misses, it's the Holocaust."

Jack Newton shook his head as he gazed out from the hotel at the rust-red rough. "They've taken everybody out except for what I call the par accumulator," he said. "Some bloke like Lee Janzen."

Magee didn't have the record, although he seemed to possess the sense of humor to do well. Elkington had the pedigree and seemed to have his game in order, until you noticed how poorly he'd done in third and fourth rounds since his last illness. As for Zane Scotland, you only hoped he could avoid a truly embarrassing score. But some survivor would figure out the game.

Perhaps Scottish history provided the model for the coming tournament. In 1396, one hundred years after Wallace, the Scots were feuding among themselves as fiercely as they'd battled the English. To settle an intractable dispute over land or castles or cattle, King Robert III ordered Clan Chattan and Clan Kay to choose thirty men each to fight to the death. Fourteen pounds and change were dipped from the royal treasury to build a wood-and-iron gladiators' arena in a meadow in Perth, just thirty-five miles up the River Tay from Carnoustie. A huge crowd appeared to watch the slaughter, including the king and his court.

The Chattans enjoyed a good day with axes, swords, and daggers, and in time only one member of Clan Kay remained standing. You imagine this man with blood on his face and the smell of blood in his nostrils, cornered, outnumbered, panting, spectators screaming, and all his allies dead. So the last Kay did the only sensible thing: he climbed the wall and swam the Tay.

That flexible attitude seemed to be just the thing for the Carnoustie battlefield 603 years later.

CHAPTER THREE

Maurice Flitcroft,
Professional Golfer

Some of the regular players are neighboring lairds who have driven in dog-carts from their homes in Fife; others from farther afield, like Colonel Fairlie from Prestwick, having an eye on the seduction of Tom Morris; some are teachers from the university; some are men of business from Edinburgh like Mr. Blackwood, who has now and again to go back and look after his famous magazine, thus, to the horror of old Mr. Sutherland, "Wasting a Monday"; others like Clanranald and Carnegie, the poet, who described them all in cheerful verse, have homes in St. Andrews from which to play golf.

—*Bernard Darwin, describing the scene at*
the Old Course in 1848 in
A History of Golf in Britain

THE HISTORY OF the British Open is like a Bernard Darwin sentence: filled with commas, detours, subordinate clauses, and people you've never heard of. But unlike Darwin's writing, the 140-year-old Open is still fresh and alive.

The Open survived two world wars, a virtual boycott by the nation with the most and often the best golfers, and equipment changes as profound as the bamboo-to-fiberglass evolution in the pole vault. The late-coming Americans arrogated to themselves the three other majors—and invented the very concept of majorhood—but the original Championship was not diminished, except in the eyes of the Colonists.

The Open prospered partly for the things it did not have to endure. Other sports franchises have had to wink and spin past drug and cheating scandals, corrupt owners, and players who couldn't care less how they are perceived. And does the National Football League executive call twenty-one of his friends on autumn Fridays? "I'll bring the anabolic steroids, you find the white vinyl go-go boots for the cheerleaders, get Chuck to hire the referees. In the Sheep Meadow at noon." You may regard the R and A as a bunch of gouty old farts, but its members play the game themselves, on the same courses as the heroes inside the ropes, with the same clubs, the same balls, and by the same rules. The lawyers, cynics, and marketers running the other sports ultimately hollow and cheapen their games. R and A and the USGA have the lawyers—in spades—and a growing cadre of beady-eyed beancounters, but their participation in the game they administer ennobles their efforts.

Two other things have helped make the Open the longest-running major sports event, and both are as foreign to the United States as room-temperature beer. First is the club system in the United Kingdom. In the United States, the golf-course real estate *is* the club. Not so Over There. At Carnoustie, for example, clubs called Dalhousie, Caledonia, Carnoustie, and Ladies have their own clubhouses near the course, their own tournaments, and their own lore and history. Thus you will read that Carnoustie Club was founded in 1851, but that golf has been played in the town at least since "the zeir 1547 or thereabouts," according to one old record, and there is no contradiction.

So it has always been. A club calling itself The Honourable Company of Edinburgh Golfers played at Musselburgh for fifty-five years; when the more pleasing golf ground down the coast at Muirfield became available in 1891, they simply abandoned Musselburgh. The St. Andrews Society of Golfers was at heart just another bunch of guys who liked to play golf and drink together. When in 1834 the club's secretary convinced King William IV to bestow his royal patronage—and a new name—the Royal and Ancient Golf Society of St. Andrews began to achieve preeminence.

The rota system—a fixed list of host courses—is the Open's other unique strength. Of the eight proud hosts, five are in Scotland: Carnoustie, Muirfield, St. Andrews, Troon, and Turnberry. The other three—Birkdale, Lytham, and St. George's—are in England. Administrators in the United States cannot bring themselves to imitate it. The Masters, of course, never moves from its Georgia hillside. And the USGA and the PGA believe that secretive competition gets them more money, so site selection for their championships has a cloak-and-dagger air. Sometimes members at a potential host course simply don't want to be bothered. "But can you imagine anyone at Troon wanting to turn down the Open over worries about parking?" asks Dallas golf pro and historian Gilbert Freeman. "Tradition is so powerful there, and so is the anticipation of hosting the Open every seven or eight years."

And so is the disappointment of falling out of the rotation. When Muirfield permanently replaced poor little Musselburgh as the Open host in 1892, the jilted Musselburghers hosted their own mini-Open a week before the real thing. But Bob Ferguson's home course had only nine holes. Not enough. The Open had gotten big.

CENTURY-OLD IRON DRAINPIPES snake along the exterior wall at the back of the clubhouse, the side facing the street. Tracks from the Glasgow and Southwestern Railway hug the right side of the first fairway, and you could throw a ball from the train station and knock off someone's hat on the first tee. If you're not hearing a train, it's because the scream of a jumbo jet is drowning out the clickety-clack; there's an airport on the other side of the tracks. Salvaged railroad ties—"sleepers," in local parlance—are the main building material of the exquisitely hand-made course. The locker room is a musty rabbit warren with bad light illuminating wooden locker fronts so brown they look like they've been rubbed with tobacco spat from Old Tom's mouth. The lockers date from 1882; in those days they called them "boxes." Not a lot of pretense at Prestwick, the host of the first twelve Opens. But its history is as thick as Scottish fog.

Out of the fog stepped a refugee. Things had gotten uncomfortable for Old Tom Morris in his hometown of St. Andrews. He worked for Allan Robertson, the original golf pro, who derived a crucial part of his income from the tedious manufacture of leather-and-feather golf balls. In or around 1848, someone asked Robertson to try one of the new high-tech gutta-percha balls. He topped it on purpose and announced that you couldn't get the damn things in the air. Molded from the rubbery sap of a Malaysian tree, guttas cost a fraction of a feathery, so Robertson bought as many as he could and threw them away. When he discovered his apprentice actually playing one of the despised pellets on the links, they had words. And Old Tom quit, or was fired, depending on who told the story.

The introduction of a cheap, durable ball, the greatest-ever advance in golf equipment, led Morris to Prestwick. Between the ball and the Industrial Revolution, the sport was enjoying its first boom. Golfers began to outnumber soccer players, shooters, and wheelbarrow-pushing seaweed pickers (good fertilizer for the garden) on Prestwick's multipurpose grounds by the sea. Let's have a golf club! someone said, probably Colonel James Ogilvy Fairlie, from nearby Coodham. The new Prestwick Golf Club invited Old Tom to build and maintain a twelve-hole golf course on its links land, which had been a gift to the city from King Robert the Bruce. Morris, Sr., accepted, and in 1851 moved from the east coast to the west coast with his wife and infant son. And he named his next son James Ogilvy Fairlie Morris.

As its hiring of the best golfer in Scotland proved, the Prestwick men were go-getters. In 1856, they proposed the idea for the first-ever tournament for professional golfers. No one got behind the idea, not the R and A, not the Honourable Company, no one. Four years later, Prestwick decided to go it alone. Again, J. O. Fairlie led the way. A letter he wrote in September 1860 hints at the reason for the lack of enthusiasm from the lords and gentlemen: "In regard to the entry of players and to avoid having any objectionable characters, we think that the best plan is to write to all the secretaries of all the golfing societies requesting them to name & send their two best professional players—depending on them for their Characters. This will make us quite safe. . . ." Professional golfers then were almost always also caddies. Caddies drank.

Fairlie announced that the winner of the National Tournament would be given "a highly ornamented Belt . . . to be challenged for every year—until won by the same player three years in succession when it becomes his property." The club paid £25 to an Edinburgh jeweler for the red leather belt with an ornate silver buckle.

Just before noon on Wednesday, October 17, 1860, the eight competitors in the first Open met in front of the Red Lion Hotel across the street from the club. They heard a speech about the rules—"the game to be thirty-six holes or three rounds of Prestwick Links, the player who succeeds in holing his ball in the lowest number of strokes to be the winner." The players signed a sheet of paper indicating their acceptance, then walked across the street to the course. They carried a bit of pine pitch in their pockets, and applied it to their palms to keep their clubs from slipping. With their whiskers, rough tweed jackets, baggy pants, and substantial boots, the players crossing Links Road resembled lumberjacks more than golfers. But the October wind off the Firth of Clyde and the litter left everywhere by the club's mowers—sheep—dictated their dress.

Tom Morris, Sr., the host professional, hit the first shot.

A good-size crowd followed the four twosomes around the course. Morris and Robert "the Rook" Andrew of Perth attracted the most wagers, but Andrew didn't have it that day and suffered through a 191.

Willie Park of Musselburgh shot 174 to win by two over Morris. They moved fast: teeing off at noon, the entire field played thirty-six holes before dark.

At Prestwick's Autumn Meeting the next year, the club resolved that "the Challenge Belt . . . shall be Open to all the World." But even with gentleman amateurs participating, only eight players competed in 1862. Increased prize money in 1867—up to £7 for first—swelled the field to ten. Why so small? Partly because the idea of an open tournament was so foreign. Run-of-the-mill players had their club competitions, and the gods—named Morris, Park, Dunn, and Simpson—played challenge matches for big stakes, two against two.

Young Tom didn't help. His dominance, like that of his father (four wins) and Park (three), discouraged his rivals. Tommy began playing in the National Tournament at age fifteen, and finished ninth; by age seventeen, he was unbeatable. He would hit a long putt and start walking toward the next tee, saying to his caddie, "Take it out of the hole, laddie." He ended the Belt era by winning three consecutive times on the links where he grew up. In the third of these, in 1870, Young Tom won by twelve shots, a mind-boggling margin in a thirty-six-hole event.

Tommy's 149 that year broke the tournament record by five shots, and may have been the best performance in a Prestwick Open. His win the previous year qualifies as one of the Open's most unusual denouements, because he didn't actually lead at the end by himself. He and his pa tied at 154, but Tommy took the Belt, presumably because he had the lower final twelve holes, 52 to Old Tom's 53.

But Prestwick would be known as the home of disaster, not of triumph. Harold Hilton's 9, James Braid's 8, and John Henry Taylor's 7 became stories to tell over a glass of whisky, the stories spiced by mention of the Pow Burn, the Cardinal Bunker, the Alps, and the Himalayas. And Mac Smith's final round in 1925 may have been the saddest, slowest train wreck in golf history. An out-of-control gallery wrote part of that story; Mac, an expatriated Scot, thought the throng wanted him to lose. It didn't. But there were so many of them, and the golf ground was so small. . . . Prestwick never applied to host the Open again.

"Altogether it would seem that some gremlin haunts Prestwick," wrote Darwin three years before his death in 1961. "[It] drives unfortunate golfers to play fatal, almost moonstruck shots. There must be some greatness about a golf course which can produce such catastrophes."

No OPEN WAS held in 1871—Fairlie was dead and Tommy had retired the Belt—but it was the key year in the history of the tournament. Representatives from Prestwick, the Royal and Ancient, and the Honourable Company decided to resume the Open (though no one called it that yet). Each club would kick in £10 for prize money, and another £10 to buy a new trophy, the Claret Jug. Against the advent of another Tommy, the committee decreed that no one could retire the Jug, no matter how many times in a row he won. More important, the organizers decided that henceforth the big event would alternate between their home courses: Prestwick, St. Andrews, and Musselburgh.

To no one's surprise, Tommy Morris won the first Claret Jug Open. The next year, the tournament left Prestwick for the first time. The St. Andrews era began.

Thousands of small towns around the world huddle around a village green. In coastal Scotland, the green equivalent is a golf course, and the Old at St. Andrews is its purest expression. But the Old is more than the gray town's heart. It is its arena, its agora. Just as football owns the soul of small-town Texas, golf rules St. Andrews.

A hundred things make it unique. If you're a touring golf pro—let's say you've won a U.S. Open—approach the starter's box and ask to play the Old Course for free. "Sorry," the starter will say, "we make no accommodation." Look to your right as you approach the home hole green and see the house where the Morrises lived, and the room where

Young Tom died. Raise your eyes higher and observe the University and churches half a millennium old. Eyes left, and there's the stained stone fortress of the Royal and Ancient. It's a relatively new building, constructed in 1861.

A melodrama of damnation and redemption lurks in the names of things at St. Andrews. You play next to the Eden Estuary, aim for the Elysian Fields, and avoid if you can the Hell Bunker and the Valley of Sin. Almost a hundred years before the gutta boom, they were a golf club. Of all the golfing societies in Scotland, the R and A had the best clubhouse, the most appealing rituals, and the most medieval town as its headquarters. They even had the most striking club uniforms, worn to distinguish themselves from the dog-walkers on the free-for-all of the early links. Regular members wore scarlet coats with yellow buttons; committeemen, authorized to advise the procedure when a ball came to rest in a wheelbarrow full of wet seaweed, wore blue velvet capes behind their red coats, and on the capes were embroidered a club and a ball of silver.

Lord, they were keen. During a club competition in 1948, J. F. Gilliat collapsed and died on the first fairway. What to do? After milling around for a few minutes, one of the survivors worried aloud about being penalized for slow play. So the remaining three continued their round—without poor Mr. Gilliat, of course, for whom nothing more could be done.

The R and A loved its dinners and drinks and its intramural competition for the William IV Medal, but it became much more than a golf club. According to the club, when the Honourable Company "suffered a temporary loss of cohesion" in the mid-nineteenth century, "the R and A, without conscious exercise of authority, gradually acquired the status of premier club." They took over the administration of the Open, and of the Amateur. They interacted with the smaller organization, the USGA, which had only two client countries, the United States and Mexico. They institutionalized the rules and wrestled with problems great—such as the size of the ball—and small, such as Maurice Flitcroft. Mr. Flitcroft decided he should like to attempt to qualify for the 1976 Open at Royal Birkdale. Problem: he had never actually played golf before, having confined his efforts to playgrounds and parks. But he paid his fee, pronounced himself an unattached professional, and was given a spot. A walk around the qualifying course the evening before may have saved him a stroke or two; he shot 121 at Formby the next day, with one par. Why did he bother? a reporter asked his mother. "Well, he has to start somewhere," Mrs. Flitcroft said.

Despite such highlights, the crumpled postdiluvian ground of their golf course held far more intrigue than the club. The links inspired some men to poetry:

> *Ah! Seaweed smells from sandy caves*
> *And thyme and mist of whiffs*
> *In-coming tide, Atlantic waves*
> *Slapping the sunny cliffs*
> *Lark song and seas sounds in the air*
> *And splendour, splendour, everywhere*
>
> —*"Seaside Golf" by John Betjeman,*
> *from* Collected Poems

But others most sincerely hated it. "Terrible," said U.S. touring professional Scott Hoch of the Old Course. "Worst piece of mess I ever saw." Hoch is no historian, but neither were his outraged critics, who did not remember that Harry Vardon, Bobby Jones, and Sam Snead felt pretty much the same way. Sainted English golf writer Peter Dobereiner referred to it in print as "a sad old bitch of a golf course." Vardon won the Open six times, the most ever, but he never broke an egg at the Old. Jones was an angry young man of nineteen when he quit on the eleventh hole of the second round of the 1921 Open at St. Andrews. Snead looked out the train window and asked the gentleman in the next seat, "What abandoned golf course is that?" The man got huffy.

"I'll have you know that is St. Andrews, sir!" he said. Snead didn't know when to quit: "Is *that* where they're going to hold the British Open?"

But Dobereiner recanted, and Jones got religion. He won the 1927 Open at St. Andrews, and came to love the inscrutable Old Course above all others. And St. Andrews embraced Bobby like a favorite son.

The earliest winners of the St. Andrews Opens were particularly anonymous, and their scores—even allowing for their wood-shafted clubs and sap balls—were terrible. Take Tom Kidd. Please. Kidd, a caddie, won with the highest winning score of the thirty-six-hole era: 179, one under nineties. Jack Burns, a plasterer who resembled the actor Richard Dreyfuss, tied two others for first in 1888—or did he? As he and Ben Sayers and Davie Anderson prepared to play off the next day, someone added up the cards again. *Um, you won, Jack, the* someone said. Let's have a drink. Burns had come out of nowhere, then went directly back there. Bob Martin, a former shepherd, shot a snappy 176 in 1876, tying Davie Strath. But in the final round, Strath's third shot to the seventeenth had hit a civilian on the green, which some said aloud was not cricket. He should be disqualified, they said. The championship committee waffled. Their nondecision was that the play-off should go on the next day, but without the protest having been decided. Strath didn't show up. Martin did. He walked around the course by himself and was declared Champion Golfer.

John Henry Taylor won in 1895, beginning a nearly unbroken run of distinguished Open champions at the Old. Kel Nagle, a minor star, won in 1960, but that may have been the most important Open of the modern era. Nagle edged the charismatic Arnold Palmer, who had already taken the Masters and the U.S. Open. Interest in that and all succeeding Opens skyrocketed. Gate receipts doubled those for 1959, and the R and A realized a profit of £6,600. But the most memorable event at St. Andrews could prove to be a recent one, the 1995 event won by John Daly. Long John waited by the final green with his then wife, Paulette, watching as Costantino Rocca of Italy tried to make a tying birdie. Rocca, forty yards short of the green with his drive, hit an unforgettably bad second, a subterranean chunk only halfway to the hole. The tournament leader and his third Mrs. exchanged grins and a warm embrace. Then Rocca holed the sixty-foot putt through the Valley of Sin and fell to the ground in ecstasy. Daly's reaction was deliciously nonstoic.

Rocca got in trouble in the Road Hole bunker and Daly won the four-hole play-off with ease. Before he and his handlers departed for a celebration in Amsterdam, he delivered one of the greatest Open quotes. A high-profile drinker, he'd won the PGA Championship in 1991 while pouring a six-pack down his neck during the final nine holes. But he didn't tipple on the Old Course. "To win a major sober is unbelievable," Daly said.

Musselburgh, the poor relation of the three original Open courses, hosted the tournament six times. With only nine holes and almost completely surrounded by gray stone houses, it was the coziest of major championship venues. And the worst.

A round at Prestwick may remind you of the movie *Citizen Kane;* both were strikingly original productions, destined to be copied or imitated by countless golf architects/filmmakers. But no one consciously duplicated Musselburgh. Because what was it, anyway, a golf course or a race course? In 1816, the town fathers, who always seemed to favor the ponies over the golfers, ringed the links with a wooden railing to delineate the path for racing horses. Today the railing is made of hideous white PVC. Looking like a section removed from the Yale Bowl, the stair-stepped back of the starting-line grandstand doubled as the Honourable Company's clubhouse.

Musselburgh owned several compensating virtues, however. Antiquity, for one: Mary Queen of Scots teed up there in 1567, shortly before her long imprisonment and her brief beheading. The course charmed visitors with its view of the Firth of Forth and the River Esk, and so did the sight of local fisherwomen trudging home across the links from the mussel beds, their backs bent from their full creels. Mrs. Forman's hotel and restaurant dispensed Welsh rarebit and bread and cheese by the third green. Musselburgh also owned the best-named bunker in golf, a huge pit on the fifth called Pandemonium. And five Open champions played out of Musselburgh: the Old and Young Willie Dunns, Bob Ferguson, Mungo Park, and David Brown.

Forty-eight players entered the final Musselburgh Open, in 1889, and a thousand people watched. For the first time, slow play was an issue; competitors who were well behind after twenty-seven holes were offered five shillings each to quit. The tournament was held on November 8, so the day was short.

Young Willie Park and Andra Kirkaldy tied at 155. In the thirty-six-hole play-off the next day, neither of the combatants was more recognizable than Park's caddie, Fiery, a little man with a face like a walnut. With the silent, florid Fiery reading the putts, Park won with 158, five better than his opponent. Afterward, a local pro saw the unhappy runner-up on his way to the pub and made a snide remark. Enraged, Kirkaldy picked the man up and threw him in the river, "and I telt him tae gan fushin' an' droon himsel'!"

L EO DIEGEL WAS literally a jumpy man. He often hit a shot and hopped into the air like a boy on a pogo stick in an effort to determine the ball's fate as quickly as possible. Really fast surfaces made his hummingbird heart beat faster, and the greens at Muirfield for the 1929 Open shone like the skin on a bald man's head. Diegel watched disgustedly as a worker mowed an already-shaved green. "Why don't you iron it now?" he asked.

Diegel's emotional opposite—and the man he frequently lost to—was Walter Hagen. Nothing bothered him. "I love to play golf with Walter," Bobby Jones once said. "He goes along, chin up, smiling away; never grousing about his luck, playing the ball as he finds it. He can come nearer beating luck itself than anybody I know."

A silk-and-cashmere man among the rough-hewn former caddies of professional golf, Hagen's magnificence matched that of Muirfield. The fourth course in Open history could make you forget the third, and possibly the first. There was some contemporary whingeing that the holes were not close enough to the sea, but Muirfield sprawls regally on a secluded meadow above the Firth of Forth, and features some of the best work by a great architect, Harry S. Colt. In contrast to its predecessors in the rota, which are as much a part of their towns as the local chemist, Muirfield stands alone, hidden from the street by evergreens and a long driveway. It is the favorite Open course of Jack Nicklaus, who won his first Open there in 1966; not for nothing did he name his own course in Ohio "Muirfield Village." And at midday they lay out a feast like the one the Ghost of Christmas Present put before Ebenezer Scrooge. One of the specialties is:

SYRUP SPONGE

¼ pound butter
¾ teacup of sugar
8 tablespoons maple syrup
two eggs
1½ teacups of self-rising flour
½ teacup milk

Cream together butter and sugar. Add eggs and milk. Pour ½ cup of flour into mixture and mix well. Add rest of flour and beat well with hand. Pour syrup into bottom of pudding bowl. Add mixture and steam for two hours.

It's a dessert fit for a king, or for Walter Hagen, who never counted calories or drinks. Leaving the nervous Diegel in the dust, Sir Walter shot a memorable 67 in the second round in '29 and found himself with a ten-shot lead with nine to play. He lost a few shots during his victory lap on that cold, gray afternoon, and he missed a gimme on the final hole, but his grandeur never left. He gave his first-place money of £100 to his caddie, a teenager named Hargreaves. "The real payoff for us in those days was the glory," Hagen would recall, "and getting our names on the mug."

Hagen got his name on the "mug" four times in the Roaring Twenties, a decade that seemed to have been invented for him. His first win, in 1922 at Royal St. George's in Sandwich, England, was the first ever by an American-born player. When Hagen again won at Sandwich in 1928, he naturally drank a few celebratory cocktails afterward, delaying the presentation ceremony. Walter's breach of protocol annoyed the presenter, the club's new captain, His Royal Highness the Prince of Wales. Hagen accepted the Claret Jug from HRH with a 500-watt smile. But the Prince glared at the cheeky American and balled his hands into fists.

Royal St. George's aimed to be the St. Andrews of England. It was conceived and built during the golf boom at the end of the nineteenth century, when the number of courses in Great Britain tripled in fifteen years. Known by most simply as Sandwich, Royal St. George's is London's links, and a course of such quality that it remains on the rota. Today it's about a ninety-minute drive from Big Ben to its huge dunes and bunkers on the English Channel, a fraction of the train-time endured by the incoming Scottish professionals a century ago. But it was worth the trip. "The best course in the world," wrote Harry Vardon in 1905. "No faintness of heart, no doubtful stroke, will ever in the result be flattered." Even seventy-three-year-old Tom Morris showed up to watch the 1894 Open, the first one not held in Scotland. When four players scratched, the committee convinced Old Tom to play. He shot 100 in the third round, and retired from the tournament forever.

As with any of the old Open venues, Royal St. George's has stories to tell. For example, there was the crisis in 1899, when a faction of the professionals threatened a boycott. An extra £30 in the purse quelled the rebellion. But its saddest, sweetest tale involved Hagen, Gene Sarazen, and a caddie. The story begins in 1928.

The two golfers sat in the smoking room on the *Berengaria,* drinking Scotch and talking about golf while the big ship glided through the North Atlantic to Sandwich. Not for the first time, Sarazen declaimed about his fervent desire to win the Open. Hagen nodded at the waiter who'd just placed a new glass in front of him. He sipped the golden liquid. "Gene, you can never win the Open unless you've had caddies like the ones I've had," Hagen said wisely. He'd won the Open twice and would win it twice more. "I'll tell you what I'll do. I'll loan you my caddie, Skip Daniels."

Daniels turned out to be a man of sixty with a trim gray mustache, a shiny black suit, a plaid cap, and a limp. Off the course, he was never without a cane, but when Sarazen hit practice balls, Skip ran out to retrieve them, and ran back. "I've never seen Hagen hit the shots as well as you're hitting them, sir," the caddie said. After dinner, the American and the Englishman would stroll onto the golf course with a dozen balls and a putter. While Sarazen got to know the greens, Daniels would point to the spots he'd patrolled against German invasion during the Great War. He knew every blade of grass, every bunker. By the time the tournament began, Sarazen knew he'd made a great friend, and that he'd listen to everything the old man said.

But he didn't. In the rough on the par-five fourteenth in the second round, Sarazen hit a three-wood when Daniels recommended a safe shot with an iron. He topped it only twenty yards. Furious, Sarazen stomped to the ball and swung again before the caddie could stop him. Another dribbler. The resultant 7 would be the difference. As Sarazen finished the final round the next day, a long black limousine rolled slowly up on a maintenance road. In the backseat were Hagen, wrapped in a luxurious polo coat with mother-of-pearl buttons, and the royal he would soon keep waiting, the Prince of Wales. Hagen would win by two over Sarazen.

"We'll try it again, sir, won't we?" Daniels said after the presentation. He had tears in his eyes. "Before I die, I'm going to win an Open Championship for you."

Four years passed before the big event returned to the south coast of England for the only Open ever held at Prince's. Waiting at the gate was Daniels—same suit, but a different man. Grayer now, and slower, with a more pronounced limp and a shaggier mustache. "And his eyes," Sarazen recalled, "they didn't look good." So though he could hardly bring himself to do it, Sarazen told old Skip that he would be looking for another caddie. Business was business, and Gene still hadn't won the Open.

"Righto, sir, if that's the way you feel," Daniels said.

Although he had other offers, Daniels would not caddie for anyone else. Instead, he watched Sarazen and his new man in the practice rounds, and avoided making eye contact with his old employer. Two days before qualifying began, Gene had a surprise visitor call at his hotel room, Lord Innis-Kerr. "I was talking with Skip Daniels today," he said. "He's heartbroken, you know. It's clear to him, as it's clear to all your friends, that you're not getting along with your caddie. Daniels thinks he can straighten you out before the bell rings." Sarazen agreed; he'd been feeling awful about dismissing Skip. At seven the next morning, the golfer and his old caddie reunited.

They made beautiful music together. With a final-round birdie on his nemesis hole, the fourteenth, Sarazen shot a tournament record 283. He won by five shots. He asked the R and A if Skip could stand with him while he received the Claret Jug. The officials turned down the request—"not traditional," they said—but Daniels wasn't there anyway. When finally he appeared, on his bicycle, with a grandson on each handlebar, Sarazen let the ceremony begin.

They hugged and cried a bit afterward. Sarazen gave him his coat, and said see you next year at St. Andrews. The happy caddie put on the new garment and pedaled away. Sarazen watched his receding figure. He could hardly swallow.

Four months later, Skip Daniels died. They buried him in that coat.

P RINCE'S HOSTED JUST one Open; nearby Deal, two; and Royal Portrush, one. Those courses would be the answers to a trivia question, but they were not trivial. That the Open established so strong a hold in England showed its strength; that only one American showed for the 1951 Open at Royal Portrush in Northern Ireland revealed its major weakness. Arnie and television still lay in the future.

Glorious championships at great courses remained dim because they preceded the TV age. Peter Thomson's five Open championships were underappreciated, because all but one of them occurred during the days before the tube. Hoylake—Royal Liverpool—would be the Peter Thomson of Open courses. Gary Player believes it to be the toughest course in the rota. It was the home course of the fabulous Harold Hilton, an English amateur who won the first seventy-two-hole Open, at Muirfield in 1892. When his club hosted for the first time five years later, Hilton won again, often hitting shots with a cigarette in his mouth. In 1930, another amateur won the Open at Hoylake. That, of course, was Bobby Jones in his Grand Slam year. But only aficionados even know that Hoylake exists, because TV covered only one Hoylake Open, the last one, when Roberto de Vicenzo won in 1967.

I N 1958, THE BBC gave its viewers only an hour and a half of Open on Saturday and another ninety minutes on Sunday, paying a piddling £450 for the privilege. When that event resulted in a tie between Peter Thomson and Dave Thomas, Henry Longhurst worked the play-off for the BBC—alone. His nasal drone was the only voice you heard. The TV era really began in 1960, the Centenary Open, starring Arnold Palmer, and the money to complement the more comprehensive coverage began to flow in 1968. The elfin Roone Arledge of the

American Broadcasting Company had made a startling suggestion to Wilbur Muirhead, the chairman of the Championship Committee. How about a TV contract, separate from the BBC, for ABC? Done. As a result of the influx of American television rights money, the R and A funded all its championships for the year, increased the prize money for 1969, and showed a nice profit.

More riches flowed to Fife when the Committee hired Mark McCormack to negotiate its TV deals. McCormack, whose company IMG is the world's biggest player agency, made ever-bigger TV deals with Japan, Australia, and ABC. McCormack explained the genesis of his deal with the R and A. "We began representing Wimbledon in 1968," he said. "I asked if anyone had thought about a film [of each year's results]. They hadn't; with sponsorships, the film became profitable. Then we asked about foreign TV.

"In 1970, we went through a similar dialogue with the R and A."

TV changed everything. It made the R and A rich. It ratcheted up the popularity of the Open, and made media stars of its champions. It allowed Americans the rare sight of brown grass and golf on a fast surface. And it made eight magnificent links part of golf's collective unconscious. The courses became seldom-seen, grown-up children. St. Andrews was the oldest. Turnberry was the pretty one. Royal Birkdale's sand-dune mountains gave it a playful quality. Troon was remote and forbidding.

And Carnoustie? Carnoustie in 1999 looked like it had been working out. And had joined a motorcycle gang.

CHAPTER FOUR

Tommy, Gary, Henry, and Mac

I predict one score above one hundred and one suicide.

*—Andrew Magee, the day before the first round
of the 1999 British Open*

EDGINESS POURED DOWN like rain from Carnoustie's pewter sky.

On the day before what would be the most bizarre tournament in Open history, John Philp's face sagged from lack of sleep and excess of responsibility. Helen Philp, worried about her husband's frantic pace and the cross fire of criticism of his golf course, remained at home, scanning the newspapers for positive stories. Barbara, their nineteen-year-old daughter, drummed her blue-painted fingernails on the blank spaces of the sign-up sheet in the starter's booth next to the first tee. A surprising number of players had decided not to play a final practice round. Annoyed and fretful about the test to come, they mingled on the putting green and the practice tee and told one another horror stories.

Magee's caddie, Eric Meller, told a typical anecdote. "So I said, 'Jesper, how you playing?' 'I'm six-over, and the other guys are seven- and eight-over. And we're playing *great*.' And they're on fourteen—they haven't even played the bogey holes!" Stuart Appleby announced that he'd shot an 85 in his practice round Tuesday, and had to play his tail off to do it.

At midmorning the wind picked up and the day darkened. Those who retreated to the big tents had to shout to be heard over the snap and pop of canvas and the metronomic clinks of metal buckles against the stays. The racket seemed to heighten the tension of the press conferences held behind the flapping walls of the Media Centre. Defending champion Mark O'Meara responded to a Ryder Cup pay question by suggesting with out-of-character sarcasm that if he had to donate his time and earnings, then perhaps "all of you media people should donate your money to a charity that week too." Have you come here in good form? David Duval was asked. "You'll find out tomorrow," he replied. Is the course too hard? "I can't define too hard, too easy, unfair, fair. It is what it is." What is it? "You tell me."

Duval told the writers in affectless tones that the on-the-ground pinball game he'd expected seemed impossible, with hard, narrow fairways bordered by voracious rough: "It looks to me like we're playing an event that is based on target golf on a links layout." With the course set up as it was, Duval said, "a lot more luck has been brought into play."

Greg Norman took the stand. He testified in his first words that what the press was hearing from the players about the course "was minor compared to what we're actually saying on the putting green and the driving range . . . I think 'brute' has been used a lot. I think trying to hit a driver into my hotel room would be another analogy I could make; that's about the width we've got to hit it into." Carnoustie far exceeded the infamous bumper crop of rough on Turnberry when he won there in 1986, Norman said. "At least at Turnberry, when you went off the fairway you could advance the ball a little bit. . . . A lot of luck is going to come into play."

R and A officials Hugh M. Campbell and Sir Michael Bonallack, O.B.E., ascended the little stage and sat behind a table, two red-faced gentlemen of late middle age wearing dark blue blazers, gray trousers, and ties striped silver, blue, and red. Campbell and Bonallack assumed defensive postures in armless chairs as twenty-nine of the thirty-two Q's in their Q and A concerned the perceived unfairness of the golf course. Two of the other questions were "Do we have a detailed [weather] forecast?" and "Any more questions?"

They deflected, they dodged, they danced a little two-step, and they wouldn't admit what seemed obvious: they wanted a high winning score. Nor would they confess to going overboard in toughening Carnoustie, whatever their motivation for doing so. Campbell conceded the importance of weather on a links course, but added that weather was not taken into account in the course setup. Bonallack claimed not to have heard any comments from players about the course, only what he'd read in the press. And though he had won the British Amateur five times and knew better, Sir Michael said he didn't believe that high scores would bother the participants. "I think they realistically will say, 'Anybody else would have done very much higher scores than that.'"

Campbell felt compelled at the end to state that "there was no way in the world that we set out to embarrass the best players in the world."

Later in the week the administrators continued to try to distance themselves from their most important job, providing a championship golf course. "Growing grass is not exactly a science in Scotland, as it is in the States," an R and A official said. A number of publications printed that Duval had gone to tournament officials to mend fences over some critical comments that got splashed like mud in the Scottish newspapers, and had been told by one of the Royal and Ancients that the whole mess was due to "an out-of-control greenkeeper." Meanwhile, John Philp continued to defend the course to anyone with a notebook or a golf club.

But the superintendent of the links didn't feel hung out to dry. He was enjoying himself.

E LKINGTON FINISHED WORK early. He hit full shots for an hour and putted for almost that long, but didn't participate in the whingeing. He, Derek Carr, and caddie Martin Roy stood on the runway between the hotel and the first tee and huddled around his big black golf bag, an unmistakable sack because Elkington never uses head covers. Philp happened by, walking quickly in his black steel-toed boots, as usual carrying a walkie-talkie. Here is the man to complain to, someone said.

"I'll take responsibility," the superintendent said cheerfully, shaking Elkington's hand.

"Fairways can't hide from a straight ball," replied Elkington with equal cheer.

"That's right," said the super. "I'd like to see 72 become a good score again."

"I've always liked 72," Elkington said. Philp's walkie-talkie crackled, and he waved his good-byes. Carr departed with his friend's golf bag on his shoulder; he would lock it in the boot of his car, with the bagpipes, because Elk does not trust bag storage.

Roy remained. He had made the grade; he'd be caddying in the Open tomorrow. "The one thing that stands out about Steve is his golfing intelligence," Roy said. "There's nothing he's asked that wasn't pertinent. But he can't care less where Hogan hit it in 1953. He's meticulous. And very confident. He doesn't think there's anything he can't do."

That attitude had served Elkington well the last two times a golf course on the U.S. tour had caused a firestorm. In the PGA Championship in 1995, the new greens at Riviera turned brown and almost died. Others looked at the uneven surfaces and saw a two-dollar haircut, impossible to navigate. But Elkington used the towering spike marks as targets for his putts, and won. The pros despised Raymond

Floyd's orgy of bunkering in his redesign of Doral, but Elkington won there, too, five months before this Open.

While the Australian whistled past the graveyard, Magee entered the lobby of the new hotel, his streaky hair still wet from the shower. Elegantly casual in running shoes, white denim trousers, and a black sweater, Magee bought a few newspapers, then strolled into the dining room. Eleven o'clock dining presented him with his biggest decision of the day: breakfast or lunch? He chose the latter, a complicated sandwich called the Bookmaker, with french fries and a Coke. Eight pounds sixty.

Jerry Pate spotted Magee at his table overlooking the eighteenth green and accepted an invitation to sit. Pate, the 1974 U.S. Open champion, would be analyzing the tournament for the BBC. He's succinct and folksy on the air, as was his predecessor, the late Dave Marr, and the Brits enjoy his Alabama accent just as they enjoyed Marr's Texas twang. But without a producer telling him to pipe down, Pate chattered without pause. Magee listened with his mouth full of sandwich and polite murmurs.

Inevitably, the conversation turned to numbers, the golf pro's obsession. What would be the winning score, the thirty-six-hole cut, the worst score for eighteen holes, and for thirty-six? Someone asked Magee if he would sign his card if he shot 90 or worse. He shrugged. "Sure I would," he said. "It's only a game of golf."

He wrote "A. Magee Room 125" on his bill, and bid adieu to Pate. Exiting the hotel on the golf course side, he turned right and walked past the eighteenth green, the north grandstand, and a litter of roped and guarded portable buildings. He crossed the busy street—Links Parade—and found International Management Group's small rented house two doors from the Hogan House Hotel. Magee has employed IMG since his career began, not least because the agent assigned to represent him is his college golf coach. A pretty employee confirmed the plan for Sunday: two hours after the completion of play, a chartered jet would take Magee, ten other pros and their families, and caddies from Leuchars Royal Air Force base in St. Andrews to Copenhagen. A bus would transport them from the hotel to the airfield. As Magee absorbed the logistics of his departure, you had to wonder if his mind was more on Sunday than on Thursday.

The perambulation continued to the huge retail tent, one of a series of marquees perched on the Buddon, the golf course next to Carnoustie's championship links. He browsed for a minute at Rhod McEwan's bookstore; felt the wool at Pringle's sweater emporium; ignored the golf equipment; and paused at the Irish Tourist Board's booth. He ran a finger up and down a map: "From here we went to Royal County Down, then over here to the K Club, and to Portrush..."

The constantly changing weather had calmed when Magee got to the practice tee. Midway through his two-hour practice session, he stood back and looked to his right. A few random shafts of sunlight illuminated the amber waves of grain gently swaying next to the first fairway. "So the superintendent says he hasn't watered the rough, huh?" he said. "Then ask him why the grass is so high around the sprinkler heads. That's a dead giveaway."

As Magee continued to drill, Zane Scotland finished a practice round with Per-Ulrik Johansson. Then he and Instructor Cranfield walked to the Media Centre for the last formal press conference of the day. While other interviewees had to listen to some rather pointed questions, the press lobbed home-run pitches to Scotland. His wide-eyed honesty charmed the writers, who began by asking if he was enjoying all the attention.

"I don't mind it at all," he said. "I'm just going to take everything as it comes, really, just go and play a bit of golf, have a bit of fun, really."

Zane, how daunting is it playing with professionals who have obviously been your idols?

"I don't think it's daunting at all. For me I'm just going to go and play golf like I normally do and let everyone else be themselves and get in the zone, yeah."

And the best part of the experience so far?

"Just being able to walk into the practice ground and use the facilities you have here. You have people like Greg Norman walking up next to you. Darren Clarke is hitting balls behind you, and Gary Player . . . This obviously is where I'd like to reach one day. So being able to see it all now is brilliant, brilliant. And, obviously, getting the shoes as well. Getting all the gear, that was good."

SUMMER VISITORS TO northern latitudes often become disoriented by the endless twilight, the fleeting curtain of darkness, and sun peeking through the window before five A.M. About the time your body clock tells you to eat dinner, it's ten P.M., every decent restaurant has closed, and you're stuck with pub grub. Or, for in-town guests during the 1999 Open, there was the Carnoustie Chippie, an open-until-midnight fish-and-chips joint with food so deep-fried it seemed to be coated in papier-mâché. Many decide it's better to subsist on liquid carbohydrates. So they have a pint or two. And seemingly sixty seconds later, the rooster crows.

Zane Scotland had none of these problems. He ate well. He didn't drink anything stronger than Orangina. Virtually his only physical problem was the blisters his new shoes had rubbed into the heel of his right foot. He didn't dissipate, spending his pretournament evenings cleaning his clubs and putting on the carpet. And although he resides at fifty-one degrees latitude and Carnoustie lies at fifty-seven, his mother had to give him a firm shake to get him up at ten-thirty on Thursday morning. He'd slept ten hours.

At five minutes to four, Scotland walked by himself from the hotel dressing room toward the first tee. Fans watching the passing parade from the elevated patio gave the dark-haired young man in an off-white sweater a "Who's that?" look. But like a fighter going from locker room to ring, he gave them no look at all. Finally his inward focus turned outward, when his eyes again beheld his caddie/nutritionist/morale officer, Ron Cuthbert. "Let's do it," Cuthbert said with a grin, grasping the fingers of Scotland's right hand in an upraised-thumb, soul-style handshake. They walked onto the sunlit center stage. Scotland shook more hands, those attached to scorers, rules officials, the starter, the bunker raker, and his fellow competitors, Lee Thompson and Warren Bennett, both of England. Cuthbert whispered something that caused his golfer to smile. Thompson hit; the announcer clicked on his big silver microphone. "Zane *Scotland!*" he said, as if calling out the identity of the next quiz show contestant.

The teenager looked relaxed as he addressed his first shot in the Open. Blustery wind blowing directly in his face emptied the tee area of sound except for the rush of moving air. Two big, waist-high waggles preceded a long, unhurried back swing. Titanium met space-age plastic—*threek*—and the ball seemed to get very small very fast.

The 139th Open Championship was almost nine hours old by the time Scotland teed off in the second-to-last group at 4:05. Bernie Scotland had studied the scoreboard while Zane warmed up, and asked his son if he'd like to know some of the scores. And did you hear what Sergio shot? No and no, Zane said. I don't want to know.

"I spoke with Seve earlier," Bernie said in parting. "He wanted me to tell you that par is 78 today. Be patient."

Early in the day it appeared the scores would be high, but not as astronomical as Ballesteros and others predicted. The gentlemen in the second group off the tee, for example, Rodney Pampling from Australia, Bernhard Langer from Germany, and Steve Pate of the United States, scored 71, 72, and 73, respectively. But then the bodies started to pile up. "The wind is blowing around and the course is drying out and the landing areas are very severe," said Sandy Lyle. "The hardest course I've ever played by a long, long way. . . . It has probably set me back six months. All the hard work I've been doing getting my swing organized and it's just torn it apart." And a final, bitter comment: "They were fertilizing the rough and watering it when I was here playing about two weeks ago. I think it's just a joke now." The 1985 Open champion had just shot 85.

Defending champion Mark O'Meara, whose steadiness is his strength, shot 83. So, too, did Fred Funk, the straightest driver on the U.S. Tour.

Which was six shots better than the card of golf's newest young star, Sergio Garcia.

What compares to an 89 by a world-class golfer? The prima ballerina slipping during the pas de deux like a fat man on an icy driveway? The pop music star forgetting the words to the national anthem before the big game? Nineteen-year-old Sergio, an ebullient, charismatic young man and one of the hottest players in golf, was reduced to a strangled "No comment" after his disaster. He walked away from the green-painted plywood scorer's enclosure with his head down and his mother's arm around his shoulder.

While Sandy and Sergio got lost in the rough, Elkington did all he could to keep the ball in play. He patiently hit three-woods and a de-lofted two-iron on the front nine par fours and fives, which often left very long second shots. But there was no stress-free strategy, and he and playing partners Ted Tryba of the United States and an Englishman, Neil Price, fought to keep their composure. For not only was Carnoustie the longest Open course in history at 7,361 yards, and not only did the fairways resemble thin green snakes lying between high brown and green rough, but now a steady twenty- to thirty-miles-per-hour wind blew in from the west-southwest. Despite his cautious strategy, Elkington shot 41 on the front, five over par. He'd finish his swing, watch his ball go a little off line, and look down at his feet.

He took the driver from his caddie, Roy, on the tenth, a typically terrifying Carnoustie par four: 466 yards, bunkers right, out-of-bounds left, a burn—sort of an organized creek—short of the green, and a vigorous crop of rough all around. A two-car ScotRail passenger train rattled past on the nearby rails as he stepped up to the ball. He flexed his abdominal muscles. The wind billowed his pants. With a slightly raised left shoulder, he tried to hit a little hook into the cross-wind but overdid it, and his ball burrowed into the wiry rye. Wedge out, wedge on, two putts, and Elkington had a classic Carnoustie bogey. There would be hundreds more like it in this Open. And scores of scores even worse on the last four holes, the toughest finish in golf.

By the time this threesome reached the final tee, they'd been squinting into the bright sun for five hours and five miles. Add the wind, and their unhappy relationship to par, and a 487-yard par four with trouble everywhere was exactly what they didn't want to finish the day. Elkington had scrambled from bunker and rough for one-putt pars on sixteen and seventeen; with a four on the final hole, he'd have a 77, not good, but no disgrace on this day. Instead he demonstrated another Carnoustie classic, the double bogey, with a ball in the burn.

As Elkington put glove, ball, and tees into his golf bag and extracted wallet and watch, Lisa, Derek Carr, and five writers encircled him on the walkway between the hotel and the first tee and eighteenth green. The watchers from the shoulder-height patio looked down curiously. Elkington repeated a writer's question: "What was the hardest thing today? Hitting the fairways." He spoke briefly about clubs he'd hit as the writers scribbled away. The 300-yard two-iron and 228-yard seven-iron he'd played onto the fourteenth green indicated how much the wind had complicated every distance equation.

Carr, resplendent in so much authentic tour gear given to him by Elkington that he looked like a pro himself, stood looking slightly stunned. He'd vowed to play "Waltzing Matilda" on his pipes on the final green if Steve ever won the Open, but suddenly that looked disappointingly unlikely for this year. Roy, exhausted, leaned heavily on the bag. "Carnoustie was four shots harder today than I've ever seen it," the caddie master said. Price and Tryba walked by after their brief greenside press conferences. Elkington had seemed resigned to his score; Price appeared to be faintly pleased with his 79; but Tryba, with an 80, looked ready to kill.

Tragedy is hard to sustain in summer sunshine, but anyone could sense a pall over Carnoustie. Golfers walked from green to tee with the pinched faces and slumped shoulders of schoolchildren taking and failing a big math test. The deep, manly roars for which British Open crowds are so famous stayed in the spectators' mouths. Such huzzahs require some foreplay, some progression of excellence, which no one could provide. Elkington and Tiger Woods, for example, birdied only one hole each. Muted applause for pars and the scattered hand claps of aficionados for hard-won bogies were carried away by the wind.

By the end of the day, two players faced the question that had been posed to Magee the day before. Tom Gillis, an American from Lake Orion, Michigan, who was making a living averaging 73 on the European Tour, shot 90. Prayad Marksaeng of Thailand, his card dotted with five 7's, shot 91. Ninety is the Mendoza line of golf, with hackers on one side and the competent on the other. Would poor Tom and Prayad rip up their shocking scorecards and pretend this nightmare had never occurred? They would not. Both signed, but Gillis discovered an injured wrist and withdrew from the event the next morning. It was his thirty-first birthday. Fred Funk also junked.

Magee took the tee at 12:35 P.M., an hour before Elkington finished, in the company of Kim Jong-Duck of Korea and David Howell of England. At least ten friends swelled the Magee gallery, including the lovely Susan, Gary and Judy Hewson, and David and Michele Glenn, two couples who'd been on the Ireland trip, and J. Douglas Trapp, M.D., an impotence consultant from Augusta, Georgia. These and other friends of Andrew walked and talked about restaurants, Ireland, golf, shopping, and Viagra, with pauses to watch their man hit.

The pauses quickly became too frequent. He three-putted a good birdie chance on the first green, then drove his ball into a bunker on the second. Two-over after two. A six-iron and an eight-iron got him on the long, peanut-shaped green on the fifth, a 411-yard hole. But then, against the wind, on Hogan's Alley, his best wind-cheating driver stayed well short of the first bunker. With a four-iron, a wedge from the jungle, and a full six-iron, he finally reached the surface.

Magee looked furious after a bogey on the eighth, an annoyingly difficult par three with a hard plateau green surrounded by bomb-crater bunkers. Five over now, he stomped toward the ninth tee with his peculiar high-knee-lift walk. As he reached the yellow nylon gallery ropes, he noticed two local lads regarding him worshipfully. "How are you guys doin'?" he asked with a smile and a wink. The children, both about ten years old, were too awestruck to reply. One of the gods from the other side of the ropes had spoken to them! They left their post to watch their new favorite golfer for a few holes.

Magee continued to punctuate his effort with gallery interaction. Walking up the twelfth fairway, he took the driver out of his bag and handed it to Glenn. "Here you go, I don't need it," he said, a joking reference to the fact that the longest course in Open history was also possibly the narrowest. Several of the Scottish spectators stared at this crazy man giving away his golf clubs and looked quickly away, as if he were handing out end-of-the-world literature.

The day seemed unsettled, almost surreal. As Kim Jong-Duck prepared to hit from the thirteenth tee at 3:59, the wind died completely. Six minutes later, it resumed at twenty miles per hour. At 4:17, spitting rain mixed with the wind, then abruptly stopped within ten minutes. Magee had hit a hooking two-iron on the tenth, which kicked dead right into a bunker, and he loudly asked the ghost in charge of such things what kind of a bounce was that. On the seventeenth, Island, he hit a driver way left and a long-iron way right. From the tall grass by the dark green gorse he lobbed over a dune as big as a moving van to the unseen hole. When his ball stopped three feet from the flagstick, the gallery roared like so many Scottish lions.

Magee's 77 would inspire no poetry; he'd avoided bad trouble, not much more. But one player in the field seemed to court disaster instead of skirting it: Jean Van de Velde, a journeyman pro born in Mont de Marsan, a little town south of Bordeaux and west of Toulouse in southwest France.

While most players risked the big stick three or four times, Van de Velde hit his driver on holes one, two, five, six, seven, nine, ten, eleven, twelve, and even fourteen, a par five playing dead downwind. The daredevil strategy worked for a while, until bogies on the back nine pushed his score up to a 75. Did he know something no one else had grasped? Although he'd had only one practice round, he knew the risks. Playing partner Bob Charles demonstrated the trouble lurking on every tee shot. The 1963 Open champion drove his ball in the rain-forest rough on the first hole, and he had to swing very hard—twice—to get it out. He shot 83. The next day, Charles again hit his first drive into the jungle, and again he had to hack two times to get the ball back in play.

"But I tend to disagree with all the whingers," said Charles. "I've been playing in the Open since 1958 and this is far and away the best-conditioned golf course we've ever had from tee to green. I've seen the fairways as narrow, at Troon, though the rough there was always wispy. It's traditional that they don't manicure the deep rough at the Open.... No, I've never played a more difficult course."

Charles is sixty-three, soft-spoken, cerebral, a New Zealander. If books were covers, you'd assume this thin steel-gray man banked or accounted, and in fact he did work in a Christchurch bank for seven years before turning pro. Van de Velde is thirty-three, darkly handsome, and as dashing as Charles is staid. You'd cast him as the French race-car driver who doesn't win the race but gets the girl. "Just the nicest guy in the world," Charles said. "He never got upset when things didn't go his way. A pleasure to play golf with.

"When he missed a fairway, he pitched out. But the most important part of his game was not the driver, it was his putter and wedge. One of the best putting performances I've ever seen. He didn't miss one under eight or nine feet." Here was significant praise, because for twenty years Charles, who popularized the arms-only stroke, putted better than anyone in the world.

An hour after Van de Velde, Charles, and Mathias Gronberg began their journey, Zane Scotland swatted his first tee ball into the left rough. And though he'd gotten praise all week for not being Earl Woods, Bernie Scotland immediately did something even Tiger's high-profile pop never tried: he walked right up the fairway, trailing ten yards behind his son. Amazingly, he got away with it for a third of the round. On the sixth, a rules official gently put Bernie back outside the ropes. "I know you have a special interest in this match," he said. "But you must keep to the side or it'll be me who gets in trouble." He complied for a while, until parental enthusiasm again compelled him to sneak up close for a better view.

Most of the Zane Show took place off the fairway, however. Predictably for a young gun in this terror-filled situation, his ball spent a good deal of time off course. But what no one in the gallery of fifty could foresee was the mature way he handled the bunkers and bad bounces. Somehow he managed to never curse, never slap his head or slam a club or hang his head in Tiger-like disgust and loathing. And his composure did not have a hypercoached quality; he didn't seem to have to try all that hard to keep his keel even. Golf is not war for Zane Scotland.

Nor was it a thing of beauty this day. On the ninth hole, he quick-hooked a drive, but was saved from deep trouble by bouncing his ball off a young man with a pierced eyebrow and a huge X carved into his hair. From there Zane smashed a high, drawing seven-iron from about 190 yards to the green. "A career shot," he said to Bernie, "and I'm still twenty-five feet from the hole."

He followed a birdie on the thirteenth—"Scotland's finest hour," quipped one of the spectators, Brian Hewitt of *Golfweek*—with a sideline conference with six of his mates from back home. It was now nearly eight P.M., and though the sun was bathing Carnoustie in golden light, the breeze remained and the temperature had fallen into the low fifties. One of Zane's pals asked to borrow a sweater. Scotland cleared the loan with the rules official, Tony Hill. "Just so long as he doesn't give a sweater to you," Hill said.

Golf can be a funeral, a funhouse, or just a game with a stick and a ball. And sometimes golf can be the canvas on which romance is painted, as two Carnoustie girls in the Scotland gallery demonstrated.

"He's lovely. He's gorgeous," quoth the shorter of the two admirers, the one with red hair, and freckles on Camay-white skin. "He's got a lovely bum." She and her taller, darker friend had dressed for comfort, not for style, in long-sleeved shirts over T-shirts, and baggy denim. Somewhere during the back nine they left the premises, only to reappear next to the sixteenth tee. Shivering, because while everyone else on the grounds had put sweaters and jackets back on—if they ever took them off—the young lasses had changed into formfitting pants and sleeveless blouses. When young Scotland came well out of a bunker on sixteen, their voices were among the loudest: "Well done! Brilliant! Excellent!"

Glowing light and backlit clouds lent a theatrical feeling to day's end. As Scotland's group trooped to the eighteenth tee, concessionaires pulled their tent flaps down and Philp and his men buzzed around distant holes, raking, watering, and mowing. With a four on the final hole, Scotland would shoot 80, just two above Seve's par. But with his gallery swollen to perhaps seventy on the eighteenth hole, Zane showed his worst. An over-the-top swing resulted in an ugly pull-hook. His ball entered an outstandingly large and healthy gorse bush, and stayed there, the first sad step in a triple-bogey seven.

Yet the mood felt anything but grim afterward. The girls helped; urged forward by Bernie, they shook hands with the young man they'd been freezing for. They giggled. He asked their names. He signed golf balls for them. Goose bumps stood at attention on their bare arms. But with a crowd of adults watching this vignette, Zane could hardly act interested, and the girls giggled again and ran off.

"That was probably the toughest course I've ever played," he told the inevitable circle of writers, family, and friends. "The pars felt like birdies." He looked okay with everything, not exhausted, not depressed. Sensing that he required no consolation, his intimates did not pitch a lot of "you did all right" motivational talk. Zane had been as good as his word: he'd taken everything as it came, just played a bit of golf, just had a bit of fun, really.

The grandstands had emptied and the hotel lights were on. "Who's leading?" one of Zane's group asked.

"The superintendent," someone replied.

THE AMERICAN ENTERTAINMENT industry has given the world its two dominant images of keepers of the green. First is Carl Spackler, the slack-jawed delusional in high rubber boots from the 1980 movie *Caddyshack*. As played by Bill Murray, the Bushwood Country Club superintendent fantasized aloud—to himself—about winning the Masters, killing a gopher, and getting in a clinch with a member's wife. Murray, a former caddie at a club in Chicago, ad-libbed the part for director Harold Ramis, who admitted he knew nothing about golf. A step behind Carl trudges Groundskeeper Willy, the flame-haired maintenance man on *The Simpsons*. A mental giant compared to Carl Spackler, Willy made millions of dollars in software but lost it at the track, and has to settle for mopping the floors and tending the award-winning playing fields at Springfield Elementary School. Willy, interestingly a native of Scotland and burdened by voice actor Dan Castellaneta with a comic Scottish burr, also has significant social problems. His father was hanged for stealing a pig back in Glasgow. Women do not find him attractive. He has violent impulses. He washes with scouring powder and lives in a shack. He wears nothing under his kilt.

Superintendents have found notoriety only as fictional idiots. In real life, the preparers of even championship golf venues have few lines to speak. The Golf Course Superintendents Association of America dutifully supplies writers with the name, phone number, and credentials of the man in charge at each of the events on the PGA, Nike, and LPGA tours. The handout also includes the types and heights of grass on the course, sprinkler capacity and manufacturer, the year the course in question was built, the designer, and the kinds of wild animals that roam its acres at night. But most writers do not avail themselves of the opportunity to talk hybrid grasses and growing cycles and how is your armadillo problem; thus, in the history of golf, the warden of the course never became part of the tournament story. Never, that is, until the 1999 Open.

John Stanley Philp came to golf in the traditional way, as a caddie. While carrying gentlemen's bags at Pitreavie Golf Club—near the Forth Bridge, in Fife—the twelve-year-old decided he'd like to give the game a whirl. He tried it, and liked it, but sensed a better long-term opportunity in working on the course than in baggage handling. So young Philp went to work, scything thistles from the Pitreavie rough, at age fifteen. "When an employee got to push the Certes [human-powered] mower over the greens and tees, that was a real privilege," Philp recalls. Sometime in the mid-sixties the club finally bought a mower with an internal combustion engine.

Philp stayed with golf, and with growing and mowing. His boss, Len Jamison, liked to sit on a sack of seeds and talk to young John about the time not too long before when he'd begin his day at 4:30 A.M. He'd push open the creaking barn door and put padded shoes over Old Mary's hooves. While the horse ate her breakfast, Len would go home for his own. On his return he'd hitch Old Mary to a gang-mower and off they'd go to trim the fairways the old-fashioned way.

Old Len's stories and the smell of new-mown grass got Philp thinking about a life in golf. "I was quite a competent player, with a two-handicap, when I was offered the head pro job at Pitreavie in 1970," Philp says. "They'd never had one before." He accepted the new position while keeping the old. Old Mary was long gone, of course. "We had one tractor, an old petrol-paraffin Fergie 35. When you got to ride that, you were the bee's knees." After the mowing, he changed into his golf-pro hat, giving lessons and looking after his small shop.

Within months, the head greenkeeper, Peter Ogg, died of emphysema, and his twenty-four-year-old assistant stood at a crossroads. Should he take Ogg's job or pursue the golf pro's life? Philp knew he couldn't do both. And though by now he and golf shop assistant Helen

Watson were courting, he took the road less traveled by, and that has made all the difference.

"That was quite an experience, becoming a head greenkeeper at a very young age," says Philp. "With three full-time employees and one part-time, we rebuilt four greens and a few bunkers with no input from architects." Stimulated by the leap to sculptor from just the man who polishes the sculpture, Philp studied the arcane details of golf-course architecture. His work drew good reviews, and his enthusiasm and ability to express himself drew further notice. In 1979 his career took a quantum leap, when Walter Woods, the head superintendent at St. Andrews, hired young Philp as his deputy. "I was quite delighted to be offered the job," Philp says, "and quite delighted to be back in Fife."

While Newmarket sprinkled only its eighteen tees and greens, and only locals played it, St. Andrews consisted of eighty-one holes, a putting course, a sophisticated fairways-greens-tees irrigation system, and the most famous and popular golf course on earth, the Old. After six years, and after again demonstrating his abilities to maintain and to build, John Philp's future and that of Carnoustie became linked. By extension, Arnold Palmer and microwaves also affected their fates.

After Hogan's win at Carnoustie in 1953, the Open slid back into its postwar funk, because except for Frank Stranahan, Americans didn't play in it. "How da fuck you go to da British Open unless you was rich?" asks Al Besselink, no scholar, but expressing a common sentiment of his peers on the post–World War II golf tour. "Even if you won, you lost money." And before Hogan, unless the Walker Cup or Ryder Cup teams were in town, there was scant American participation in the Open. Byron Nelson, a meticulous financial diarist, calculated that his Ryder Cup and British Open adventure in 1937 cost him at least eight hundred dollars.

Television galloped to the rescue like a pony, and on its back rode TV's first and still greatest golf celebrity, Arnie. Palmer's star had risen in 1960, when he won the Masters and the U.S. Open—on TV—with a great deal of telegenic smoking, emoting, and charging. After a runner-up finish in 1960, he returned to try again for the Claret Jug in 1961, at Royal Birkdale on England's northwest coast. A gale blew in off the Irish Sea and rain like bullets pelted Birkdale; the tented village near the clubhouse shuddered, then collapsed. Conditions got so bad that Friday's third round was scrubbed, an important point because it made the tournament run over to Sunday. This allowed another day of TV, and another day of Arnie.

As the low towers holding the TV crews swayed in the still-lusty gales on Saturday, announcer Chris Schenkel almost had to shout to describe the wondrous performance of the man from Latrobe. Arnie shot 32 on the front nine of the third round; the next best score was 38. A wonderfully inventive player, Palmer was gripping his one-iron down to the steel to scoot shin-high shots to the greens. His low-ball technique got him the lead, as well as Sunday morning newspaper headlines back in the States. Golf's greatest thespian wore a funny little wool hat for the final round, but he did not disappoint the viewers back home. Arnie won by one shot over Dai Rees.

By any reasonable measure—prize money, quality of field, or public awareness in the country with the most golfers—the Open had been reborn. The first-place checks at the Carnoustie Opens fairly charts the trend: £100 for Armour in 1931 and for Cotton in 1937; £500 for Hogan in 1953; Player got £3,500 in 1968; £7,500 for Watson in 1975, and the 1999 winner would have £320,000 electronically transferred to his bank. The pounds flowed because Arnie's victory in 1961 made the Open a valuable television property. People with money would watch it, and advertisers with money would pay to get in the way while we tried to see the golf. Each year the stakes went up. No longer could the Open tolerate a backwater venue with no hotel. And if the condition of the field of play fell too far from perfection, that golf course would be dropped from the rotation. So good-bye, Carnoustie.

Which was where John Philp came into the picture. In the 1970s the course had deteriorated badly. They'd tarted it up for the 1975 Open, but they couldn't hide the truth: Carnoustie was as tattered as a vagrant's undies. Bureaucratic bumbling had allowed the ground to compact and weeds to overrun the great links; County Angus owned the three Carnoustie courses, so the decline had to be laid at the municipal door. That tax revenues were down in hard economic times mitigated the blame slightly, as did the failing health of Bob Falconer, the strongest advocate for golf within the local government. As Falconer's assertiveness waned, so too did the Carnoustie maintenance and equipment budgets.

When the local golfers' disgust with the course conditions reached critical mass, Carnoustie's renaissance began. The owner of the course, the Angus Council, agreed in 1980 to accept a Links Management Committee as tenant and operator. Of the two committee representatives elected by each of the clubs, one man stood out above the others: Jock Calder. A physically powerful and charismatic man, Calder accepted the chairmanship of the Committee in 1982, and made it his mission to bring the Open back to Carnoustie. The first big step in his plan was hiring Philp away from St. Andrews.

"A very assertive and forthright man was Jock," says Philp. "Very competent in many spheres, and equally good at speaking to people above him and below him, and commanding their respect. He was a civil engineer by training and was a director for Bett's, a big construction company. And a former military man. The Black Guards."

Calder knocked down the other big obstacle between Carnoustie and the Open by finding a hotel developer from Dundee.

"When I arrived, they had one spiker for three golf courses," recalls Philp. "And the other equipment was a load of scrap. They'd used lime to make the lines for spectator fairway crossings in 1953, and someone noticed how the grass came up a lovely green under those lines later on. But that was meadow grass, which turns white with seed heads and is difficult to hit golf balls from. Unfortunately, they spread that potato fertilizer everywhere. By the time I got to Carnoustie, the local golfers were fed up with the conditions."

Calder talked on occasion with the new superintendent about the glories of Opens past at Carnoustie, especially the one in 1953. He spoke fondly of those days when Armour and Cotton and Hogan walked the earth, giants they were, so different from the current crop of whingers shooting next-to-nothing on ridiculously easy courses. But even Hogan had to fight to tame Carnoustie. Soon, securing a spot on the championship rota became Philp's crusade, as well. Recognizing his unique ability to sell himself and his ideas, Calder put his new man in front of the county council to solicit more money to restore the course. The chairman trusted him in any situation. The R and A began to take the Carnoustie initiative seriously in 1987, and sent its consulting architect, Donald Steel, to see what was happening on the course. Philp took the crucial meeting. Steel liked his proposed changes and suggested a couple more.

Although Calder died two years before his dream came true, he would continue to speak through Philp during Open week. Not that the younger man had been so impressionable; rather, they just agreed on many important issues. "[The contestants] are all geared up to hit shots precise distances. They can tear up the yardage charts here," Philp told *The Irish Times.* "They're not prepared for this type of game. They thought they would come here and rip the guts out of it. Who the hell do they think they are? This is very special. This is serious.... Required to hit a half-swing seven-iron, they're mesmerized. There is so much money in the game I think they're losing touch with reality. A lot of them have made no preparation for the world's greatest event. They thought it would be just another venue with the winner finishing nineteen-under. I don't think so."

But on Thursday night, and for the only time all week, he felt the weight of being the principal defender of the playground. The R and A had invoked Philp the entire week, partly because they agreed with what he said about these pampered modern golfers, though they felt constrained from saying so themselves. But their arm's-length stance

gave the whingers a face and a name on which to focus their complaints.

"They're after my hide," he said sadly. "The players say they're
looking forward to links golf, to the run-up game, except when they
actually get to do it." He'd stopped his green utility cart near the fifteenth green. Turning to his left, he watched the players and caddies in
the second-to-last group wander uncertainly around a gorse bush. To
his right, two of his fifty employees raked long, broken leaves of grass
into impressive mounds of green and beige. Every day the gallery's feet
cut down another crop of bent and rye, which Philp's crews harvested
every night.

He restarted the cart and drove over a maze of crushed-seashell
roads to the second fairway, where he came upon six young men, each
carrying a three-gallon plastic bucket of mixed soil, sand, and seed.
"How are we doing, lads?" Philp said. "Good, good," murmured the
troop of divot fillers. Up at the second green, Philp coached another
employee in the application of water and Aqua-Doc wetting agent.
"Over here a bit more, Angus," the superintendent said. "This area is
not really defective, but it doesn't look good on TV."

Fatigue showed around his eyes. For several months now, he'd
been arriving for work at four-thirty A.M., and returning home around
six P.M. "Shall I pick up a video?" he'd ask his wife and daughter. Three
times in a month he rented *City of Angels,* badly overacted by Nicolas
Cage, according to his daughter, Barbara, and three times he got in his
chair in the corner and slept all the way through it. Then he'd return to
the course, to take care of his "bits and pieces," as Helen called it. He always returned from his nocturne between eleven and midnight,
whistling. Something corny, usually; early in Open week his song had
been "Happy Heart," by Andy Williams.

But he wouldn't whistle tonight. Philp climbed back into his
dusty green Jacobsen cart and continued his patrol. Preoccupied with
high scores and the hurricane of complaints, the garrulous man fell
silent.

F RIDAY, SEVEN A.M. Coffee and tea were free in the little mess section in the Media Centre, compliments of Town and Country Catering. Writers, photographers, and broadcasters from many nations prepared their caffeine drinks, bought their cheese-and-onion sandwiches, their meat pies, their Mars Bars, and their roast-beef-flavored potato chips, entering and exiting so often during the week they stopped noticing the six four-foot-high photos to the right of the cafeteria door: the five Carnoustie Open champions, and the current holder.

On the far left was Armour, big-nosed and gangly, not yet the handsome man he would become when he gained a bit of weight and his hair turned silver. But he wore an elegant double-breasted suit that afternoon in 1931 when he accepted the Claret Jug from tartaned and kilted Lord Airlie. Next to Armour, Cotton, nicknamed The Maestro. Cotton held the Jug while wearing a silk tie, a knowing smile, and a beautiful camel-hair overcoat, borrowed from Henry Longhurst. The action photos of Hogan, Player, and Watson revealed less than the formal poses of the first two champions. But the close-up of Mark O'Meara after his play-off win over Brian Watts in 1998 spoke eloquently with a universal message. O'Meara kept his hat on for the presentation. And on his black cap, in white capital letters: TOYOTA.

Clothing etiquette? Americans don't get it. "*Surely* Mr. Lehman will remove his Dockers hat during the presentation?" Bob Blyth had said aloud to his telly in 1996 when Tom Lehman won the cup but failed to doff his lid. Blyth, Carnoustie's Hogan correspondent, had muttered a similar plea to Mark Calcavecchia in 1989, when the new Open champion kept his Titleist cap on in the aftermath of his win at Royal Troon. "But Justin Leonard [hatless during his victor's speech in 1997] was just the opposite, a super person."

Even away from the solemn joy of the final act of the Open, golf retains a lot of its traditional formality in the British Isles. Visitors to Muirfield, for example, should treat the day as an outing at a church with a golf course attached. Coats and ties, please, from the moment you arrive and at all times in the clubhouse. A guest at Moseley Golf Club in Birmingham finished his round and walked to the bar, remembering to remove his hat. Having won, he bought the beer, but in a moment of insanity, transferred his hat to his head while trying to carry four lagers to a table. Immediately, voices rang out: "Your hat, sir! Kindly remove your hat! No hats allowed, please!" Many clubs have both a bar and a stud bar, the latter not requiring manliness, but allowing shoes with studs, or spikes. But even studs better remove their bloody hats when they enter.

At Sand Moor Golf Club in Alwoodley, Leeds, the club secretary, B. F. Precious, posted a notice which left nothing to chance. "Smart casual wear is permitted in the clubhouse at all times, but this should be a change from that worn playing golf. If gentlemen wear shorts whilst playing, they must be tailored, and full-length stockings with turnover tops must be worn. Shorts may not be worn in the clubhouse by Ladies or Gentlemen after 6:00 P.M." Military service is the classic background for club secretaries.

Just as appalling to the traditionalist as the impolitely hatted heads were the commercial messages attached thereto. There are deep meanings, to be sure, in the fact that it always seems to be a Colonist who violates the rules of taste. But the deepest meaning is money. Some players do not get paid, or paid as much, if they win but remove their endorsement hats in the afterglow of TV lights and flash photography. Not that the Europeans have so much room to talk. The signage at their tournaments often makes the area around each tee look like an outfield fence at a minor-league baseball stadium. And today touring pros from every country advertise one to five or six products on their persons.

An American refrigerator company started it all in the mid-sixties. "We were trying to build a distributor network, but we couldn't compete with the big guys, GE and Whirlpool," recalled Lou King. "They gave away trips." The senior vice president of marketing for Amana gave away rounds of golf with touring pros, and hats on which he'd had sewn—why not?—the Amana logo. To King's surprise, now and then the pros wore their free hats during competition, not just to wash the boat. Possibly the key moment in logo history occurred at the PGA Championship at Pecan Valley in 1968. With the TV cameras on him and the San Antonio sun beating down, Julius Boros pulled a white Amana bucket hat from his bag and put it on his head. Eureka! To encourage this ridiculously cheap, effective, and accidental campaign, Amana began paying fifty bucks, an amount equal to a tournament entry fee, to any pro who'd wear the hat all during a tournament week. In 1980, Amana distributed over a million hats. Between 1958 and 1982, the company's sales increased fifty-fold, and it wasn't all because of the new Radarange.

Just once you'd like to look at a golf pro and not get a commercial. But that will never happen again. The space on a top-thirty player's hat, sleeves, chest, and bag rents for hundreds of thousands of dollars a year, too much to pass up. Magee, as usual, would speak honestly about the implication. "None of these guys will admit it, but we play for the money," he said while relaxing behind a beer on Wednesday evening. "Maybe not all of us; I don't know about Tiger and Duval. But my motivation is having to send quarterly checks to the IRS. The only things I'm not paid for are my iron shafts and my underwear."

If the portraits by the media cafeteria reminded you how much money had changed things, the images also hinted at golf's timelessness. Armour was old enough to have known Old Tom Morris; Old Tom apprenticed as a feather-ball maker under Allan Robertson, the original golf professional and the first formal designer of the ten-hole Carnoustie links. In 1872, twenty-two years after his mentor's primitive dirt work, Old Tom expanded the course to eighteen. Hogan, several years dead and forty-six years removed from Carnoustie, feels so present in 1999 it's as if he's entered in the tournament. When Henry

Cotton won his first Open, at Royal St. George's in 1934, he left the presentation ceremony as soon as it was seemly and walked to the nearby Guilford Hotel. Went to a room and knocked on the door. He entered and then gently placed the trophy in the lap of an old man who'd been too ill to watch that day. And tears streamed down the face of Harry Vardon, the greatest Open champion, whose name had been engraved on the Claret Jug six times. Vardon died two and a half years later.

EVERY CARNOUSTIE OPEN produced a great champion, strange weather, and certain bizarre subplots. The greatest unifying characteristic, of course, was the course itself. Even seventy years ago, a round at Carnoustie was like giving up smoking: hard at first, then more difficult, and finally damn near impossible. But Carnoustie in 1975 was doable, more like giving up dessert. Because of the drought that turned Carnoustie into a runway and tee markers set way up where the members play, many look at the '75 Open as an aberration. For not only was the winning score nine under par, the man who shot it had never played a British Open before.

"Shortly before the tournament, Tom Watson came to me and said, 'Peter, tell me about links golf,' " recalls Peter Oosterhuis. "I said, 'Tom, sometimes you must land the ball twenty or thirty yards short of the green.' " Watson took the simple advice to heart; after two rounds, Young Tom II, Oosterhuis, and Andries Oosthuizen of South Africa were all at 138, one shot out of the lead. This represented the greatest performance by two double-O's in major championship history. With his long white hair in a pageboy 'do, Oosthuizen looked like a member of the pop music band ABBA. The unlikely leader was a surprised-looking club pro, David "The 'I' Is Silent" Huish of North Berwick.

"I birdied fifteen in the first round, then chipped in on sixteen," says Oosterhuis, the runner-up in the 1974 Open. "I remember that Johnny Miller was in the group just behind us. I'd just beaten him in the Italian Open, when I'd chipped in and holed a wedge. I imagined he thought, 'Here we go again.' "

No, we didn't. Miller, who'd bought a Ferrari in Italy, shot 66 in the third round. Jack Nicklaus asserted himself, too, as he always did in the disco age. His 68 took him to eight-under, two behind Miller. The scores that week were as preposterous as the clothes. An Australian chap named Jack Newton, who of all the contestants wore the shirts with the biggest collars and the widest and whitest belts, shot a third-round 65. He trailed Bobby Cole for tightest double-knit pants. As an eighteen-year-old, Cole had won the 1966 British Amateur at Carnoustie. Now, after consecutive scores of 66, the slim South African led the tournament at twelve-under, one ahead of Newton. Twelve-under for three rounds at Carnoustie!

At the press conference, someone pointed out the quality of the players just behind the leader. "Maybe they could all drop dead," Cole said with a smile. "I mean, how would you like to be in [this] position, Nicklaus, Miller, Irwin, all of them biting at your heels?"

"Watson?" prompted a writer.

"Watson, all of them," Cole agreed.

The west wind returned for round four, as did sweaters, umbrellas, and more Carnoustie-like scores. Only one man broke 70: Bob Charles, who, incidentally, does not recall his 69 or even that he played that week. Of the horrendous clichés haunting golf, "It all came down to the last few holes" may be the worst. But it all came down to the last few holes.

Fifteen slopes right, doglegs left, and is bunkered right; both Newton and Cole, first and second at that moment, bogied it. "When we got to the next tee, there were three groups waiting," Newton recalls. "Nicklaus, Floyd, Watson, Miller. A Who's Who of golf. I don't think that forty-minute wait did me any good." The sixteenth, a downhill par three of 250 yards, screams for comforting mounds around its green, something to bounce an off-line shot in the right direction. But instead of friendly mounds, Carnoustie's sixteenth gives the golfer agoraphobia. With too much of nothing to frame the shot and a bit stale from waiting, Cole missed the target way right. Newton, smoking cigarettes and chewing gum simultaneously, missed the little plateau to the left. Chips, two putts, two bogeys again. Miller, Nicklaus, and Watson were catching up.

Twice the Barry Burn snakes across the seventeenth fairway, creating the hole's landing area and its name, Island. Both the Newton and Cole tee shots clung precariously to dry land above the ditch; from awkward lies, both missed the green on the long against-the-wind par four, and both made their third consecutive bogeys. Up ahead, Watson had birdied eighteen, to go to nine-under, tied with Newton for the lead; Nicklaus had only parred when a birdie would have moved him to nine as well; and Miller, by leaving his six-iron second shot in what is now known as the Miller Bunker, also finished at eight-under. The last twosome finally hit a green in regulation, the eighteenth. Newton missed from twenty-five feet to win; Cole, his putting magic gone, missed from fifteen to tie.

Stormy weather continued off and on the next day. Almost immediately, the Newton and Watson play-off turned a bit edgy, at least from the Australian's point of view. Watson hit a full four-iron to two feet on the second hole. "Great shot, Tom," Newton called politely. No reply. And when Newton hit shots of equal brilliance, the intense little man from Kansas City said nothing. "I'd always been taught to acknowledge an opponent's good shot," Newton recalled. "Well, to hell with that if he's not going to reciprocate. I'll just keep my mouth shut."

Silent Tom chipped in for eagle on the fourteenth to go one ahead, then bogeyed sixteen—for the fifth time in a row—to fall back into a tie. Tied they remained to the final hole. An important moment, mirroring the Masters in 1958, when at the end it came down to two similarly young and talented men, Ken Venturi and Arnold Palmer. Like Watson and Newton, neither had won a major. There was not a dime's worth of difference in their golf games at that particular moment, but one man would win, transforming his self-image and his future.

Like Venturi, Newton would be the other man, the one who looks back in regret. The Aussie bunkered his two-iron second shot, and his twelve-footer for par skirted the edge. Watson made four. A few minutes later, while Jackie Newton cried into her husband's chest, Tom and Linda Watson held the Jug between them and kissed it.

Watson would become a great champion, and win the Open four more times. But he was a withdrawn, often unhappy man. In the eight years after Carnoustie, Newton would win once on the U.S. Tour and finish second in the 1980 Masters, a mediocre record compared to Watson's, but he had a hell of a good time doing it. Then his career came to a violent stop at the Sydney airport. Newton recovered with amazing speed from the accidental amputation; three major surgeries and five months later, having already completed his mourning for his lost limb, he debuted as a television golf analyst. He filled his life with one-handed golf games, family, TV announcing, a golf course design business, and a full plate of charity work. On July 13, 1975, in front of seven thousand witnesses, Watson had beaten Newton 71 to 72. But Newton didn't really lose.

CARNOUSTIE LOOKED AND PLAYED more like itself in 1968. High wind and high rough led to high scores and numerous solemn pronouncements that "this is the toughest course in the world."

Two images from the 1968 Open became part of the collective unconscious. Jack Nicklaus provided the first. By opening with five fours in the final round, Nicklaus cut his four-shot disadvantage to one. Bob Charles, Nicklaus's playing partner, Gary Player, and the overnight leader, Billy Casper, were now tied at the top. On the sixth tee The Bear decided to take the Hogan line. But he hooked the ball over the fence and out of bounds.

As a child in his backyard in Columbus, Ohio, Nicklaus had often kicked a football through goalposts formed by tree limbs, pretending to be Lou "The Toe" Groza, the field-goal kicker for the Cleveland Browns. Furious, for a second he became a boy again. To the shock of the spectators, Jack booted his golf bag so hard that it flew out of his caddie Jimmy Dickinson's hands. In some versions of the story, Dickinson went flying with the bag.

Eight holes later, Gary Player produced the second moment that time cannot erase. The South African had taken the lead with a birdie on the sixth but lost it with bogeys on ten and thirteen. The fourteenth played into a strong, cool breeze. Two bunkers on a ridge—the Spectacles—hid the green from sight. Player, as usual monochromatic in black pants and turtleneck and white glove and shoes, uncovered his three-wood for his second shot. With the most pronounced right knee forward press in golf, he began this crucial swing. Then he . . . let's let Gary tell it.

"I started at the backswing, hit, and then waited. The roar started again and I ran to the top of the hill. I said afterwards that the ball was traveling so perfectly on line, I had to lean sideways to see the top of the flag. . . . Henry Cotton [was watching] and he held his hands apart to show me I was only two feet from the hole. I leave it to others to ponder on the nature and source of such a match-winning stroke."

Player finished at one over par 291, two shots clear of Nicklaus and Charles. Michael Bonallack, the man who would be Sir, finished eleven back.

Player packaged his reminiscences of this and many other glories in his second and most recent autobiography, *To Be the Best.* Rarely has a title been so apt, because the little South African had an overarching intensity that was embarrassing to behold. During a preliminary round before a recent senior tour event, he played with four businessmen. From the first hole he reads their every putt and comments on their every shot. The four duffers are quite obviously flattered and amazed at the attention from one of golf's greatest. But he wants the pro-am experience for these men he's just met To Be the Best they've ever had.

During the round, apropos of nothing but his own thoughts, Player says, "If you're going to be a top athlete, you've got to know how to talk, how to read, how to write. You've got to take elocution lessons. You've got to be a *great* orator, not just a good orator."

The cart rolls over the flat ground of Silverado Country Club. Player groans loudly and sympathetically as one of his amateur teammates flubs a shot into the sand. "Arnold Palmer and Jack Nicklaus were really poor bunker players," he says. "You know why? They were never in them! But Jack and Arnold Palmer are the two men I admire most. You never saw them walk into a dining room with their hats on, or wear their hats back to front, or travel on an aeroplane in jeans or tennis shoes."

He shares his goal of winning a tournament after the turn of the century, which would make him the first to be a winner of a professional tour event tournament in five decades. It turns out that Gary Player is not only one of the world's greatest showmen, and sportsmen, he is also the world's biggest show-off.

"Once when we were entertaining some friends at our ranch, I did not greet them right away because I was practicing," Player says. "My wife, Vivienne, said, 'Gary, you're being rude.' I said, 'Tell them to come down here with their drinks. I must hole my fifth bunker shot.'"

Bobby Cole has his contemporary and countryman figured out. "When Gary tells you how many push-ups or sit-ups he can do, he truly believes it can help him win," says Cole. "Not the exercises themselves so much as telling you about it. He's trying to convince you—and himself. Gary was very, very tough to play against in a tournament and difficult to play with. You knew he would use every opportunity to beat you. Anything legal, that is. I never saw him play outside the rules."

Cole brings up the latter point with Tom Watson in mind, for the two Carnoustie Open champions waged a bitter and public fight after

Watson accused Player of cheating during a skins competition in November 1983. Tom alleged that Gary illegally adjusted a growing weed under his ball before playing a chip shot. Player denied the charge, of course. In his book, he insinuates that the shocking accusation may have been the culmination of years of personal enmity. "I have never warmed to Tom as a person," wrote Player. "I found him too dour. In fact, when we were both under contract to Ram Corporation, I suggested that we conduct our clinics separately because I found no enjoyment working with him. There was a sharp personal edge to be seen and at times a disregard for the courtesies that normally exist between professionals." Player had also been peeved that Tom had gone behind his back to hire away his regular British Open caddie, Alfie Fyles.

Physically strong, obviously intelligent, proud, driven, below-average height—the two men were similar in a score of ways. But Watson's parents could afford Kansas City Country Club and golf lessons for Tom, while the Player family hovered between poverty and disaster. Gary's father, Harry, made three hundred dollars a month working ten thousand feet underground in a Johannesburg gold mine, and his mother, Muriel, died of cancer when Gary was eight. Watson majored in psychology at Stanford and all that that implies; Player turned pro at age eighteen. They weren't so much oil and water as Abel and Cain.

IN THE DOG DAYS of the British Open after World War II, only one top American player could be counted on to participate. He was not Hogan, Nelson, or Snead. He was not even a professional. Nor was he a former caddie, a mama's boy, a drinker, or anyone's fool. In the entire history of the game, Frank Stranahan was unique.

The pride of Toledo and the heir to the Champion Spark Plugs fortune had the money and the game to play the biggest tournaments in the world, pro and amateur. "I'd finished second at Greensboro, second in the Masters, and second in the British Open," he says in his nearly uninflected voice, recalling 1947, one of his many very good years. "This was as an amateur, mind you. There was no amateur who could compare with me." It's not bragging if it's true: Stranahan proved it by capping his year with a win at the British Amateur at Carnoustie.

Strannie won big pro events too, such as the Los Angeles Open. "At the trophy presentations I'd say, 'I want to be the best in the world.' And those pros would glare at me."

Resented for his money and his lack of tact, Stranahan suffered a number of run-ins on both sides of the Atlantic. A misunderstanding over a conceded putt caused one British Amateur flap, a matter of firing his caddie resulted in another. But from his native generosity and his unmistakable love of the game, Stranahan became one of the boys. You can't find one of his peers from the forties and fifties who doesn't remember him with fondness. "When you'd talk to Frank, he wouldn't respond right away," says Mac Hunter, a club and touring professional from Los Angeles. "He always thought someone was trying to put one over on him, and usually they were. But he handled that real well—amazing, given his background and theirs [the golf pros]."

Of all the great and nearly great golfers in the United States, only Stranahan, Hogan, and Lloyd Mangrum entered the 1953 Open. "I liked Carnoustie because I could fly the bunkers," he recalls. Forty years ahead of his time, Stranahan lifted weights and ate a strange but relatively healthy diet—sometimes nothing but steak, or nothing but grapefruit, or huge doses of honey. Rich, impeccably groomed and dressed, and possessed of bulging arms that made the young girls sigh, Stranahan occupied one of the centers of attention wherever he played. One other thing added to his romantic stature: he hit home runs.

"I was thirty yards past Hogan in the practice rounds," he recalls. "I was using the Dunlop 65, an eighty compression, because it was so cold. But Hogan's using a one hundred compression ball. I asked him why and he said, 'Frank, over here the ball hits the green and just keeps rolling.' He dropped one of his hundreds and it hardly rolled at all.

"I asked him to take a look at my swing and he said, 'I would never even begin to try to help you. Take what you have, do the best you can, and make your own decisions.' Hogan was very intelligent."

Stranahan's 70 gave him the first-round lead, and John Derr called him into his little CBS radio studio in the starter's box. To their left the hidden sea blew cold salty air over Carnoustie, and behind them a sea of automobiles squatted in front of the brownstone Bruce Hotel.

"Well, Frank, things look pretty good for you in this tournament," began Derr, cheerfully.

"It's only one-quarter over, John," Stranahan replied, dry as dust. Between Hogan, Stranahan, and the impenetrable brogues of several locals he interviewed on the air, Derr had a tough week. But young Frank was right. He slumped a bit in the middle rounds with 74 and 73. His closing 69 gave him an equal second finish with Thomson, Cerda, and Rees.

More obsessed now with fitness and longevity than with golf, Stranahan lives a quiet life in a stark white house in West Palm Beach, Florida. Stress or drunk drivers can kill you, so he doesn't go out much. Sun can age and wrinkle your skin, so he completes his workout at the gym before sunrise. He lives alone.

When Gary Player started to come to the United States in 1957, Strannie took him by the hand. Explained that black clothing was always chic. Told him a few things about eating right and lifting weights. Lent him his Cadillac; Frank always drove Cadillacs because their heavy springs could take the weight of the weights he traveled with. When in London, Stranahan always made a point to call on Henry Cotton at his club. Thus he linked two eras in the history of golf and the British Open at Carnoustie. But he's just as keen to talk about the future as the past. Stranahan is a seventy-five-year-old man who thinks he's middle-aged.

A TRIUMVIRATE RULED golf at the turn of the century. John Henry Taylor won the Open five times and finished second five times, grunting during each ferocious swing like Monica Seles hitting a ground stroke. The little man from North Devon, England, also designed golf clubs and designed and built dozens of golf courses with his partner, Fred Hawtree.

When Taylor didn't win, James Braid usually did. Lanky, quiet, and unflappable, Braid cut a Lincolnesque figure but with a monumental walrus mustache instead of a beard. No one can be as wise as James Braid looks, they said. In a ten-year run, the impassive man from Elie, Scotland, won the only tournament that mattered five times and was runner-up another three. The most durable of the three—he celebrated his seventy-eighth birthday by shooting a 74—he was also the most homebound, and never crossed the Atlantic. In the winter of 1926–27, Braid had a go at remodeling Carnoustie; his was the eighth such effort, and probably the best. It got Carnoustie its first Open.

Harry Vardon, the greatest of the three and therefore the greatest in the world, swung in time with a Viennese waltz and took divots about as often as he put down his pipe—which was almost never. His life began on the little island of Jersey, and ended with recurrent sadness. At age fifty-five, he fathered a child out of wedlock with Matilda "Tilly" Howell, a singer/dancer from Liverpool, but convention did not permit him much interaction with the son he'd always wanted. Between his remote and rural beginnings and his bitter end, Vardon enjoyed life and won the Open six times.

Their glory faded. Americans came to the fore after the armistice. One of them was as flashy as the sheen off his pompadour, another was a boy-wonder with a wondrous temper, and the third looked like he'd just stepped out of the caddie yard—which he had. Hagen, Jones, and Sarazen. Man, were they good. No Scot or Englishman compared. Then Thomas Henry Cotton came along, wearing an ascot, and driving a red 1929 Mercedes-Benz cabriolet. Like Andrew Magee, Cotton kept the top down.

He spoke French. He devised a floating golf ball driving range in front of the casino in Monte Carlo in the winter of '46. A continental man, Cotton took the job as pro at Royal Waterloo Golf Club in Belgium partly because he could afford more wine there, which seemed to soothe his chronically sour stomach. On days off, he liked to motor over the bumpy Belgian *pavé* to the smooth highways of France and on into Paris. In addition to being the only English golfer of world stature in the thirties and forties, Cotton stood out as the golf correspondent for two magazines, *Country Life* and *Golf Illustrated*. The first tournament prize ever won by Bob Charles—he and his mother were runners-up in a mixed foursome event—was a book by Henry Cotton. "That book was my real introduction to professional golf," Charles recalls. When the child in New Zealand looked at a picture of Cotton's long, supercharged Mercedes and read "I once stupidly drove 555 miles in eleven hours from Evreux to Biarritz," he began to imagine the possibilities of a life in golf.

Steve Elkington owns the same book, *This Game of Golf*. He underlined this passage in pencil: "There is no doubt that under pressure the good player keeps on pivoting and the bad player gets frightened to pivot. . . . If I have to think of any one thing to get myself into position successfully to hit a crucial shot, it will more often than not be pivot."

Cotton tied for the thirty-six-hole lead at the first Carnoustie Open in 1931, which prompted Eliot Cockell, the publisher of *Golf Illustrated*, to take the overnight train from London to help with his correspondent's final push. But Cockell "helped" Cotton to a third-round 79 and the end of his chances of winning. When Cotton finally took the big prize three years later—and brought the cup to Harry Vardon's hotel room—he was the first Englishman to win the Open in eleven years.

What the USS *Manhattan* delivered six years later guaranteed an exceptionally strong field for the second Carnoustie Open. The United States Ryder Cup team that walked down the gangplank included Snead, Ralph Guldahl, Denny Shute, Gene Sarazen, Horton Smith, and Byron Nelson, who'd never been out of the country before. Nelson "drove against" Cotton in the opening foursomes at Southport and

Ainsdale. "I put my ball inside his [on the par threes] every time, and we ended up winning," Nelson recalled. The U.S. team won eight to four, its first-ever Ryder Cup win on British ground. Then the professionals trained up north to Scotland.

A lot of them didn't like what they saw. "Too many forced carries," said Sarazen. "Why have traps in the middle of the fairway?" asked Denny Shute. "Too much importance is attached to the drive here, and I figure you might get on better using an iron off the tee." Old-timer Sandy Herd, the 1902 Open champ, called Carnoustie "a slogger's course. They've made it too long [7,135 yards] even for these big hitters." But Cotton commented in his plummy voice that he didn't care if the winning score was 312, as long as he had it.

"I forget about rain, I am so engrossed in the task of keeping my score as low as possible," Cotton wrote in a column published during the qualifying rounds. "Nevertheless . . . I find it hard to imagine anything more discouraging than the cold wind and rain which swept Carnoustie." The rain remained on the Angus plain the rest of the week.

Cotton missed most of the final day's downpour, and pulled ahead of Nelson, Snead, and all the other Yanks. But it was raining hard when The Maestro drove way right on Carnoustie's last hole, playing away from the out-of-bounds on the left. He sensed he had a lead of one or two; would he play his second shot safely, short of the burn? He would not. Cotton took out a two-iron, again aimed way right, and concentrated on hitting the ball as hard as he could. After an eternity of three seconds the ball landed on the other side of the ditch and settled in the bunker, hole-high to the right. He splashed out, two-putted, and won by two.

The rain stopped for the presentation of the Claret Jug and Cotton's stylish gray suit did not get wet.

THE YOUNG BYRON NELSON owned apple cheeks, a long, thin frame, and an unshakable belief in the Lord. Byron never fooled around on Louise or smoked or drank—well, one drink, once, but he hated it—which caused earthy Sam Snead to ask, "Just what *does* he do?" Well, no one could call it a vice, but Byron ate breakfast of a morning with very great pleasure.

As the lanky Texan prepared to wrap himself around his ham and eggs before a round in the 1939 Western Open, a Scottish voice asked, "May I join you?" Byron looked up and beheld the magnificent Tommy Armour. Sure, he said, sit down. They'd only recently met, since Nelson had signed with MacGregor Golf to play the Tommy Armour Silver Scot golf clubs. His first set came off the rack in Tommy's pro shop at Boca Raton Country Club.

Oh, to have a photograph of Byron's face as Armour consumed his pregame meal: a shot of whiskey, a gin drink, and a glass of Bromo-Seltzer. "It was the most unusual thing you've ever seen," Nelson says. "But he really handled it well. I never saw him what you'd call drunk."

Armour lived a life of superlatives, not the least of which was his heroic appetite for and tolerance of alcohol. He may have been the best golf-ball striker of his era, and the worst putter. He won the British and U.S. Opens and the PGA and twenty-four tournaments on the U.S. Tour. No nineteenth-hole raconteur could touch him, and his stories about the Great War made many a man forget to sip his drink. He owned the biggest, strongest hands of any golfer, bigger even than Nelson's giant mitts, which enabled him to tear through a deck of cards and to strangle a German soldier in France. No one gambled more at golf, or so enjoyed the give-and-take of setting the bet.

"Armour teamed up with Bobby Cruickshank, another former Scottish amateur who turned professional," Henry Cotton recalled. "They knew all the tricks. . . . Two cross-talk comedians would find it hard to keep up with these first-class kidders."

Armour wrote the best-selling book of 1953. Not the best-selling golf book, the best-selling *book*. Partly as a result of the success of *How to Play Your Best Golf All the Time* and a second best-seller entitled *A Round of Golf with Tommy Armour,* wealthy hackers stood in line to pay him two hundred dollars for a lesson, at least ten times more than what anyone else could charge. At his southern headquarters in Boca Raton, Armour delivered his wisdom from a chair behind a table under a pink and white beach umbrella, always with a gin buck within easy reach. The tutor called out, "Hit the hell out of it with your right hand," while his sweating students hit brand-new balls from the pro shop, never range balls. This added value to the lesson, and made them care about each swing. An assistant ostentatiously unboxed the balls and teed them up, further enhancing the mood.

A courtly and charming man with a full head of silver hair, Armour and amour went together like an interlocking grip. An often-repeated locker-room story takes place in a luxurious boardroom at Winged Foot or Oakland Hills, both of which employed Tommy at different times. Six committeemen sit at a large table. Their spokesman clears his throat: "Tommy, we regret to inform you that your contract has not been renewed. Feel free to seek employment elsewhere. Now, about your compensation . . ." and the club man droned on.

Finally, Armour rose from his seat. "I've screwed all your wives save one," he said. "Good day to you."

Tommy told that one himself, but not all his affairs went so well. The headlines in the London *Times* in January, February, and June of 1921 revealed one tangled web he'd weaved. THE ACTION AGAINST A GOLFER and GOLF CHAMPION AND GIRL VIOLINIST and GOLFER SUED FOR BREACH OF PROMISE; "GREATEST MISTAKE OF MY LIFE." According to *The Times*,

Mr. Thomas D. Armour, the amateur international golfer who lives at Comiston Road, Edinburgh, was the defendant in an action in the Courts of Edinburgh today for breach of promise at the instance of Marie Catherine Young, a Leith violinist, who sued for £2000 damages.

The plaintiff, who is twenty-five years old, said she was introduced to the defendant in December 1916. He seemed at once to become attracted to her, and she was also attracted to him.

Counsel read extracts from a number of letters written by the defendant to the plaintiff, all couched in affectionate terms.

The plaintiff said that Armour proposed marriage in April 1917 and she accepted him, but there was no time fixed for the marriage. In 1920 he went to America to play in the championship. In November she received a letter from the defendant, dated New York, in which he wrote: "I have made the greatest mistake I ever made in my life and already I have realized it. I was married two weeks ago in New York to a Spanish girl. . . . It was a great mistake, but she fascinated me beyond everything. I could not help it. She haunted me on golf courses until I did not know what I was doing, and then we got married. . . . I hope you will forgive me."

But Marie Catherine Young did not forgive. She had been introduced to Tommy by his sister, who played the piano in the same picture-house orchestra as Miss Young. At the time of his betrothal to the "Spanish girl," Senorita Carreras of Cuba, it had been three and a half years since the alleged engagement of Armour and Young. "Lawsuits like that weren't terribly unusual back then," says Gaylen Groce, a well-known attorney from Fort Worth. "Possibly Mr. Armour used the implication of a future marriage to gain something that Miss Young might otherwise have withheld from him."

The defendant protested that he'd only given the girl a watch, not a ring. The jury discussed it for half an hour and found for the plaintiff, though for three hundred pounds, not the asked-for two thousand. Armour moved to the United States.

All that was a decade in the past when Tommy came marching home again for the 1931 Open. The Carnoustie galleries enthusiastically supported his campaign, but they fancied another expatriated Scot more than Tommy: MacDonald Smith. Mac endeared himself to the locals by having been born in Carnoustie, the son of the links superintendent—though he was just a child when his family emigrated to California in the great golf pro exodus. History would remember MacDonald Smith as a lovable loser, but he was neither.

The Smiths of Carnoustie were the most remarkable family in golf history. Willie, Alex, George, Jimmy, and the baby, MacDonald, all became golf pros. Willie won the U.S. Open in 1899 and Alex won it in 1906 and 1910. In the latter tournament, Mac, age twenty, tied for first with Alex and Johnny McDermott, but his 77 in the play-off was third best. Mac subsequently stood too close to the cannons in France during World War I, and suffered a profound hearing loss, which led to a nickname: The Silent Scot. At some point in the teens, Smith became a drinkin' man, a bad one, and disappeared from the sportswriters' view. "Poor Mac has the jitters," Armour said. Twice, prestigious clubs hired him to be their professional, but Mac lasted at Olympic and Oakmont only one year each. He couldn't stand being nice to the members, particularly after he'd had a few belts.

His renaissance began with his marriage in December 1922 to a Mrs. Louise Harvey of San Francisco, a woman thirteen years his senior and a Christian Scientist. With his drinking under control, Mac won the North and South, the Western Open twice, and twenty or so other tournaments. Since the Western and the North and South were among the four most important tournaments of the day, Smith's reputation as a loser or as the best player never to have won a major is entirely undeserved.

But the way he lost the Open at Prestwick in 1925 stained his name forever. This was a wide-open Open, because Hagen and Jones had not entered. Smith played well, built a big lead, and needed only a final-round 78 to win. But all of Scotland seemed to follow his final trip around quirky old Prestwick, and Smith had to wait up to ten minutes for the crowds to clear so he could hit his tee shots. He overanalyzed things during the delays and suffered an appalling 82. Smith boycotted the Open for the next three years.

He returned to Scotland for the first Open in his hometown. But like Prestwick '25, Carnoustie '31 would be a loser's Open.

Partly out of duty and partly to watch some golf, royalty often visited the great annual championship, but the Prince of Wales had an unusual rooting interest in 1931. He'd taken his clubs on a recent tour of Argentina, and had practiced his swing on the deck of the *Arlanza* on the return. A golf pro who happened to be on board watched the royal hacker and said *"bueno"* or *"manten la cabeza asi abajo."* Jose Jurado and His Royal Highness became friends. A month before the Open, the shipmates became teammates in a match against the Duke of York and James Braid, and won, two and one. Although Señor Jurado spoke no English, he could play golf in any language. He not only qualified for the Open, he played superbly. With the Prince looking on, the unheralded Jurado led by three shots over Smith and by five over Armour with one round to go. Tommy was hitting the ball great as usual, but he had the yips again.

> Jurado: 76-71-73
> Smith: 75-77-71
> Armour: 73-75-77

Armour conquered his nerves in the final round and made up ground. He jerked a little one on seventeen, however, which added to the difficulty of his three-footer for par on eighteen. He knew it might be a putt to win. He put a death-grip on his hollow-headed mallet to stop his shaking hands. "The instant the club left the ball on the backswing, I was blind and unconscious," he said later. The putt fell in for a 71.

Jurado needed three pars to tie. He got the first by holing from eighteen feet after his shot from a bunker, but he dribbled a feeble iron off the seventeenth tee, an infamous 150-yard shot into the burn. He made a six. Needing a birdie four now to equal the score Armour had posted an hour before, Jurado tragically played for a five; no one in his vicinity could speak Spanish, and scoreboards didn't yet exist. So in ignorance, Jose played short of the burn with his second shot on eighteen and got the bridesmaid's par.

With three holes remaining, Mac Smith led Armour by one. Three pars to win. What happened next recalled some words philosopher and humorist Ernest Thayer wrote in 1888:

Oh, somewhere in this favored land the sun is shining bright,
The band is playing somewhere, and somewhere hearts are light,
And somewhere men are laughing, and somewhere children shout;

... But there was no joy in Carnoustie. Mac Smith finished double bogey, double bogey, par.

CHAPTER FIVE

Burns

———

Everybody's got a plan—until they get hit.

—*Mike Tyson*

P ROFESSIONAL GOLF ATTRACTS depressives, or it creates them. The ball driven three hundred yards nestles too deeply in the fairway grass. The iron shot to eight feet should have stopped within a yard of the jar, but it rolled too much because of an unseen and unseeable hard spot on the green. The gallery's applause is therefore often annoying, almost insulting. This instant feedback and relentless disappointment reinforces a me-versus-the-world feeling and the perception that the big-time golf pro is arrogant, defensive, and lacking sympathy for the safe and mundane ways others make their livings.

But then there was Andrew Magee, the Pro-Am King, playing like a dog on the first few holes of the second round of the 1999 British Open at Carnoustie. The bogies mounted on his card, but he did not darken the cold July morning with frowns or histrionics. After whacking another drive into the maddening rough on the sixth, he trotted toward the gallery ropes. "Sub!" he called out, reaching out an arm like a wrestler trying to touch the hand of his tag teammate.

Magee's caddie smiled at the boss's joke and continued his racewalker's stride down the fairway. Eric Meller complements the earnest yet fun-loving persona of his boss. He is twenty-eight, similarly blond, similarly handsome, and can talk the birds out of the trees. A flamboyant heterosexual, one of his favorite openings is to ask attractive young women for their panties, which he promises to place in a pocket of Andrew's golf bag—"to keep the balls warm." He claims a surprisingly high success rate with this get-to-know-you technique; a red crushed-velvet pair surrendered by a sweet young thing in Orlando in 1998 may be his favorite trophy. He's been on Magee's bag since midsummer of 1996. Before that he worked as a home builder, a caddie at a club in Florida, and an assistant golf pro. Before that he studied nursing, but gave it up just two or three semesters short of his degree.

Meller veered left into the rough on the tenth hole, waving a five-pound note at a friendly spectator and mouthing "I'm starving." The bill fluttered like a paper kite in the freshening wind. On the eleventh tee, the gofer delivered a ham and cucumber sandwich, a Twix bar, a Diet Coke, and his change. "Cheers, lovely, brilliant," the caddie said, in perfectly accented British.

Susan Magee looked low-key behind big sunglasses, but with each bogey she smoked another Marlboro. Lisa Elkington will raise her voice with a "Great shot, Elkie!" but Mrs. Magee hangs back, chatting quietly in her sensual alto. "The Arizona resident began his comeback with a thrilling birdie on the seventh hole," said a friend in sports writerese on the seventh hole, but Magee took bogey instead. "Carnoustie's gusty winds could not extinguish Magee's red-hot putter as he rolled in a long birdie putt on the short eighth," but no such birdie occurred. On the ninth hole, however, a fed-up attitude seemed to take hold of him. For six consecutive holes, he hit fairways and greens in regulation, and though he usually stalks and squints on the green like a surveyor getting the finest reading from his transit, now he putted after just a cursory look at the terrain. On the twelfth green, Kim Jong-Duck barely got out of the way after marking a three-footer before Magee's putt started rolling. The hurry-up offense resulted in three pars, two birdies, and one bogey, modest numbers elsewhere but a hot streak at Carnoustie. Magee loyalists resumed talking about a subject no one had raised for an hour, the possibility of making the cut. He'd need four pars to stay at ten-over, probably too high. Magee himself had dismissed the idea of playing on the weekend.

Holes have names in Scotland. Carnoustie stuck mostly to the straightforward—Ditch, Dyke, Cup, Burn, Railway—but the fifteenth owned a wonderfully descriptive handle, Lucky Slap. A 472-yard par four usually evokes an image of a wide fairway and a four-wood second shot. But the wind and the skinny corridor of wind-hardened fairway made Carnoustie's fifteenth a four-iron and a two-hundred-yard eight-iron, landed well short, because the dune-encircled green wouldn't hold a water balloon, much less a golf ball. Magee underestimated the bounce of the second shot and came up twenty yards short. But he hit a luckier slap with his sand wedge to five feet and made the putt.

Sixteen, a 250-yard par three, also played downwind. A driver for Jack Nicklaus against the wind in 1968; Magee hit a six-iron in 1999. But the wind-assisted golf ball acts like the baseball pitcher's knuckleball, and an erratic flight and roll is no bargain on a par three with a tabletop green and an absolute orgy of rough to the right. Magee missed the target to the left, putted up the shaved slope, and missed from ten feet.

With a full-out driver and a three-iron, he hit the green on seventeen, but charged his twenty-foot putt four feet past. He wiggled that one in for par. Eleven over now, one hole to play. For the last time, Magee stood on the eighteenth tee and pondered the Barry Burn. A strange hazard, more seen than felt, because the meandering ditch hid like a snake in the grass on the dead-flat plain of the final two holes. Magee decided that the burn's invisibility increased its danger and made good swings more difficult. But did its blocked banks and concrete bottom diminish it, making it too obviously man-made and sewerlike? No, he thought, the industrial-looking hazard fit right in at industrial-strength Carnoustie.

Needing a birdie now to make the cut he assumed he'd already missed, Magee drove into a bird's nest of a lie on eighteen. Two sand wedges and two putts later, his tournament ended. He signed his card for a 79 and walked toward the hotel to meet his wife and friends and any media brave enough to address another disgusted golf pro.

James Mossop, a brown-haired and amiable columnist from the London *Sunday Telegraph,* wondered if he could ask Mr. Magee a question? Shoot, said Magee. Given the conditions here, would you have trouble recommending this course and this tournament to other pros back in the States? "A lot of us will go home and tell our buddies how it was and we are not going to have too many kind things to say about Carnoustie," Magee said. "You'll have to hope that an American wins it so that he can go home and tell the folks something glamorous about it."

Someone in Magee's party noticed that a little portable bar had been set up in a corner of the hotel patio. And above it two emerald-green beer tap handles glowed like stained glass on Easter Sunday morning. The angels sang: free Carlsberg. Andrew and company settled at a front-row table with an unobstructed view of the hubbub below and an unimpeded path to the beer. The sun shone down and the hotel and grandstands blocked the wind. Magee put on sunglasses and tilted back his chair and a pint of liquid gold. Soon the turmoil and strife of competition receded. Dropouts from the parade, Magee and friends watched the world go by.

They watched as Sandy Lyle approached the final green, a stocky, erect man who looked like he'd spent his life pitching bales of hay into a loft. He'd been the bitterest of the whingers after round one, but the 1985 Open champion smiled now as he walked over the burn bridge, placed his white golf glove on the grip of his putter, and waved it to and fro in mock surrender. The crowd should have tittered at his humorous gesture, but didn't; perhaps they did not see it. Lyle holed out for an 81 to go with his opening 85.

Tom Watson made a nice putt to finish with 73, whipped cream on the dung of his opening 82. He grinned in acknowledgment of one of the loudest cheers of the day. He missed the cut by one. David Duval finished bogey–bogey–double bogey–bogey for a 75 and a 155 total, exactly on the cut line. As Greg Norman became visible on the distant eighteenth tee, Mrs. Greg Norman appeared on her third-story balcony like Rapunzel. Magee and Meller turned around and exchanged waves. Competitors walked past, some relaxed, some not. Billy Andrade was not. Marching to the first tee, trying to get into the zone, he could not hear Magee's greeting. But he got into the wrong zone and shot 84. "How'd you do, Magoo?" asked Mark Brooks. "I met the cutest girl in the pub last night," said Meller. The conversation floated like a butterfly from the possible delights awaiting in Scandinavia, to a possible visit to Stirling Castle tomorrow, to what to do about dinner.

Elkington emerged from the hotel dressing room. He glanced at the obvious beer activity at Magee's table. "Pints," he said dryly, then clattered down the steps and to the first tee without a pause or another word.

Magee had had relatively calm conditions for the first hour or two of his round, but Elkington's 12:55 start gave him a fresh breeze that would not go away for the rest of day. The weather report in the Edinburgh newspaper had predicted "bright intervals," a forecast as vague and as partly right as a horoscope. Elkington teed off in a bright interval, which turned to gloom with an immediate bogey. Nine-over now after nineteen holes, he couldn't afford many more slipups. But neither could he avoid them.

On the seventh hole, Elkington drove just one inch into the "semi-rough," but his ball nestled down like a cherry tomato in a bowl of Romaine. He had 210 yards to the green, against a gale. White out-of-bounds stakes loomed to the left, a continuation of the line from Hogan's Alley. He hated to lay up, having come so close to hitting the fairway. But if he hit it over the fence, all hope was gone. With no good options, Elkington blew the shot way out to the right and took another bogey.

Derek Carr and Lisa Elkington walked briskly along, looking for silver linings. "Good bogey," Carr said wisely more than once. "Could have been worse," said Lisa of an iron shot not too far off the green. They studied the scoreboards: might ten or eleven over par make the cut? Certainly not twelve, which was Elkington's standing with five holes remaining. "He's got to birdie here," Carr said as Elkington waited to hit from the tee of Carnoustie's only birdie hole, the fourteenth. A downwind, dogleg left par five, fourteen required just two accurate irons for most players to reach its double green. But Elkington pulled his tee shot into a nasty lie in a nastier sod-faced bunker, and he barely got the ball back to safety with a sand wedge. The resulting six and tee shots into the hay on sixteen and seventeen decided the issue. Fed up too late, Elkington bombed a driver on the last hole over 344 yards.

By the time Elkington finished, it had become clear that his 79-78-157 and Magee's 77-79-156 would miss the thirty-six-hole cut. One hundred fifty-four would be the magic number. A glittering cast stood on the wrong side of twelve over par: Phil Mickelson, furiously; Mark O'Meara, the defending champion, silently; and, incredibly, the first-round leader. With a second round of 86 to go with his opening 71, Rodney Pampling had grabbed a piece of history. No first-round leader in the Open had ever before missed the cut. Rodney P. on Thursday: "We plan to finish in the top ten." On Friday: "I had a bad hole on the ninth and a couple more—and suddenly, you have an 86." The most dismal previous first to worst had been turned in by Ted Ray in 1922. Big Ted led with a 73 at Sandwich, then fell to rounds of 83, 85, 80. Chicken feed compared to 71-86.

"I wish I hadn't come here," said Mickelson. "I was looking forward to playing one of the greatest links courses ever created. The R and A botched it. I would only come back to play Carnoustie the way it was designed."

Elkington said or did nothing revelatory after his round. Lisa had fetched the kids from day care; he hunkered down and spread his arms wide and they ran to him to smother him with, and be smothered by, kisses.

A magazine photographer asked Elkington to pose with his family. He did so, cheerfully, next to the first tee. He traded a few insults with Carr, then invited Carr and Martin Roy "to come back to the house," where he thanked the Carnoustie caddie master warmly and paid him generously. His expansiveness and good humor looked a lot like relief. The Elkingtons were on a plane back to the States at midday on Saturday.

Zane Scotland, on the other hand, wanted the week to never end. Not that his results had been so good; his Friday had been much the same as his Thursday. Even par through five holes, his ball consistently found rough and bunkers thereafter. On eighteen, in brilliant sunshine, he hit his second shot within inches of the heavy wire fence on the left, right in front of the packed grandstand. The three thousand seated spectators whispered and buzzed while young Scotland puzzled and swung experimentally with two clubs from five angles. Finally he just chipped the ball back toward the tee. He made a double-bogey six, for an 81 and 140th place, but that didn't matter to anyone.

Least of all to Bernie. Zane holed his last putt, accepted a standing ovation, then moved to the side of the green to hug his father. Another wave of applause rained down in the football stadium atmosphere. Something about this kid had hit a pleasing chord. His youth, his shy but confident smile, his name, and his lack of pretense or calculation formed a refreshing package. And he didn't whinge.

"How many guys have the guts to play their shot backward on eighteen at the Open in front of everybody?" enthused his caddie, Ron Cuthbert. "I told Zane all day, this is like a chess game. His head went down a couple of times but we had a saying: 'That's Carnoustie.' I think everybody in amateur golf should be proud of that boy today. I'm privileged to be a part of it."

The dramatis personae went their separate ways. The Magees drove to Gleneagles for dinner with friends; the Elkingtons packed; Zane Scotland and his pals went to a McDonald's and a snooker hall. The next day was his seventeenth birthday. Derek Carr departed for the pub.

A long, last look at the black-on-yellow scoreboard above the grandstands on eighteen made you think about the scores being shot and the names not there. When the average score for the best players in the world was over 78, and none of them could break par for two rounds, was something wrong with the competitors or was something wrong with the test? Nothing unimpeachable could be said for either side. Philp and the R and A felt they must preserve the integrity of par and the sanctity of the record book. The players felt deprived of hope; the spectators watched with concern instead of excitement.

The display of those who'd handled the test, more or less, revealed names strange and familiar. LEONARD and WATTS sandwiched LAWRIE in a tie for seventh at five over par. WOODS and NORMAN tied for fourth at four over. VAN DE VELDE, like Lawrie, another cipher, led the thing at one-over. One shot behind *le monsieur* waddled *el pato*. (CABRERA was known as "the Duck" back home in Argentina.)

Van de Velde had shot a 68, largely on the strength of a putting round his playing partner could scarcely believe.

"He could win this tournament," Bob Charles told his wife, "if he learns to proceed with caution."

A LITTLE LOVE BOAT called the *Clipper Adventurer* anchored a mile out in Carnoustie Bay during the championship. For between $4,495 and $7,000 each, the 122 guests on board dined regally, played "five rounds of unforgettable Scottish links golf," according to the PerryGolf/InterGolf brochure, and attended the Open. From a door in the ship that opened to sea level, the sailing golfers stepped into motorized, inflatable dinghies, which then putt-putted right onto the beach. They walked across the hard-packed sand, up a flight of wooden stairs, and there they were, at an Open entrance next to the practice range. Lovely.

But by its pubs shall ye know the Open, not its tourist ships. St. Andrews, for example, has a handful of well-known meeting places specifically designed for the after-golf conference. At times you need a lubricant to squeeze into the two most famous, the Jigger Inn and Dunvegan's. The tiny white Jigger squats hard by the green at the Road Hole, and manages to feel homey and comfortable despite its neighbor on its other side, the tony Old Course Hotel. Try the soup. Tip Anderson presides at Dunvegan's, and for the price of a drink he'll tell you why he's called Tip instead of James—an inheritance from his father, a caddie who sometimes maintained pool and snooker tables, and put new tips on the cues. Another drink might buy you knowledge of what Arnold said during the rain delay in 1960, or what Tip told Tony about the sand wedge the year Lema won with only one practice round under his belt. Mr. Anderson holds forth in a quiet, dignified way; you sense his ironic amusement at being a tourist attraction.

An Open at Muirfield requires a visit to The Old Clubhouse in nearby Gullane, or to The Quarterdeck in slightly more distant North Berwick. The Quarterdeck is a well-lit L-shaped room with three green-shaded lights overhanging the pool table. The inevitable dartboard and a chalk scoreboard hangs to the right as you enter. A sign next to the men's room toilet-paper holder says SELF SERVE, and you certainly hope so. The Quarterdeck became famous during one of the wild nights during the 1992 Open, a warm evening when an overflow of one hundred spilled out the door and onto the street, not that the pretty models from the exhibition tents had to wait outside for long. It was a night, according to an eyewitness, when "I watched John Daly put twenty pints down his neck." Mrs. Fred Couples apparently had a few, too; she climbed onto a table and did a bit of a striptease, she did. Fred's side mentioned Deborah's willful public display of her brassiere in the subsequent divorce petition.

The American cocktail lounge is an arena for intrigue and business deals, but the pub in Scotland is a place for the entertainment of conversation. For centuries the Scots have been acknowledged as the best educated, most egalitarian people in Europe, and many of them enjoy a ritual nip, a combination that makes for delightful company. In Dallas, the gentleman on the next bar stool might offer a gambit no more stirring than: "How 'bout them Cowboys." But greater efforts are made, or greater minds are at work, in the Scottish pub. In *The Scots,* author Clifford Hanley recalls once encountering "in a grubby inn among the tenement back streets of working-class Glasgow, a shabby individual who on visual inspection would not have fetched £2 on the open market, and while I was making the calculation, he said, 'The basic fallacy of Freudian theory is the silly old trout's assumption of his clinical rationality, when in fact he was a suppressed doorknob fetishist, and it's your turn to buy the next drink.' "

Similar erudition is available in a St. Andrews basement tavern half a block from Dunvegan's. Its similarity to the main set on the TV program *Cheers* is eerie. After the familiar get-to-know-you ritual of light conversation and having a drink, and then another, you pose a vague question about Scotch and the Scots. Waitresses Katherine Jefferson and Jenny Bowman respond with impressive specificity and detail. The relationship starts early, Ms. Jefferson explained. "A parent may give a child age five a bit of port or sherry if he's got a gippy tummy. You can drink a beer at age eighteen in a restaurant—or sixteen if you look old enough. The pubs open at eleven in the morning and close at midnight."

Behind the bar, a backlit shrine of whisky bottles draws the eye like neon. The labels thereon for Glen-this and Glen-you-never-heard-of testify to the popularity of single-malt Scotch. Why so many? According to Ms. Jefferson, and to connoisseurs who are probably kidding themselves, and to enterprising bottlers, water from two streams tumbling off the same mountain yields whisky of completely different flavor. You gotta taste 'em all! To some, the local Scotch identifies a town as much as its golf course. Carnoustie doesn't have its own distillery—it's a Highland thing—but Glendronach, from Huntly, is born only seventy miles away, and it's damn good.

The rise of Scotch, you learn, coincided with the birth of the Open and the American Civil War. The grape crops in France frequently failed in the 1860s; then plagues of aphids caused further disaster. Well-bred English who ordinarily drank cognac and brandy were persuaded to try Scotland's peasant moonshine. They liked it. Prohibition gave Scotch another tremendous boost and opened up the United States market. In the final decade of the millennium, Americans swirled single-malt instead of wine in their tulip glasses and squinted and sniffed and held it up to the light and talked about body, nose, finish, and palate. "It is an amusing little Scotch, but I think you will be surprised by its presumption."

Ms. Bowman, whose father, Jimmy, is a wise and weather-beaten caddie at the Old Course, continued the tutorial. "Scottish words you should know? We'll often say 'clute' for cloth, 'baffies' for slippers, 'seemit' for vest. 'Mankey' is dirty; 'minging' is dirty and smelly. 'Better watch or I'll skelp your dock,' a parent might say, meaning 'smack your butt.' 'Nithered' means very cold. What else . . ."

A bar patron gripping a pint overhears; overhearing is a key part of pub society. His contributions are of a theme: snoggin' is kissing; winching is the hugging preliminary to snoggin'; and of a homosexual gentleman, it may be said that he is "bent as a ten-bob note."

Another Scottish word in common use, "stroppy," often attaches to "American." It means rude or arrogant. Stroppiness often manifests at breakfast, according to Ms. Jefferson: "There was one the other day who wanted me to butter his toast. Imagine! Like he's a baby. And another asks, 'Can I pay with dollars?' "

Open patrons spending the evening in Carnoustie often warm

their nithered docks in the Kinloch Arms. To get there you walk north away from the beach and the huge white nylon WELCOME TO CARNOUSTIE signs fluttering above Links Parade. Ferrier Street or Park Avenue conveys you to High Street. Take a right, starting to walk uphill now, past the tiny library and the Chippie, with the four lowest denominations of United States paper currency taped to its window. On the right the Kinloch Arms presents its plain, flat face to High Street. Its right half houses a restaurant, its left, the pub. Derek Carr turned left.

The Friday night revelers included several touring pros and several famous spearmen. Fluff Cowan, Bruce Edwards, and Jimmy Johnson, caddies for Jim Furyk, Tom Watson, and Nick Price, respectively, waved and called to Carr when he entered the bar. "Derek, have you met Tom Watson?" Edwards asked, and the introductions were made. Edwards then whispered a request: would he go and get the pipes? No, said Carr. Edwards persisted, and bought him a beer. Finally Carr agreed to serenade the five-time winner of the Open.

He played "Flower of Scotland" and "Scotland the Brave" and "Yankee Doodle Dandy" for the Americans. Watson, newly married and newly happy, looked delighted. Three other pipers appeared, but they were mere pub players, fifteen handicappers on the instrument compared to Carr's scratch. Yet the four together blended magnificently. When they finished, a hundred and fifty flush-faced men and women roared in unison. Under the affluence of incohol and fired with patriotism by the pipes, they looked ready to march off to war.

ANOTHER MARCH OUT of Carnoustie began one hundred years before. The damnedest thing happened: when golf began to boom in the Gilded Age, Carnoustie supplied the world with more instructors, club builders, and caddie masters than anywhere else. Why this happened no one knows for sure. But depending on who's counting, between 150 and 300 Carnoustie carpenters, jute spinners, vitriol stirrers, ironmongers, and shoemakers left their little village between 1898 and 1930 to become overseas golf professionals, mostly in the United States. Carnoustie exceeded all other villages in Scotland in spreading the golf gospel, even St. Andrews.

MacDonald Smith's oldest brother, Alex, was in a party of five golf pros aboard a British steamship sailing for New York in March 1899. Not so fast, a union boss said. The hell we bringing in these jocks for? Looks like a violation of the alien contract laws. The ship was detained in New York Harbor until responsible parties determined that the United States really did need golf instructors. The immigration seemed to go without a hitch after that. Whole families soon got on the boat west, most notably the Smiths and the Simpsons from Carnoustie, and the Auchterlonies from St. Andrews. There was moon-faced Clarence Hackney, a big man and a big drinker, who took the Atlantic City Country Club job in 1915 and kept it the rest of his life, which lasted until 1941. And Harry Hampton, Willie Mustard, Davie Bell, Walter Carnegie, Jimmy Mason, and at least a hundred others, Carnoustie men all.

The newly minted American golf pros made about sixty dollars per month, board included; the exchange rate was five dollars to one pound. Most earned extra money teaching. A lesson then was not stand-and-hit, but a nine-hole playing tutorial for which the pro made about seventy-five cents. Some added to their wallets by building clubs or by winning tournament prize money. The average income of the Scottish American pro in the early 1900s was about £150, which dwarfed the foreman's £90 salary at Simpson's golf club factory in Carnoustie. No wonder they wanted to leave.

Many of the lads returned home for the winter, often with annoying American accents. "It is not pure American, either," said a St. Andrean, whose ears were offended by "a sort of a cross between American, English, and Fife, and with some it is a really bad cross. On the links, you hear the young pro: 'A bully fine shot, sonny.' . . . 'That one's gone some.' . . . 'What do yew think o' thaat.' . . . 'Yew putted great thaar, ol' boss.' "

A few of the Carnoustie pros in America touched greatness. Marty Cromb landed the job at the Toledo Country Club, and encouraged young Frankie Stranahan. Sam White taught Art Wall, the 1959 Masters champion, at a little golf course in eastern Pennsylvania. Stewart Maiden grew up watching the best practitioners at Carnoustie use a long, aggressive swing, a narrow stance, and a hook. Maiden copied the technique and brought it with him to his new job at East Lake in Atlanta. On those occasions when the silent little man got out of the professional's shop to play the game, the bigheaded son of a lawyer followed him around the course. Thus did Bobby Jones learn the Carnoustie swing.

You could see some Carnoustie in the hook and the outlook of another great American golfer. Carnoustie's own Ken Stewart, a former assistant pharmacist, taught the rudiments to the greenkeeper at a nine-holer in western Pennsylvania, and provided the man's toddler son with clubs and balls. The superintendent, Milfred Jerome Palmer, subsequently succeeded Stewart as the pro. He operated in the humble yet proud manner of the Scottish professional, a style embraced by Mr. Palmer's son Arnold.

The exodus of about-to-be experts might seem to indicate that nothing was happening in golf back in Angus. On the contrary, a golf-based tourist industry thrived in Carnoustie for most of two decades. The Bruce Hotel and the bed-and-breakfasts filled up from June to August, and the city fathers built a bandbox and organized a brass band to serenade the golfers as they strolled about after dinner in the endless summer twilight.

But then the winds of war blew. The Great War in 1914 undoubtedly encouraged some of the lads to get the hell out of Europe, but most stayed to fight. Scottish troops gained renown for their ferocity in battle, and for the kilts they wore to the front. "Devil women," the Germans called them, or "women from hell." But when the Boches (from the French *caboche*, "hard-head," a derisive term for German soldiers) spewed mustard gas, the poison wafted under the kilts, burning sensitive areas. The Scots fought on in pants. No group was braver, or suffered more. Ten million died in World War I, and Scotland lost a higher percentage of its population than any other country.

Carnoustie grieved for eighteen soldiers, including Corporal Bertie Snowball, a club builder for Simpson's. Splinters from the shell that killed him at Aubers Ridge also blinded Willie Richardson in one eye. Richardson was well known for having played a lot of golf with Tommy Armour. Tank Commander Armour also lost the sight of one eye—mustard gas. His monocularism would make him the slowest, most interminably waggling player in golf.

War, opportunity, and restlessness made foreign golf pros out of hundreds of Scottish lads, but the golfers were only the latest installment of a migration 150 years old. French historian Amaury de Riencourt described the first Scots in America as "inhumanly self-reliant, endowed with an ecstatic dryness of temper which brushed aside psychological complexities...they fought their own selves with gloomy energy, repressing instincts and emotions, disciplining their entire lives... remorselessly brushing aside all men who stood in their path."

The Scots and Scots-Irish picked up their pots and pans and fiddles and axes off the American dock and did what no other immigrant group did—they kept going. They pushed into Indian country, away from British colonial control, and even away from themselves; they did not form cities or towns. They made their own tools. Like the Basques in Spain, they not only tolerated loneliness, they sought it out.

The threads stretched forward to the incoming golf instructors. They worked extremely long hours, usually alone. They made their own tools (golf clubs). They were extremely polite but not servile, with political and religious views mirroring the conservatism of their members. "There are two things I hate," went a joke often told in Glasgow, "religious intolerance—and Catholics." The son of Federico and Adela Saraceni recalled the cold shoulders turned his way when he was breaking into the business in the teens. "Those old Scottish pros sure didn't want an Italian boy around," he said. "It was a closed shop." At age fourteen, the boy anglicized his name, becoming Gene Sarazen.

How closed a shop? The PGA of America had a Caucasians-only policy from 1943 until November 1961. While it's not fair to blame the institutional intolerance on only the PGA's original members, the Scottish influence on the organization—and on the culture of the golf pro—was profound.

As the twentieth century wore on, the professional's status rose a few cautious notches above bootblack or caddie. Then alcohol and gambling addictions pulled their reputations back down again. The Depression boosted several golf tours around the world because the growing pool of out-of-work pros literally had nothing else to do but compete; who could afford to take lessons? But the prefix *touring* added another unseemly quality to the perception of the golf pro. "Golfing nomads," the sportswriters called them. Read: shiftless.

Actually, the touring pros shifted plenty, because they always worked simultaneously as club professionals. All of them, from Vardon to Cotton to Hogan to Palmer, did hard time behind a counter selling Mrs. Smith a package of tees or listening to Mr. Jones talk about his slice. All of them, that is, until Billy Earl Casper, Jr., who can be thought of as ground zero for the final disconnect between the club pro and the touring pro. Casper went from caddying at San Diego Country Club to junior golf to exactly one semester at Notre Dame (too cold! too lonely!) to a couple of years in the Navy and thence to the PGA Tour. He towed a twenty-eight-foot trailer and his teenage bride from tour-nament to tournament, and produced a very good living and a very large family. Buffalo Bill was the first big-time player never to toil as a club pro.

Now it's rare to find a touring pro who has ever hit a clock in a pro shop. The best players in the world no longer teach, or sell, or repair clubs, or schmooze with members. A major part of the Scottish legacy has died.

JOHN PHILP REMOVED his good blue suit from the closet on Friday night. "Ah yes, the prince will be here for lunch tomorrow," the superintendent said. "Met him once before, on the course. Quite a nice chap. 'So you're the man the pros will want to kill,' he said to me." Prince Andrew, the Duke of York, ex-husband of the fabulous Sarah Ferguson, is the keenest golfer in the Royal Family. He arrived in the lobby at noon in a confused swirl of blue suits and without the American politician's accompaniment of stone-faced men wearing earphones and sunglasses. He walked free for a moment—he's a nice-looking chap—then the suits surrounded him in a sort of rugby scrum and off they went into the dining room. R and A people, mostly, Bonallack among them. Infiltration seemed impossible.

But if he'd wanted to, the Zelig-like Derek Carr probably could have sat at the prince's right hand. No matter what encampment he visited in the Open community, the different tribes thought he was one of them. Inside the Media Centre, it was assumed he was a journalist. He ate inside the players' dining room or visited the players' changing area, and was taken for a competitor. Even in the R and A tent, where the men looked like John Updike and the women like Kathy Whitworth, Carr moved with a member's grace. The fact that he did not have the proper credentials for any of these heavily guarded enclaves made his blending that much more impressive.

"We've got to do something to Elkie," Carr said. With his Titleist tour hat on which rested Oakley shades, the Ayrshireman vaguely resembled David Duval fifteen years from now. Surrounded at the moment by Royal and Ancients, he stirred his tea and surveyed his domain. But how to even the practical-joke score with the superconfident Elkington? Carr noted that a new line of Elk golf shirts had come out with a stylized elk logo, as if from a cave painting. Could that be exploited? Or how about his burgeoning friendship with country music superstar Clay Walker? Carr also recalled that the rapidly expanding Elkington universe now included a golf course design company. "Let's pretend to be a potential client," Carr said.

Amid a great deal of snorting and giggling, a letter of inquiry was composed. The "client" would be named Wally Bampot; a wally is a jerk or a buffoon in Scottish slang. A bampot is roughly the same thing.

DEAR MR. ELKINGTON,

Please consider this an invitation to your firm to discuss the design of my new golf course at the ruins of the Castle Lingus in Fifeshire.

You have been referred to me by my second cousin Mr. Elmore Bampot of Pumpherston Golf Club.

I am Wallace Bampot IV, until three months ago the president of Bampot, Limited, Europe's third largest distributor of hemulators, incinerators and retransmogrification devices for the semi-hazardous waste industry. Now, with the buyout of Bampot's by RAMJAC Corporation of Cuyahoga Falls, Ohio, United States, I am in position to commit up to £10 million to the project.

The site features heavily wooded but rather flat terrain. The castle ruins lie on the northwest perimeter of the 282-acre parcel. While perhaps not suitable for restoration as a clubhouse, the ruins may well provide a magnificent location for a "half-way house" or a restroom.

We at Bampot's are keen fans of your marvellous golfing ability, and would consider it an asset to have you affiliated with our project. Please let me know by return mail of your possible interest.

MOST SINCERELY,
WALLACE BAMPOT IV

If Elkington bit, Carr decided to set up a meeting at the Dunhill Cup at St. Andrews in October. He'd get some letterhead, and use a friend's address as the Bampot "office." And who would play Wally, if the ruse worked? The possibilities seemed endless.

"Let's go watch the Frenchman shoot 80," said Carr, and rose to leave the R and A tent.

L IKE THE UNEASY beginnings of a summer storm, the atmosphere at Carnoustie had changed. With the field cut approximately in half, play proceeded on Saturday in twosomes, not three at a time as in the first two rounds. The spectators were more numerous, less knowledgeable, less dyed-in-the-wool—many of those who watched the first two days had had to skip work—buying more merchandise in the retail tents and consuming a lot more beer. As the pressure on players, caddies, officials, and media ratcheted up, and the sun came out for long intervals, an exhilarating, almost circuslike feeling took hold.

The excited charge in the air did not erase the unease between players and administration, however. In addition to the weeklong jousting over the conditions of play, now there were bad reports from the lads at the practice range. Of the rudeness of the pro who demanded tees without a please or a thank-you, then carelessly left his twenty pegs on the ground after he'd hit a few drivers. Of Greg Norman, for saying he'd be up to hit balls late in the day, which required a couple of workers to remain past the usual quitting time, but not showing up. A communications breakdown or a hangover from the end of round two? On the penultimate hole of a magnificent round Norman was five under par for the day and leading the tournament at one-over. But his tee shot leaked three steps into the rough to the right. He swung with a grunt, but the ball failed to achieve escape velocity; in fact, it didn't move at all. "I'm going to have to classify it as an air shot," Norman said later. He scored 70 with a 7 on seventeen.

More than anything else, however, the rangers' feelings were most hurt by the balls in the burn. The practice fairway for the Open was a temporary arrangement, occupying what was normally the fifth fairway of the Buddon course, part of Carnoustie's fifty-four-hole complex. Way to the left of the long tee lay the implacable gray North Sea; to the right, a high fence to keep the practice balls from the first hole of the Championship course; and in front, the bone of contention, the Barry Burn. Players were gently reminded daily not to hit into the burn, which was deep and wild with grass and salty mud. Any shot over thirty yards would clear the pit, but many balls found their way in anyway. The ball pickup crew grew bitter.

As the leaders began to tee off at around two in the afternoon, the condensed scoreboard read:

VAN DE VELDE:	+1
CABRERA:	+2
PARNEVIK:	+3
WOODS AND NORMAN:	+4
LEONARD AND FOUR OTHERS:	+5

Certain old hands, finding a variety of reasons to doubt the first three names, declaimed that the "real lead" belonged to Tiger, Greg, and Justin. And of these contenders, many of the sages liked Leonard best. He'd won two years before, passing Parnevik from five back on the final day. He wore HOGAN on his hat and golf bag, and on his heart; like all members of the inner circle, Leonard refers to him as *Mister Hogan*. The possibility of a win by a Hogan man at Carnoustie seemed too appropriate to ignore, so a writer asked him about it on Saturday night. "I've got enough on my shoulders as it is without putting Mr. Hogan on there as well," he replied.

Earlier in the week, Bob Blyth had waylaid Leonard and spoken to him for twenty minutes about his hero and pen pal. Leonard feared the enthusiastic Blyth was going to have a coronary. Hogan was hard to miss at Carnoustie, least of all for Justin.

The sincerity of his playing style earned him a reputation as the U.S. Tour's greatest grinder, a backhanded compliment. "Grinder" is not a word that attaches to tall, chiseled types like Norman and Woods, but is reserved for the little guy who can take nothing for granted. Hogan was a grinder, too, in a different way. If they'd traded short games, Ben would never have lost and Justin would never have won. And the reverse is true. With Hogan's long game, Leonard would be the king; if Hogan had had to make do as the sixty-sixth-ranked greens-in-regulation man on the tour, he'd have made his living fixing Buicks.

Both were meticulous neat-freaks, unfailingly gracious in public, and from north-central Texas. But the lower-middle-class kid from Fort Worth dropped out of high school; he was a caddie from a one-parent home and no world-beater until he practiced his way to the top. Justin, blessed with two successful and involved parents, was a college man and a star at every level, and possessed the wherewithal to *hire* caddies. In conversation with either man, a writer would be impressed by intelligence wedded to a determination not to say too much.

Leonard gave a virtuoso performance of avoiding the negative after his third round of the Open the year before, in a gale at Royal Birkdale. He was the defending champion and justifiably proud of it, and the 82 he shot that day plainly humiliated him. He faced the press behind the final green with eyes moist from the wind or emotion. His voice was flat, and he looked like his dog had died. "There's no trouble out there if you play on the fairways. The trouble was I wasn't on them too often," he said. "If I hadn't putted well I would have shot 90." For about five minutes he spoke. At the end, he tried a small joke: "I'm going to turn this score in and get my handicap rating changed." The writers laughed, murmured thanks, and dispersed. Leonard went to his parents and exchanged hugs. The tears more prominent now, he said, "That was the best interview I ever gave in my life."

For the mostly sunny and breezy third round a year later, Leonard selected a white sweater, shirt, and visor, taupe trousers, and brown-and-white shoes. He's a Ralph Lauren Polo man, a clothing endorsement as perfect for him as Coors Light is for Andrew Magee. He and Len Mattiace teed off at two-thirty, five groups ahead of the final pairing of Van de Velde and "El Pato" Cabrera. The group ahead, Kyung-Ju Choi and Paul Lawrie, crested the hill on one. "Game thirty-three," announced the cheery, amplified voice of Ivor Robson. "Justin *Leonard!*" Enthusiastic applause for one of Scotland's favorites, and a tip of the hat. Justin rocked into his unique, wrist-free swing, and creamed it down the middle. Larry Leonard, Justin's father, walked along the yellow nylon ropes to the left.

Hitting the ball like Hogan, Leonard staked three iron shots on the front nine: five-irons to a foot and a half on the fourth and to six feet on the sixth, and a six-iron to five feet on the par-three eighth. All day he putted well, struck the ball solidly, and strategized like a chess player. His even par 71 was one of the best rounds of the tournament. But the most shocking thing happened, or kept happening. Like a stain that no amount of scrubbing would erase, the name Van de Velde would not fade from the top of the leader board, and at the end of the day Leonard actually lost a shot to the leader.

Songs will be written about *le grand* Jean's third round at the 1999 British Open, if poets can find words that rhyme with "one-putt." Perhaps a composer of religious music can do something with it, because divinity dwelt in the way Van de Velde rolled his ball on the Carnoustie carpets. Certainly he looked and felt godlike when he lined up every putt, from any distance, and had a pretty good idea that it was going in. Someone estimated that he made 180 feet of putts.

On the other hand, the loser's glib and bitter accusation that all the other guy did was make putts is seldom completely true, and it held no water in this case. Van de Velde had something more going for him than that, something profound that made all those putts meaningful: self-control. His decision-making had no flaw. If his lie in the rough or bunkers looked less than perfect, he pitched out, and laid up. He continued to hit devil-may-care drivers from the tee, but reached just as many fairways as a lot of the more cautious players, and—duh—his driver got him further along than a two-iron would. And when Van de Velde missed a green, he was missing in the right places, precisely the strategy Leonard relied on.

He seemed to make a significant putt on each hole—or an unbelievable one. From eight feet for a birdie on the third, erasing a bogey on the second. From twenty-five feet on the seventh for another birdie. In a voice John Garrity of *Sports Illustrated* called "sort of an Yves Montand purr," Van de Velde described his Houdini pars on ten and eleven in the crowded Saturday night interview room. "Ten, I drove it in the left bunker . . . but the ball wasn't sitting very high so I decided to chip it short of the water and left myself about ninety-five yards and I hit it to five yards and made the putt. Then on eleven I dropped it in the jungle and I find the ball, chip it back on the fairway to what— seventy-five yards from the flag—and I hit a nice little pitch shot there to six feet, made the putt." But Van de Velde's adventure on eleven deserved a little more explanation.

No analysis in the perspiring arts is complete without a finding on the Turning Point, and the eleventh was the big fork in Van de Velde's road. By then Carr had retreated to the hotel bar, and was taking his ease with a lager and a TV screen. But the BBC did not show Jean's little drama with R and A rules official Michael Lunt. ABC TV did, however, and they had their best man on the scene, walking reporter Bob Rosburg. On the air and in the airport bar the day after the championship, Rosburg called Lunt's ruling the worst he'd ever seen.

No one expected Van de Velde's wild-right flight path on the eleventh tee, and no one could pick his ball out against the gray sky. But a spotter thought she saw something, and walked quickly to a seldom-visited area between the ten and eleven fairways. She peered into the underbrush and waved back to the tee; she'd found it. The ball had burrowed into the kind of lie from which Greg Norman had swung and missed. "A *horrible* lie," recalls Rosburg. "I didn't think he'd be able to hit it more than two feet." Jean's only hope, it seemed, was to play diagonally into the fairway. But on one particular vector back to the short grass stood the metal scaffolding of a ten-foot-high TV platform. A ladder leaned against it, and a camera and cameraman perched on its plywood floor. An ugly structure, and in the field of play. And it's in my way, maintained Monsieur Van de Velde: "I asked the referee, if I needed to—if I could get a relief, or if I played it—if I kill the cameraman, what would happen?"

Request granted by Lunt. The golfer plucked his ball from the tangle and dropped it a few yards away into a much better lie. He hit it out, hit it on, and made par. But the free drop had been a complete mistake. Only the Temporary Immovable Obstructions *in a direct line* between the ball and the hole can fairly be called "in the way." If a player was free to declare that any such obstacle in the vicinity blocked his nonlinear path, the resultant free drops would multiply and smell like subterfuge.

"I certainly didn't blame him for asking for a drop," Rosburg says, and Van de Velde's reputation as a fair competitor did not suffer. On the air, Frank Hannigan, Curtis Strange, and Rosburg wondered aloud about the wisdom of using amateur officials in such an important event, when there were gentlemen available from the European Tour and the PGA Tour who dispensed golf justice every week. While walking up the fairway a few minutes later, Lunt approached Rosburg and said something pleasant. "Made me feel kind of funny," Rossie said, "since I'd just blasted him on the air."

On the par-five fourteenth, the only birdie hole, Van de Velde seemed to blow a chance to pad his lead. Three mediocre shots left him in three-putt territory, about thirty steps from the hole. "Fourteen was funny," he told the press. "I made the putt. That was a good bonus, yeah. And eighteen, I hit a two-iron and nine-iron to forty-five feet and it went in. Great." Great God!

With one round to play, the condensed scoreboard read:

Van de Velde:	even
Leonard:	+5
Parry:	+5

WOODS:	+7
NORMAN AND CABRERA:	+8
LAWRIE:	+10

With the lead and the spotlight all day, Van de Velde had shot 70, one under par. His lead of five shots left many in openmouthed wonder, but the way he handled the fame that had been avoiding him his whole life was just as incredible. The dark, handsome man in black pants and a too-short-in-the-arms lavender polo shirt strode into the interview room in the press tent looking like he'd looked all day—utterly at ease. This was hard to understand. Didn't he realize the gravity of the situation? Then he explained himself with a combination of wit, good cheer, and fatalism the press had never heard from an elite athlete. He seemed charming, but he sure as hell didn't sound like the heir to Armour, Cotton, Hogan, Player, and Watson.

A questioner wondered if Jean would be a bundle of nerves on Sunday, despite his obvious relaxation now. "No matter what, even if I bring 90 tomorrow, I'm going to enjoy it," he said. "Because maybe people will say 'Oh, he blew it' or whatever. Maybe I'm going to blow it. It is the first time I am ever there. What do you expect? You know I'm not number one in the world. . . . I'm number one hundred fifty-something. . . . My knees are gonna touch each other on the first tee tomorrow, [but] let me tell you that I will enjoy it. I will force myself to enjoy it."

Additional questions emphasized the extraordinary fact that the third-round leader of the biggest tournament in golf was almost totally unknown to the world and the world's press. Someone asked when and how he became interested in golf. Van de Velde replied that he first played golf at age six and a half but thought of himself as a skier and a rugby and soccer player as much as a golfer. Even when he made the junior national team, golf was only a once-a-week activity. His final turn to golf seemed to occur during his mandatory army service at age nineteen. He had to endure only six or seven weeks of hut-*deux-trois-*

quatre; the rest of his year in the army was spent "detached," and practicing his sport. He had no coaching to speak of, but he progressed. "So I said, 'Well, you know, you're twenty years of age . . . if you think you can—you're improving—then maybe you keep on going. If you don't, well, you know, you play on the weekend, be a weekend player and start something, law or be a doctor or whatever.' "

Van de Velde looked his questioners in the eye when he spoke, a continuation of his unusual manner on the golf course. He'd hole a putt or nail a chip, someone would applaud or yell, and Jean would thank the yeller with a direct look, a nod, and touch the bill of his white visor. No one looked at him and was reminded of smoldering types like Hogan or Player.

His response to an inquiry about his life away from golf revealed what the note takers already knew but did not realize: he is French. "Well, I definitely enjoy my food," he said. "I love eating. I love drinking wine. I love skiing. I spend about thirty days on my skis every year. And, you know, I enjoy being around with my friends, with my family, with my kids, and with my wife. I play golf with my friends. If I can invite twenty people to a barbecue I definitely tell my wife at eight o'clock in the evening, 'We're gonna be twenty tonight,' and she's pretty happy with that. I try to be myself. I was . . . no intention of being someone else."

He had spoken twice as long and twice as entertainingly as Woods or Leonard, his predecessors in the press conference. It was after nine when the still-puzzled writers retreated to their computers and the golfer strolled out of the tent and into the night.

THE MYSTERY OF Jean Van de Velde could not be resolved in one or two free-for-alls with the press. But in the fullness of time, details illuminated his portrait. He'd met Brigitte, his wife, when he was five; her brother Patrick was a playmate. As the youngest of a family of five brothers, Jean had learned competition and how to get along from the cradle; Jean Michel, Christian, Bertrand, and Pierre had made sure of that. But none of his siblings or parents had the slightest interest in golf. "We had a summer house in southwestern France," Jean says. "I didn't enjoy waterskiing or the beach; there was a golf course nearby, and that's what I asked to do, two thousand times a day. So twice a day someone would take me to adventure golf—what you call miniature golf?—and finally to the real course."

The great minds in the pressroom and the pubs looked for Van de Velde's fatal flaw, for surely this man would pop like a balloon tomorrow. Tragic, but inevitable, and tragic *because* it was inevitable. Probably his putter would fail him, which would provide the symmetry the philosophers wanted.

But they couldn't be sure. The big question remained: were we about to witness the crowning of a champion golfer from *France*? In 127 previous British Opens, there had been only one French champion, Arnaud Massy, in 1907. Most of a century later, the former caddie and sardine fisherman from Biarritz remained the greatest French golfer ever. *Le Golf,* a beautiful volume from the thin library of French golf history, reports that Massy, a swarthy, powerful Basque with the requisite turn-of-the-century mustache, left France in 1902 at age thirty-five to complete his golf education in Scotland. He studied under Ben Sayers at North Berwick links and played—very well—in the Open. Arnaud finished tenth on his first try in '02, fifth in '05, and sixth in '06. When he came through the next year, he became *"le premier vainquer non britannique du British Open."*

Le Golf does not address the paucity of *vainquers* of major golf tournaments, other than to reproduce a chart that confirms an intuitive truth: few courses equals few players equals few Open champions. France and Grand-Bretagne had similar populations in 1988, the year the book was published, about 56 million. But 1.34 million British golfers roamed on 2,020 golf courses, while only 121,300 French players made do with just 191 *parcours.* Van de Velde claims that 300,000 of his countrymen and -women play the game now, still a trifle compared to the neighbors across the channel. Others put the number at 200,000.

Was it the game's inherent masochism that they had no taste for? Its plaid pants? The fact that the English liked it? Perhaps it comes down to grapes. Golf courses require land that might bring the world more pleasure as merlot vineyards.

Their lack of interest did not result from lack of contact with Scotland. For centuries the French allied with them against the English; the Scots referred to the relationship as "the Auld Alliance." Mary Stuart, Scotland's most famous queen, lived in France from age seven to nineteen, spoke French, and referred to herself as Marie. Her skeleton proves she stood nearly six feet tall, which would have given the red-haired queen quite an arc; she played golf. A variety of plots against her prevented that particular golf connection, but France had adequate exposure to the golf virus over the centuries. It was immune.

They liked other things. The Tour de France bicycle race, for example, is a national mania. "There is a French fascination with the wheel that relates the national consciousness to a two-dimensional, Ptolemaic universe," writes Sanche de Gramont in *The French,* perhaps putting too fine a point on it. "Whereas the sports madness of England and America is concerned with Copernican spheres, the cricket ball and the baseball." And the golf ball. Van de Velde, with one win in his life on the European Tour (the 1993 Roma Masters) has been France's best player for a decade.

Gramont, the son of a French diplomat, tells the story of a Paris tobacconist who on Sundays rented a tiny inner-city lot and stocked it with forty pheasants—with clipped wings. The owner of the *tabac* and his friends would arm themselves and dress in the knee-high boots and feathered hats of the veteran hunter. Then they'd stalk their prey in the well-fenced enclosure—bird dogs are not mentioned—and always enjoy 100 percent success on their hunt. A Frenchman, writes Gramont, feels "the urge to be a sportsman without taking a risk."

"I think golf is the wrong sport for them," says broadcaster/author Ben Wright, who is also an occasional golf course architect. Once he designed and built a course, called St. Cyprien, in extreme southern France between the Pyrenees and the Mediterranean. Lovely country, fit for an artist, and, in fact, Pablo Picasso grew up in the nearest town, Perpignan. "One of the worst experiences of my life," says Wright. "The French were duplicitous in the extreme. Really impossible to work with. They would line up on the runway and wave when my plane took off, then scurry back to change everything. By the time it was over, the man I had on-site was ready for an asylum.

"They liked to pretend they knew everything about golf. Quite ludicrous, because they're so backward in that respect." Adding injury to insult, Wright did not receive all of his fee for almost two years.

Other European countries built courses and developed world-class players in the last decades of the millennium, but St. Cyprien would not be the opening blast in a French golf boom. "We had some great players with good potential in the early eighties," says Van de Velde. "But those guys were too comfortable. They leave home on Wednesday for the pro-am and come back on Sunday evening. We lost a whole generation. I never had this kind of vision; I like to play with the best player." Van de Velde's win at the 1993 Roma Masters was the first Euro Tour victory by a Frenchman in twenty-three years.

If you skate the thin ice of generalizing about national character, you'll find a score of French traits that seem all wrong for golf. They're too pessimistic. French fiction and films seldom deliver a happy ending; but like people who marry a second time, golf requires an optimism that triumphs over experience. Their obsession with form and fashion looks great on the cover of *Vogue* but clashes with a game that prizes adaptability and doesn't really care how you look. The corollary is that the Scots, who invented golf, have been the most inventive people on earth. The French know in their bones the superiority of their culture and their language, but no pastime can do more damage to the smug than golf. Napoleon, de Gaulle, and Pompidou achieved imprecise perfection as intellects, while American presidents unashamedly used their leisure time to play a game with a number grade. Their numbers were never very good.

So Van de Velde stood on the verge of ultimate success as a golfer despite his country's antipathy toward the sport. But the *way* he was doing it mystified observers as much as *that* he was doing it. Not the touched-by-god putting; there were precedents for that. What was hard to fathom was his relaxed air when as a low-ranked qualifier he should have been nervous, and his wonderful politeness when he was supposed to be French.

Perhaps genes outweigh history, and Van de Velde's relaxed exterior mirrored an inner calm. He seemed simply to be a very pleasant man determined, as he kept saying, to enjoy the experience. But maybe in his heart of hearts he felt like an impostor or a gate-crasher, trying to smile and bluff his way past the host until the party was over.

CHAPTER SIX

The Day of Glory Has Arrived

———

Even the Scots like a man who
is prepared to think big—as long as
he is punished for it.

—*Clifford Hanley*

How can anyone govern a nation
with 238 different kinds of cheese?

—*Charles de Gaulle*

"M EET ME ON the tenth tee tomorrow morning at six,"
John Philp said on Saturday. He'd changed out of his lunch-with-the-
prince suit and into a rough sweater and work clothes. "Bring a putter
if you like." Observing the selection of the targets for the final round of
the Open would, one guessed, have a surrepetitious and sacramental
quality, like watching from behind the curtains as Father Fred de-
canted the wine.

Majesty attends the Cutting of the Cups. Even on a deserted muni
course, the rubber-booted maintenance man who changes the holes
isn't merely doing a bit of drudgery that will keep the green from wearing out in one spot; he is locating the goal for everyone who plays the
game that day. Probably this subject best suits a baseball writer, who

would have a field day probing the transcendence and symbolism of roundness and of holes. While golf has mostly left the Big Metaphor and tinhorn musings on spirituality to the nine-man game, this little ritual really does feel special.

Part of its pleasure—and its pain—is the early hour. "How beautiful the vacated links at dawn," wrote the Canadian Arnold Haultain in 1908, in the final paragraph of *The Mystery of Golf.* "When the dew gleams untrodden beneath the pendant flags and the long shadows lie quiet on the green; when no caddie intrudes upon the still and silent lawns, and you stroll from hole to hole and drink in the beauties of a land to which you know you will be all too blind when the sun mounts high and you toss for the honor!"

Carnoustie town had the dew, the silence, and the beauty, but no open establishment selling the coffee and the Tylenol that would help you appreciate them. No wind stirred at five-thirty, but the sun lacked enthusiasm and a chill gripped the torso. From the hills on the west side of the village you could peek between houses and down alleys and see the North Sea and the *Clipper Adventurer* dozing in the cold water. Nothing and no one moved as you neared the golf course except the eyes of the security officers who wondered what to do with this red-eyed writer chap walking onto the grounds so early, and with a golf club; the club being a driver, not a putter, a refugee from the trunk of Clark Dennis's rental car six days before.

"There you are." Philp rumbled up on his utility cart near the sixteenth green. The 8.2-degree Callaway and a blue nylon briefcase were tossed in the back with some dirty gloves, a metal-tined leaf rake, a shovel, and the tools of the hole-changing trade, and off he went toward the tenth green. This was the last day in a fourteen-year odyssey for Mr. Philp. The news was good: he'd had off-the-record assurance that the Open would be returning to Carnoustie. This was a triumph for everyone involved, including the late Jock Calder. The hotel, the spacious grounds, the well-organized spectator flow, traffic that was not *too* bad, the superb condition of the playing surface, and the course itself—all of this had trumped the bitter complaints about the rough.

The cart sped along, leaving behind rooster tails of seashell dust in the air. "Hogan." Philp calls the name into the wind like an incantation. "Hogan came here two weeks early to prepare. And for winning got paid five hundred quid. He *worked* for his money."

Philp brakes at the tenth green and sees that the others have already gathered for the final session of this ritual. How many men does it take to change a British Open hole? Five, counting Philp. R and A representatives Rodney James and Robert Burns are handsome gents, shaved, shirted, and tied even at this hour. But they shake your hand with something less than warmth, and you immediately abandon any hope of putting on the tournament greens with the new Bertha. The rest of the crew is Philp's young assistant, Paul O'Connor, and Herb Gibson, a volunteer from the links committee.

You try to break the ice by asking the obvious question of the deputy chairman of the Championship Committee. "No relation that we can confirm," says Robert Burns. "He left no male heir—that he admitted to." Yet the poet's biographers state that of the nine children he had with his wife, Jean Armour, several were boys. Strange.

The first nine having been reholed late Saturday, only the back nine remains. As the party of five gets down to work, it's obvious they've been together too long. Burns, second in command in the Championship Committee, had been the only R and A man on this prestigious detail early in the week, but he had called in experienced reinforcements, in the person of James. Between them, they are a match for the enthusiastic and forceful Philp. While the superintendent evinces no unhappiness, the committee approach clearly irks Philp's deputy, a sleep-deprived young Irishman with an uncanny resemblance to William Wallace's wild Irish lieutenant in the movie *Braveheart*. Paul O'Connor finds the officials to be emotionless, formal, and too slow.

At the Open's sister major, the Masters, the target selection ritual has a different feel. Early birds in Augusta can observe a cadre of officious-looking men as they walk from green to green grasping hole charts and computer printouts. There's a great deal of murmuring and gesturing. Someone hits a few putts at a possible hole location. The decision made, a wizened black man from the maintenance crew cuts the new cup. With an artist's tiny brush and a steady hand, the local jeweler paints the dirt above the cup liner to increase the hole's visibility for golfers and TV, and another hand provides the crowning touch, a trim with a pair of cuticle scissors.

The Open's cup cutters employ a style that is both more seat-of-the-pants and more rigid. James's preoccupation with equalizing the number of front, back, and middle hole locations annoys Philp, as does the R and A man's related obsession with yardage. He wants to adhere to the published total of 7,361 yards, as if someone besides him is counting. Their British reserve showing, James and Burns murmur and gesture with less animation than the Masters men. No putters; Burns merely rolls golf balls underhand, as if playing boccie.

From one green to the next the wise men travel in the gathering daylight. Philp walks onto the surface and within a few seconds places the cup cutter on the spot where he thinks the new hole should be cut. He'd stand there, not defiantly, but with an air of "show me something better." James and Burns either indicate tentative acceptance by rolling golf balls at the device or talk to each other inaudibly and scan the surface for other options. Several absolutes have to be kept in mind—holes can not be placed on severe grades, or closer than ten feet from the edge of the putting surface, or in the same vicinity any two days of the four. On the double green, four/fourteen, the flagsticks should be planted in opposition to each other, and as far apart as possible.

When finally there is a meeting of the minds, Philp lifts the lever-action cup cutter by its wooden handles and punches it into the turf. The T-shaped cutter looks like a pogo stick for a very short, very heavy person. The superintendent twists the handles in a steering-wheel motion while pressing the sharp edges of the heavy cylinder at the bottom of the stick straight down, trying not to rock back and forth, which might ruin the hole's symmetry. This has become more of a workout each day, because the greens have grown hard and fast from the wind and dry conditions. After bottoming out at seven inches, Philp bends his knees like a weight lifter and straightens, extracting a perfect plug of dirt and grass. This he deposits into the old hole, while Deputy Paul finishes the new.

Kneeling on a board so as not to indent kneecap shapes into the green, Paul inserts the six-inch cup liner, shakes a can of white spray paint, and inserts it upside down in a little fixture he's placed on top of the hole. He presses down on the top of the can, depressing the nozzle, and slowly sprays 360 degrees. Two small problems: the dried-out, one-inch circles of dirt below the lips of the cups are absorbing about triple the usual amount of paint, and Paul wonders if they have enough cans to finish the job. (They do.) And though the first one-eighth inch of earth just below grass level is supposed to remain bare, the white is spreading outward like a coffee spill on a paper towel.

The links superintendent inspects for quality before christening the hole with a pole. Just as at Augusta National, the finishing touch is a trim with a tiny pair of scissors.

"Bet you're a good putter," you say to Robert Burns as he bowls three golf balls at the cup cutter on fifteen.

A sidelong glance and an uncomfortable pause. "Quite awful, actually," Burns finally replies. "Haven't made one all week." This thought inspires him to keep rolling until he sinks a ten-footer with his eighth try.

The four-vehicle caravan proceeds to sixteen and seventeen, and the hotel and the big Rolex come into view. The place is coming to life: as gallery marshals walk slowly to their posts, food vendors throw up tent flaps and fire up the grill and put change in the till, and a few patient pilgrims park in prime spots in the grandstands on eighteen, five hours before the first group will finish.

Deputy links superintendent O'Connor is moving too. His five-day ordeal almost at an end, he feels a joyous madness. He commandeers the forgotten club, the briefcase with the golf balls inside, and the writer chap. "You're not ..." you say, but he is. O'Connor skids to a stop at the eighteenth tee, puts a ball on a peg, and cuts the air with a few ferocious practice swings. But the ball seems not to understand the violence the club intends. His first shot dribbles into the burn fifteen steps in front of the tee, and his second cuts softly 230 yards into the right rough. Not bad, but no screamer. Like to see you do better, Paul says. Up past the fairway bunkers, the rest of the caravan has stopped and its members are looking back toward the tee. Burns and James stand next to their cart, their heads tilted back. Hitting practice shots on the home hole before the last round of the Open? Not done.

You take the driver from the crazy Irishman because a dare is a dare and the law is three hundred yards away, and because it's easier to get forgiveness than permission. You look down at the teed ball and notice that your hangover is still a category five. Then you look up toward the putative target and discover with alarm that there is no fairway. Wait—there it is, that diagonal stripe of green between the hay and the bunkers. Your two shots duplicate Paul's—a pathetic grounder into the burn and a girly-man flare toward the right rough and the ditch.

Two lessons accrue from the experience. First is a gentle reminder of what pressure feels like and what it can do to an already addled brain. The second has to do with the hole itself. The eighteenth tee is too low; you can hardly see the target, and the burn not at all. With its high rough, its length, its lack of bail-out room—and wind against for the first time all week—the eighteenth at Carnoustie is the most uninviting hole in the world.

J EAN AND B RIGITTE Van de Velde dined Saturday night at a modest home in Carnoustie that had been rented by the French

168 / CURT SAMPSON

Tourist Board. In the house were assorted friends and countrymen; a French chef, who whipped up a paella; wine; a good deal of laughter; and a TV replaying Open highlights, most of which featured the sensational man from St. Martin. *"Allez,* Jean!" his friends said as another televised putt rolled toward the cup, and in. The Van de Veldes went back to the hotel and to bed shortly after midnight. But Jean could not rest.

"On Sunday I rode with him and his caddie in his cart from the practice tee to the putting green," recalls ABC TV golf analyst Curtis Strange. "As you know, that trip must be half a mile. We had enough time for me to get to like him—he's a perfect gentleman—and for him to tell me he'd had a sleepless night." Strange had perhaps purposely forgotten meeting Van de Velde nine years before, when they were opponents in a Dunhill Cup match. The Frenchman won.

And his night hadn't been *quite* sleepless. For several hours he tossed, turned, and "rolled from side to side in the bed like toast in the oven." But, Jean says, "from three to nine I slept like a baby." When he awoke, six hours remained before he teed off in the last group.

T HE SELECTION OF the hole location on the final hole went on as before, but with the breakfast crowd watching. Burns took control, taking half steps this way and that, while for some reason looking frequently at the hotel. Finally he bent to mark a spot, straightened, and looked toward the left side of the building. "That's about right," he said. "I should be able to see that from my room."

Philp went out to stick the flagsticks in the front nine holes and to do a final sweep. He pointed out a little one-yard square of metal stakes and yellow rope near the back left side of the second green: a lark's nest. The hole location had been adjusted to get the baby birds out of play. He had second thoughts about the hole on number three, cut only eight dangerous yards from Jocky's Burn. And on the fourth green, at about the spot from which Van de Velde holed his ninety-footer, he discovered a divot hole. "Say again please, John," the voice on the walkie-talkie said. "Yes, a divot," Philp confirmed, "such as might be made by an angry golfer." Who? How? No one bothered to ask. The superintendent used the hole cutter to transplant turf from the fringe to the wounded green.

"We've blown it on six," Philp said, pausing on the hill behind the tee. The new bunker had had no impact; with the wind against it all week, it simply had not been in play. This was a correctable situation, of course, but the Rigid and Ancient would not move the tee markers forward to create an opportunity for some macho. Instead of the hoped for threes, fours, sevens, and eights, Hogan's Alley was just another bogey hole on a course filled with them.

And they blew it on seventeen. For months Philp had lobbied to shorten the Island hole so that a gambling or desperate player could have a go at flying over the last crossing of the burn. Nicklaus did exactly that in 1968 and had only a sand wedge to the green. Though Jack didn't make his three and he didn't catch up to Gary Player, it had been thrilling to watch him try. But the R and A seemed to have no sympathy for those go/no-go situations everyone else enjoys. The tee markers stayed put and no one even dreamed of driving over the wicked Barry Burn.

"I take the questions about the fairway width as a valid criticism," Philp said. He'd stopped to watch his workers harvest another huge crop of grass cut by the gallery's feet. "The semirough should have been wider. But you can't adjust too late; if you cut down high grass, the remaining stalks look white and stark. As for the tee markers, the R and A don't want to be seen as bending to pressure."

AFTER BREAKFAST, Van de Velde put on shorts and running shoes and worked out for an hour and fifteen minutes in the hotel gym. Treadmill, bicycle, and StairMaster for the legs, heart, and lungs. Sit-ups and crunches for the abdominals. He's five-foot-ten and 168 pounds, and fit but not chiseled; he doesn't care for any weightlifting. His swing requires the torso strength and flexibility he was building in the fitness center, not bulges in the biceps. "My swing thoughts always vary between two and three," Van de Velde says. "During the Open, I'm trying to turn my shoulders and keep them on top of my hips [that is, turn, not sway back and forth]. I want to keep my shoulders the same distance from the ball all through the swing. And I want to keep my right shoulder very high at impact."

After the workout, Van de Velde stretched for an hour. He showered, shaved, ate lunch, "and boom, it was ten minutes to two, time to hit balls. Filling up the time before I teed off was not a problem. I was used to it, since I played late three out of four days."

Christophe Angiolin waited by the bag storage in the hallway between the front desk and the players' changing room. Van de Velde's caddie was a thin, hip-hop-looking dude with a high forehead, cheap white denim cargo pants, a flat snap-brimmed hat turned backward, and whiskers on the underside of his chin so wispy it looked like you could easily pull the whole patch out, like a weed. In short, Christophe was a beatnik from Central Casting. He'd been on Jean's bag only four months; when his previous employer, Fabrice Tarnaud, lost his European Tour card, he called and asked for the vacant Van de Velde caddie position. Christophe showed up and kept up, mapped the yardages, got on well with the boss, and offered strategic opinions when asked. He played the game a little himself, had a nine handicap. But "the key to hiring Christophe was that he spoke French," says Jean's London-based agent, Jamie Cunningham. "It's tiring to speak another language, as I know from speaking French.

"Christophe had a helluva good Open. He didn't do anything wrong. Jean made 98.9 percent of the decisions."

As Van de Velde entered the practice ground, he passed Zane Scotland exiting. Zane had been so enamored of the Open experience that he'd stuck around for two days after missing the cut, hitting balls and going into the equipment trailers like a kid in a candy shop. "We were in the Mizuno van yesterday, and they asked him if he wanted a one- and a two-iron," said his instructor, Scott Cranfield. "And he looked at me like, 'Can I do that?' And I said, 'Yes, he wants a one- and two-iron.' I want him to stay just like that, never expecting that everything will be done for you.

"The main objective is for him to always see the good in his game, that everything will benefit him in some way. The tour is actually a very negative place. Many players are always complaining about something, but notice players like Tiger haven't been this week. I don't want Zane to become a whiner, a bitch."

Now a man of seventeen years and one day and with an Open under his belt, Zane sat in one of the big upholstered chairs in the hotel lobby and talked about the big picture. He's decided that his models would be the doomed Payne Stewart and the absent Fred Couples, players he admired for their cool, unperturbed style, guys who stayed in their game no matter what. "Physically, I learned these guys are not light-years away from me. I've been out competing against the best players in the world. I guess I always thought the U.S. Open was the toughest, but this must be the toughest course ever set up.

"Gamewise, I can compete with these guys. I've learned so much this week. Right now I'm at the point where I think this game is one hundred percent mental."

A bit later, out of his son's hearing, Bernie Scotland let his pride show. "He grew in my eyes," the father said. "There is no bigger circus than this one, and to have performed like he did . . . I've been proud of him before, but not like that, not like that. At the end of his round, I saw him throw a ball to a kid and then walk back to his bag, and I thought, 'What's he doing?' He came back to the fence with two more golf balls and he tossed them to two handicapped kids in wheelchairs. You should have seen their faces."

Fifteen minutes before the final starting time and the leader didn't feel right. After hitting a few practice putts, he knew what it was: the pants. Specifically, the pockets of his beige trousers, which stood out in irritating little tents when he assumed the position with his Z/1 Delta model Never Compromise. Van de Velde handed the putter to Christophe and went back into his first-floor hotel room to change into black pants.

He returned in time to hit a few more putts. By ones and twos the practice green had emptied like the hallway outside a courtroom during a big trial; only two players had yet to testify, Van de Velde and Craig Parry. The spectators encircling the fenced enclosure two-deep searched the leader's face and studied his stroke. The face looked composed, almost serene, and the putts went in or rattled the edge.

Van de Velde had owned his magic black-and-gray putter for all of eleven days now. "I was trying it on the putting green at Loch Lomond," he recalls. "Instead of the fifteen minutes I expected to practice, I'm there two and a half hours. It felt comfortable right away. I always had my hands behind the ball [at address] and then used a strong forward press. With this putter, I don't have to forward press so much.

"The rep says, 'Perhaps you'll use it one day?' I said, 'I'll use it tomorrow.'" With the new wand, Jean shot 69-68-69-72 at Loch Lomond; two 67s to lead the Open qualifiers at Monifieth; and 75, 68, and 70 to lead the Open by five with one round to go. He'd putted only about twenty-four times per round so far at Carnoustie; on the greens, in other words, he was thirty-six under par. Unofficially, he would have the best putting performance in the history of golf's four majors.

Like it or not, every golf tournament is a commercial, and the advertisements on the leader's bag and body have the most value and get the most attention. COBRA (golf clubs) adorned Van de Velde's white visor and his big black golf bag. The little crocodile on the left side of his chest told observers that his royal blue shirt was a Lacoste garment. BLUE-GREEN on the other side of the shirtfront indicated an affiliation with a consortium of thirty French courses. The left sleeve is a key piece of billboard because it shows up so well on TV when the golfer is actually hitting a shot, and here stitched in white was the symbol of Jean's most unusual endorsement deal, with Disneyland Paris. "He represents the park, not the golf course," says agent Cunningham. "He genuinely enjoys it, and he and Brigitte and the kids [Alexandra, age seven, and Anne Sophie, two] go there ten or twelve times a year."

The day was gray and just right for a light sweater. The wind blew lightly off the blue-gray mirror of the North Sea, in the opposite direction from the first three days. Sixteen and eighteen would be against the breeze, seventeen with it. On the first tee, a wonderfully odd sight: a formal wooden table, and on the table the antique silver Claret Jug, glowing dully against the green background. Gray-haired George Nicholson of Group 4 Security stood at attention a yard away with a look that said, No funny business. Funny business came anyway.

Four different players would lead the Open by day's end and the three who didn't win all should have. All four hit shots that shocked everyone who watched. The day would end in near bedlam; grown men would cry openly as the winner walked across the eighteenth green to accept the Jug.

The most bizarre day in the history of the British Open was about to begin.

For the last time, the cheerful, do-re-mi voice of Ivor Robson: "On the tee, *Jean Van de Velde!*" Most golfers react to applause with a touch of the brim of the hat and a nod, but Van de Velde acknowledged his first-tee cheers expansively, like a politician on the stump. His drive showed a trace of nerves, bouncing out of the short grass and into an awkward lie near the fairway bunker on the right. But after experimenting with stances and a minute or two of discussion with Christophe, he punched an eight-iron that landed over the bunkers in the rough short of the green, then rolled up to twelve feet. A beautiful shot, and he almost made birdie. Then the round stopped.

David Frost had duck-hooked his drive into an it-goes-without-saying nasty lie close to the service road on the second hole. Frost contended, ad infinitum, that since his only shot was to the left, and aiming to the left got his left heel on the road, he was entitled to a drop under the local rule permitting relief from pavement. Of course the road was not his problem; he was hoping for a technical dropout. He demonstrated the extra-wide stance he'd have to employ for his planned attack. "I don't think that's a reasonable shot," said rules official Michael Lunt, the same Mr. Lunt who'd blown the Van de Velde call the day before. The R and A had had to admit that mistake and no one wanted another screwup.

"Am I standing on the path?" asked the South African golfer rhetorically and repeatedly. "Then I'm entitled to relief if I'm standing on the path." The situation differed from the Van de Velde ruling on Saturday but the principle was the same: if you're not aiming straight at the hole, you get no free drop from an obstruction.

ABC put rules expert Frank Hannigan on the air to explain the dispute as it dragged on. His gassy analysis didn't seem to clarify much, but whatever transparency it offered was stirred to muddy confusion by the next voice heard. "So the rule then prevents *protracted* play, not toward his target but merely to take relief?" Steve Melnyk may as well have said "protractor" or "prophylactic" for all the sense that made.

After fifteen minutes of indecision on the one hand and badgering on the other, Frost lost. "I'd have disqualified him," Rosburg said. Meanwhile, the final pair of Van de Velde and Parry just stood there on the second tee, all keyed up with nowhere to go. When at last they could play, the fireplug Aussie made a routine par, but the dashing Frenchman missed a four-foot putt and bogied. "No, the delay didn't bother me at all," Van de Velde says now, but you have to wonder. His lead over Parry fell to four.

On the third, Carnoustie's only short par four, Jean drove into the rough, pitched out, pitched on, and missed the putt. Another bogey. Parry played the hole perfectly with a mid-iron, a sand wedge, and a short birdie putt. Now Van de Velde led by just two.

The collapse everyone expected continued on the fourth. After hitting the ball three times on the par four, Jean had still not made the putting surface. He took the putter from the bag and Christophe pulled the flagstick out. After a 360-degree survey and three practice swings, he tapped his Titleist 4 through the fringe and down the hill. Three seconds later the ball fell in so squarely it was like he'd putted from two feet instead of twenty. The lead remained at two. Sprinkles of rain began to fall.

Derek Carr, meanwhile, searched for the low Scot. He'd had lunch with Andrew Coltart in the players' dining room, so he watched the man from Dumfries for a while. But Coltart couldn't keep it in the fairway enough and lost ground. Besides, he was paired with Tiger Woods, whose huge, adhesive gallery made watching difficult. Carr noticed from the scoreboard that a chap from up the road in Aberdeen had made a bit of noise on the front nine with a two under thirty-four, so he tracked him down. At about the moment Van de Velde made his long par putt on the fourth, Paul Lawrie hit a seeing-eye second shot on the long, brutal twelfth. His ball landed fifty yards short and skipped gaily to within three feet. The resultant birdie put Lawrie three-under for the day and seven-over for the tournament. Five behind Van de Velde, six away from Parry. Lawrie would need some bogeys out of them. They made birdies instead.

On the par-three eighth, Parry hit a beautiful shot to six feet and made it, while Van de Velde uncharacteristically three-putted from the front edge. The final pair was tied for the lead now, at three-over. In eight holes, Jean had lost his entire five-shot lead. Made you think about Carnoustie's own Mac Smith when he had led the Open by five in 1925. Then poor Mac shot 82 in the last round at Prestwick and lost, which seemed a fair prediction for Jean. Before they drove on nine, the sprinkles became a drizzle. The leaders both put on sweaters—light brown for Jean, charcoal gray for Parry—and unsheathed umbrellas.

But Van de Velde would not leave the stage. He killed a driver down the middle, snuck an eight-iron in to twelve feet, and pumped his right fist in milking-the-cow fashion as he walked to the hole to remove his made birdie. He had the lead back, plus two to Parry's plus three. Justin Leonard was five-over.

Parry birdied ten from twenty-five feet; tied again. Van de Velde scattered the ball around on eleven and bogeyed. Parry now led, and for the first time since Friday afternoon, Van de Velde didn't.

Up ahead, Carr watched as Lawrie birdied the seventeenth to drop to four-under for the day, six-over for the tournament. Now the BBC and ABC began to notice him and mispronounce his name. It's "lorry," like the British word for truck, not something rhyming with "dowry" or "bowery." Lawrie thus replaced John "Phillip" as the most abused phonetics at Carnoustie.

Before the leaders hit on twelve, Lawrie played his second shot on eighteen—and got the biggest break of the tournament. From the left rough and a decent lie, he hit an iron sadly short of the burn. But before he could get a dry ball out of the bag or even say "Aw, shit," an unexpected concatenation of physics caused the ball to hop over the twelve-yard-wide ditch and into a happy lie in the left front bunker. From there he hit a very good shot to six feet and made the putt. The leader in the clubhouse was in with six-over, and happy as a clam. The R and A's media liaison escorted the low Scot to the Media Centre.

Seven holes remained for the leader at plus two, Craig Parry. The little Australian lists his dimensions as five foot six and 170 pounds, but he looks shorter and stouter than that. A beetle-browed man with a short stride and feet that pointed east-west when he was walking north or south, he seemed to deserve the duck nickname more than El Pato, Angel Cabrera.

He peered through the cleavage of two breastlike mounds of gorse flanking the fairway a hundred yards out. What to hit? The twelfth's a

479-yard par four, straight, narrow, wind against, with Carnoustie's usual complement of terrifying rough. Most spectators walk forward on the left to watch the drives land, so not many observed as Parry hemmed and hawed then pulled a long iron from his quiver. But he teed his ball at driver height, went back to the bag, and exchanged the conservative club for the aggressive one. He was about to make a triple bogey.

Like a chain-reaction car wreck, disastrous holes require one big, bad decision or the intricate interplay of several little ones. Parry's mistakes were little ones. His driver flew high and right and stopped in a luxurious growth of bent grass, soft and thick enough for a sweater. He wedged out too far, across the fairway and into the worst Carnoustie had to offer, an equally healthy patch of ryegrass. If the bent was cashmere, this was a hair shirt. He swung a mighty swing—and moved the ball only two steps forward. A third wedge rolled over the green; a fourth wedge stopped six feet short; a discouraged putt, a tap-in, and Parry had his seven. With a routine bogey, Van de Velde had the lead again.

When Justin Leonard birdied the fourteenth a minute or two later to tie Jean, the Open had its third leader of the day. At about five-thirty, the top four were:

LEONARD AND VAN DE VELDE:	+4
PARRY:	+5
LAWRIE:	+6

Justin wore navy blue Polo and Hogan mojo. Counting the four iterations on his umbrella, the relentless Texan had seven script HOGANS on his bag and his person, and nine more on his clubs. But he lost the lead as soon as he'd gained it by missing the fairway and the green on fifteen. And when Van de Velde played the par-three thirteenth and the par-five fourteenth in par and two-putt birdie, the heir to Arnaud Massy led Hogan's man by two.

VAN DE VELDE:	+3
LEONARD:	+5
LAWRIE:	+6
PARRY AND CABRERA:	+7

Jean had taken Justin's role; his steadiness was making the other guys give up. You could see it in the desultory bogey-par Parry made on thirteen and fourteen and you could hear it in Lawrie's remarks to the writers. No, I have no chance to win, the Aberdeenian said, but fourth or third or even second would be lovely. He'd drawn fifteen souls into the two-hundred-capacity interview room. He reminded the modest congregation that he'd shot four under par the last nine of the qualifying tournament at Downfield just to make it into the Open by two shots. "This is the best round I ever had," Lawrie said. "To shoot four under around here is lovely."

He wore a baby-blue shirt and a sleeveless sweater. Five eleven, 180 pounds, thirty years old, dark hair, a good-looking man without his white Wilson golf cap. Lawrie was sleeping in his own bed this week, he said, which was lovely. Waiting for him at his home an hour's drive away in Kingswells, on the outskirts of Aberdeen, were his wife, Marian, and their two sons, Craig, four, and Michael, seven months. Before the kids, Marian had caddied for her husband. They'd met when both were employed in the pro shop at Banchory Golf Club. The head professional, Douglas Smart, was like a second father to Lawrie. His suicide in July 1993—he was ill with cancer—still stung deeply. "He gave me my chance in life," Paul said. "Just a great guy."

The world's 152nd ranked player, the biggest of his two European Tour wins had been the 1999 Qatar Masters. His previous best finish in the Open had occurred in 1993. On the seventeenth hole of the last round at Sandwich, he'd holed a full three-iron for an eagle. This gave him a 65 and a from-out-of-nowhere tie for sixth.

Carr retreated to the hotel bar for the big finish. Naturally, he wasn't supposed to be there; the room had been reserved by ESPN

Radio for its affiliates and advertisers. But the Ayrshireman looked so much like *somebody* that he, as usual, walked right in. Seven times in the next hour revelers brought him pen and paper. The first one was a bit of a problem: who the hell did this guy think he was? "Just your name, please, Dave," the man said, so Carr took a flyer and scrawled "David Duval" in a flamboyant hand. He didn't dare speak because his accent sounds nothing like Jacksonville, and he kept his black Titleist hat on because he doesn't look twenty-seven—or that much like Duval. The autograph seeker thanked him effusively. Carr muffled his laughter in a glass of beer.

Outside in the gloom, El Pato missed a fifteen-foot birdie putt that would have taken him to six-over. The encircling crowd in the grandstands groaned with him, but this small misfortune didn't seem to matter much. A top ten for Cabrera, well-done. Seems a nice chap. Can you see Leonard on seventeen yet?

No one knew, of course, that The Duck might have won the Open if he'd made it.

The leaders had reached Vitriol Corner. Before its first Open in 1931, comments were made about the weakness of Carnoustie's finish because the final four holes measured 339, 335, 150, and 365 yards, and terrified no one. The Golf Course Committee took the criticism to heart in a big way; they eliminated the short seventeenth; the new seventeenth was the old sixteenth plus a hundred yards. The new eighteenth was the old one plus a hundred. Now the final holes at Carnoustie measure 472, 250, 459, and 487, which only hints at their difficulty.

On sixteen, Justin slapped an unHoganesque one-handed hooked one-iron. The ball skittered along the fairway and through a few yards of rough until it stopped in an unlikely spot, hanging at eye level on the edge of a bunker. But with his feet in the sand, Leonard used a T-ball swing to pitch to ten feet. With a perfect putt he saved par. Still two behind and desperate, Leonard hit two solid shots onto the seventeenth green, but his birdie putt didn't scare the hole. He walked wearily up to tap in. One last slim chance remained.

Van de Velde's tee ball on fifteen sailed so far right it ended in a bunker on the *fourth* hole, about fifty yards right of his target; he hit a provisional in case he couldn't find it. But he followed this atrocious drive with a brilliant iron to about fifty yards short of the green. He pitched to six feet below the hole. Christophe lay on his stomach in the push-up position to line up the putt; with three bogey holes still to play, this putt was huge. In silence, the golfer putted. When the ball fell gently in, a small chorus of Gallic-sounding screams mixed with the larger roar of the gallery. "That's unbelievable," said Bob Rosburg on ABC's air. But Van de Velde did not take part in the celebration. No fist-shaking.

On sixteen, an almost preposterously difficult hole—250 yards to a coffee table—he nailed a long-iron, which missed the green left, hole high, on the shaved bank. Now he faced a putter shot of twenty-two yards with not much break, but thoroughly complicated by the circumstances and by the five-foot elevation change from ball up to hole. Christophe tended the flagstick, standing on the golfer's left. And the mystical communion continued; invisible threads connected Van de Velde's hands, putter, and golf ball with the hole. Four practice swings, a forward press, a confident strike; the ball skidded twelve yards up, almost ten yards across, and died two feet from the goal. "Unbelievable," said Rosburg's TV colleague Ian Baker-Finch, as Van de Velde finished off his par.

Van de Velde:	+3
Leonard:	+5
Parry and Lawrie:	+6
Cabrera:	+7

Leonard waited on the eighteenth tee and didn't hit. He wanted to see what the leader would do on seventeen first. The Texan looked across the plain at the gaggle of little figures at the base of a packed green grandstand, a still-life watercolor in the gray light. Two caddies, two golfers, a policeman in a blue-black uniform, the match referee, a cameraman, a soundman. At the back of the tee, the one in a white visor and a royal blue shirt stood motionless. If Justin had been thirty feet away instead of three hundred yards, he would have seen Van de Velde purse his lips and exhale cleansing breaths, like a skier at the starting gate. Spectators scooted across the fairway far up ahead. Christophe and the bobby waved them away and Jean waited until they cleared. Finally he hit, a duplicate of the solid long-iron on the previous hole. The ball stopped in the middle of the Island fairway in perfect position. Leonard teed up his ball.

As Van de Velde and Parry walked up the parallel, penultimate fairway, Leonard drove. Trying to reconcile the need for distance and the necessity of hitting the fairway, he hit a three-wood, pulled it a little, and missed both objectives. His lie in the fluffy bent grass looked pretty good, but the moisture in it added a complication. If he didn't catch the shot perfectly, the wet rough would be like cooked pasta between the club face and the ball. Two down, one to play, and Jean safe on the Island; even though Leonard had 254 yards to the green, he had to go for it. Or did he? Again, Justin waited and watched as Parry and Van de Velde played to the seventeenth green. From his slightly lower vantage point, he wouldn't be able to see where Jean's ball would finish, but the crowd reaction would tell him enough.

Parry, his edge gone, hit a nothing shot that somehow stayed out of the bomb-crater bunkers in front of the green. The spectators' group groan and slightly surprised "ohhh" told the story. The leader's turn to hit from about 230, with the wind helping.

"*Quatre, je pense.*" Four-iron, I think, said Jean.

"*Ça va, ça va. Allez.*" That's good, that's good. You go, boy, said Christophe.

Van de Velde's upright body through impact and ticktock rhythm gave him by far the prettiest swing of the three actors still in the drama. He crunched the four-iron. Leonard could mentally trace the ball on the ground from the crowd's acoustics: a yell, a roar, an "awww," and applause. The ball had cleared the bunker, rolled up to the flagstick, past it, and stopped thirty-odd feet from the hole. "We've got to try to make three," Leonard said to his caddie, Bob Riefke.

He choked down a bit on his three-wood and aimed for the big clock on the distant white hotel. It was twenty past six. A high, hard cut would have the best chance of flying over the Barry Burn and bouncing up somewhere close. But Leonard hit the ball microscopically "fat" and the ball landed short, bounced four times, and fell into the burn. Watching in the Carnoustie bar, a fat man with a red face started to sing:

> *Allons enfants de la patrie*
> *Le jour de gloire est arrivé*

The comedian looked around. No one had laughed. Didn't anyone recognize "La Marseillaise," the French national anthem? Hadn't anyone seen *Casablanca*?

Christophe tended the pin on seventeen, standing on the golfer's right. Jean putted to one foot. Then Parry, who'd mis-hit his chip, three-putted from fifteen feet for a double bogey. The revelers had stood at the windows and cried out together in disappointment when Leonard hit into the burn and made bogey. It was all but over now—a three-shot lead!—and the buzz in the room dropped a notch or two. Carr silently signed another autograph.

Van de Velde:	+3
Leonard:	+6
Lawrie:	+6
Cabrera:	+7
Parry:	+8

At six-thirty P.M., Jean Van de Velde reached the eighteenth tee.

CHAPTER SEVEN

Gang Aft A-gley

———

The offensive alone is suited to the temperament of
French soldiers. . . . We are determined to march straight against
the enemy without hesitation.

—*Clément-Armand Fallières, president [1906–13] of France*

The terrible Ifs accumulate.

—*Winston Churchill,* The World Crisis

W HAT WAS HE thinking?

The only clues to the spinning gears in Jean Van de Velde's head
were the only ones a spectator ever has: body language, a golfer's vague
understanding of another golfer, and the been-there comments of the
TV guys. "I turned to Mike Tirico [off the air] and said, 'This is gonna
be good, this is gonna be a great win for French golf,'" says ABC's Curtis Strange, one of the men in the booth and twice the winner of the
U.S. Open. "After Parry tripled and he got the lead back, Jean played
great. I was proud of him. When he walked onto the tee I started setting up the situation with Rossie."

Rossie—Bob Rosburg—owns a PGA championship and the dead-
pan pessimism of a golf realist. Strange asked him on the air what Van

184 / CURT SAMPSON

de Velde should hit. "Curtis, he knows he has a two-shot lead," Rosburg said. "He does not know he has a three-shot lead. I've gotta play an iron. I think the only thing that can get him in any trouble is if he drives it in the burn."

Christophe Angiolin had reached the tee before the others. He stood by the bag, head down, studying the yardage map. His boss moved confidently onto the little stage to put the ball on a peg. Did he remember at that moment that he'd owned this hell of a hole all week, playing it in 4-3-3? He said later that no such thought crossed his mind. Was he beginning to gasp for air, for composure? He says no, and he didn't look it. But he teed the ball very high. And to many experts, here was the first sign of a brain starting to seize up from the pressure.

Another of the professional mind readers sat in the BBC booth, and if Peter Alliss is not the best talker of the bunch, at least he is the best writer. He had been a golf champion in his day, with a career distinguished enough to warrant a memoir at age thirty-two. In *Alliss Through the Looking Glass* he discussed the amusing, disturbing thoughts of the professional golfer under duress. "You line up the ball and you see these feet, all these feet watching you. All you have in your mind is the thought 'go away, go away, go away.' . . . If you are playing well, the crowd generates an irresistible, communal electricity, [but] the crowd is very ruthless and it discards you without mercy." Something in that would apply to Van de Velde in a few minutes; some of the audience that had learned to love him was about to turn on him.

At Jean's direction, Christophe pulled the black head cover off the driver and handed the stick to Jean. "Boy, I tell ya," said Rosburg incredulously. "Any kind of a two-iron out here and a five-iron short and a pitch and you go home the winner."

What were you thinking, *monsieur*? That the last time you'd hit this club, on fifteen, it had flown to hell and gone to the right? No. That you'd done something crazy and lost a big lead once before? No, that had never happened to him but he had seen it up close. In the French

PGA one year he himself had been the rabbit. Six behind with seven holes to play, Van de Velde made five birdies and a par and won on the first hole of sudden death.

"I'm thinking, 'I'm gonna hit a driver,' " Jean said later. "I just want to play the seventy-second hole like any other." He owned momentum, in other words, and did not want to interrupt the inarguable success he'd had attacking this impossible golf course. "I felt very comfortable, I didn't feel any pressure. Why would you? You're three ahead and you have one hole to play. I felt very calm and happy being there and I was enjoying the moment."

He was also thinking that safety lay not in caution, but in playing aggressively. "It is very easy to make six or seven or eight on this kind of hole," Van de Velde said. "Forty yards is water left, water in front of you, and water on the right on the tee shot. If you hit a driver you take the water from the left out of play. That's what I think, whatever. And then you know if you miss the fairway with your driver, whatever the lie you have, you're going to hit a sand iron or wedge and you're going to leave yourself one hundred yards from the hole."

A final factor in the decision did not even cross his conscious mind. "I couldn't live with myself knowing that I tried to play for safety and that I blew it," he said. "That's not in my nature. So I made my choices."

As her husband lined up a target for this crucial drive, Brigitte Van de Velde repeated her mantra, the little chant she always uses before her husband hits a shot: "*Allez*, Jean." Literally, "You go," but the definition of the idiom she had in mind was "Go for it."

The leader swung. And started an odyssey that would take twenty-seven minutes, time for a sitcom and a couple of commercials. His journey had an epic quality, a grandeur that exceeded all other final-hole performances in the history of the Open, possibly in the history of golf. Jerry Pate's miracle five-iron to win the 1976 U.S. Open? Great shot, but that's all it was, one great shot. Pate's first was an ordinary pushed drive, his last was a tap-in, and he won by two. Van de Velde would exceed that particular drama by a factor of six, which was the number of times he was about to leave the audience limp and exhausted. Palmer lost the Masters by one in 1961 by skulling a bunker shot across the final green. A short, sharp shock, that, but no Van de Velde.

Except for the heroic Nicklaus versus Watson duel at Turnberry in 1977, no Open finish in the TV age could compare. But there is romance in tragedy, and tragedy in romance, and the travails of the doomed, flawed hero affect us more deeply than someone's big win. Someday the tape of Jean at the eighteenth at Carnoustie will be the Zapruder film of golf.

The conspiracy between fate and physics began when Jean hit his drive dead right. So dead right it flew over his own fairway, his own rough, and the burn, and landed high and dry in a lovely lie on the hole he'd just completed. Van de Velde laughed as if the gallows rope had broken just in time. He covered the TV camera lens with his gloved left hand.

"Where did he hit it?" someone asked in the bar. "Way the hell right," someone else answered. During a delay, while Jean waved a section of gallery who never dreamed they'd be in the way out of the way, Derek Carr wormed up to the window. The 2,700-capacity grandstand on the golfer's right partially blocked his view.

"Big squawk going on regarding the grandstand placement, or bleachers, as you call them," John Philp had said two months before the Open. Of the fourteen thousand bleacher seats on the course, half would be clustered in a group of three—two left, one right—around the eighteenth green. Philp, David Hill of the R and A, and a representative of the contractor, Championship Structures, agreed on paper where each of the stands would be built. But the planning proved to be far simpler than the execution. "[The contractors] don't care about the turf as much as the greens staff," said Philp. "They're driving their forklifts too fast and in the wrong places. You have to stand over them with a whip. There's no space at all on the golf course. And the Barry Burn is causing an extra problem." The set of seats impinging on Van de Velde's path to the green straddled the burn like a big green mill house over the old mill stream.

"He's got two hundred thirty yards to the hole," Rosburg said. "Curtis, I don't know whether he ought to take a shot at this one, either."

But how could he not? For the same reasons he hit the driver from the tee, Van de Velde did not even consider laying up. Momentum, his up-to-now successful policy of aggression, and his own DNA would not allow him to hit an eight-iron back to the fairway. "The only thing I'm thinking about was hit it past the water," Jean said. "I'm only 189 yards. I can do that easily with a four-iron." One other factor sealed the deal: his perfect lie in the short rough near the members' tee on seventeen. Like his tee shot *not* going in the burn, the inviting, hit-me look of his golf ball was bad luck disguised as good. Had he been in the burn, or in the high rough, his next shot would have been from a spot where he'd have to play short of the burn. A perfect lie on seventeen . . . made you think about the most famous pre–Van de Velde disaster at the end of a major, a little tragedy involving, of all people, Ben Hogan.

In June 1960, at Cherry Hills Country Club near Denver, the phantom of Carnoustie came to the seventeenth hole of the final round of the U.S. Open, trailing Arnold Palmer by one. Playing his usual precise, calculating game, the forty-seven-year-old Hogan laid up short of the water on the par five. He had a three-quarter wedge left to a tight pin on a rock-hard green, and a lie so good, the Hawk said, "I could [have] hit with a driver." Hogan might have played to the fat part of the green, perhaps would have if his ball wasn't sitting so well. But his violently spinning shot straight at the flag landed a hair short of where he intended, sucked back off the green and into the pond.

Hogan removed his right shoe and sock—the crowd roared when it realized he was going to play it from the muddy water—and splashed the ball onto the green. He two-putted for a bogey. Palmer won.

"*Allez*, Jean." After calculating the yardage and handing over a two-iron, Christophe gave the boss the rallying cry of Team Van de Velde and stepped back. The golfer dressed in black and blue looked so alone; he must have been one hundred yards from the gallery ropes on eighteen. A long, breathless moment before he hit from where Henry Cotton hit in 1937, with the same club and a similar lead. Cotton landed in the bunker; Van de Velde did not. Not yet. Gary Player also did the eighteenth from the seventeenth when he won in 1968. But there was no "*Allez,* Gary" in that one; with a two-shot lead over Nicklaus, he turned sideways and played way right from the tee with a four-iron, pecked away twice more, and reached the green while minimizing his risk of a burn. Nothing wrong with that.

Jean swung that beautiful swing. The acoustics of solid contact told you he'd accomplished job one, getting the ball over the burn. But the damn thing drifted right a little bit, struck a two-inch diameter galvanized-steel scaffolding tube ten feet up on the mill house grandstand, ricocheted back toward the tee, bounced off the top concrete block on the far side of the burn, vaulted all the way over like Lawrie's ball in reverse an hour and a half earlier, hopped once on the ground in the right-hand rough, and disappeared into the high grass like a mouse. The crowd reacted with excited confusion or confused excitement, and you heard the sound of thousands of mouths falling open. Van de Velde held his follow-through for a long moment, a blank look of astonishment on his face.

He walked over a footbridge and into the arena like the leader of the Olympic marathon entering the stadium but starting to cramp. Crazy not to just bunt it back into play, they said in the bar as the dark-haired man came into view. Tempting fate, he was, said a Scot. Where the hell was his caddie? an American wanted to know. That goddamn Maynard G. Krebs should have given him a short-iron and walked away. But the best-informed experts disagree on this point. Bob Charles and Ben Crenshaw, for example, say that with a three-shot lead and a perfect lie they would have proceeded exactly as Van de Velde did. Bobby Cole would not have, and he says an older British caddie would have made damn sure Jean laid up. Rosburg, although adamant that Jean should have played the eighteenth on the installment plan, does not fault Christophe. "I like to have a caddie agree with me," he says. "I want him to give me confidence."

Angiolin was an agreeing sort of caddie, without the age, experience, or temperament to take charge of the situation. "I made a choice and I take full responsibility for it," said Jean. "I don't think [Cristophe] could have stepped in my way, saying you're going to hit a nine-iron off the tee, or a five-iron, because I would have felt even worse missing the fairway with a five-iron."

Van de Velde walked briskly to his ball and bit his lip. By tradition, spectators are allowed to fill in behind the final pairing on the last hole of the Open. The surging crowd behind the golfers and caddies looked like a battlefield scene.

As Jean examined his predictably horrid lie, other debating points arose. Analysis began with the offending grandstand. According to some, the one on the right sat too close to the green; a hole so long should have a bit of bailout room. Cotton certainly didn't have to bother with such a monstrosity in '37. But greenside spectators and grandstands almost always make golf easier. Arms, legs, and torsos make dandy backstops and a three-or-more-deep gallery cannot usually move fast enough to avoid a speeding golf ball. Sometimes a pro will purposely aim at spectators or bleachers; sometimes a fan will purposely take a hit for his hero. Balls contacting limbs or chests usually stop dead, but heads are dangerous for a player; a ball off a skull sounds like it hit a coconut and can rebound a great distance. With no room to run and hatted heads muffling the big bounce, the packed grandstand straddling the Barry Burn should have absorbed Van de Velde's shot like a sponge. Had his ball stayed up there in someone's lap or backpack he would have been given a free drop. That it struck one of the few hard surfaces that could bounce it a good distance backward was strange luck. The grandstand faced the green, after all, not the fairway.

"I think we could say that I was pretty lucky," Jean said later, "because I can stand there all day trying, even aiming at the grandstand, and I'm not sure that ball would come back." The 1.68 diameter ball had struck the dead center of the two-inch diameter tube, a railing support, just a foot or two above the stand's eight-foot-high plywood facing. Again, this was luck in a Halloween mask; as it turned out, he'd have been better off if he'd gone in the burn.

Due deliberation determined that sixty-three yards of Scotland lay between Van de Velde and the Robert Burns flagstick. The survey also reminded him how easy it would be to hit this ball out-of-bounds if it came out hot. Probably that thought doomed him. When the leader chunked his third shot fifteen yards squarely into the middle of the Barry Burn, he sent the 128th British Open into bedlam. Strangers hugged each other in disbelief. The stadium exploded with a strange keening. "I can't believe this!" shouted golfer Jim Furyk to Derek Carr in the bar. "I'm so nervous it feels like it's me out there!"

"If there was one shot I could play over, that would be the one," says Van de Velde. "But the lie was so bad, I didn't know if I could make it back to the fairway."

Carr hurriedly drained his pint of bitter and exited the hotel to watch the train wreck in person. The security guards behind the eighteenth green waved him to the front. A gentle rain fell. Van de Velde stood on the opposite bank, staring at his ball six feet below. It perched delicately on a bed of mud and slimy seaweed, and its top third protruded above the shallow salt water. He paced back and forth on the opposite shore like an expectant father with a full bladder. The crowd could not settle down. He clambered down the mossy, stair-step sides of the burn for a closer look, moved back up to the top, sat with his feet down in the burn, and began to untie the laces on his white shoes and take off his black socks. The crowd roared when it realized he was going to play it from the water.

The paved sides of the Barry Burn give it a man-made appearance, but it has meandered the seven miles from Carrot Hill and through the towns of Barry and Carnoustie to the sea for centuries. Its rough paving prevents erosion. The rows of concrete blocks on its sides are stepped back four inches each to accommodate a golfer's foot; the burn bottom in front of the eighteenth green is lined two-deep with permeable bags of concrete mix. On top of that, pebbles; on top of that, sandy silt. This portion of the burn is shaped like a flat-bottomed V, like the square grooves in an iron club, so there's sometimes room to swing. Since the Barry Burn communicates directly with the North Sea, at high tide it fills up and at low tide it drains. If the tide had been in, Van de Velde could not have even considered playing his ball.

Barefoot, Jean padded gingerly down the sides of the Barry Burn and stepped into the chilly water. He peered at the ball, his feet now in an inky cloud of liquid mud. Two photographers ten yards downstream slipped into the ditch at about the same time. And something—a seagull landing in the harbor, the six wet feet ankle-deep in the water, or the concentric rings from the raindrops—caused the ball to waver and then fall entirely below the surface. Only marginally playable before, now it was hopeless. For a long minute, Van de Velde stood there with his pants above his knees, his sand wedge in his left hand, his hands on his hips, and the photographers snapping. The crowd cheered, yelled; a vocal minority chanted, "Go, go, go, go, go!" Finally, he picked the ball out of the water and threw it up to Christophe.

The leader climbed back up the stairs in three athletic steps, Christophe handed him a blue-and-white-striped towel, and he sat on the black Cobra bag and dried and reshod his feet. With the penalty for lifting from the hazard, his next swing would be his fifth. He could still win if he could make a six.

Such theater! The average hole requires about twelve minutes; this morbidly fascinating production of *Calamity Jean* was about to double that. But twenty-odd minutes of watching the improvisational ineptness of the leading man irked Curtis Strange. ABC's analyst had built a career on superior thinking, strategizing, and self-control, and this display was making him crazy. While Van de Velde searched in vain for short grass in which to drop his ball, Strange cleared what he was about to say on the air with his producer. "The more I think about it," he said, "and you hate to be harsh on somebody—but the game is played not only physically but between the ears as well. This is one of the most stupid things I've ever seen in my life. . . . He's got the Claret Jug in his hands and he throws it away—or he's trying to throw it away."

Character is destiny, the ancient Greeks believed. And to many people—at Carnoustie and elsewhere, then and now—Van de Velde's unfolding disaster looked like an unmistakable expression of French style: cavalier, ironic, and more concerned with style than with substance. He seemed to be treating the beloved Jug like a chamber pot. Hints of anti-French bias bubbled to the surface: *This is why they can't play golf. Serves him right for his lucky ruling and his lucky putting. They always choke in the rugby World Cup, too.* "*Je ne sais* squat," wrote John Garrity in *Sports Illustrated.* Editors at *SI* and elsewhere would deem it okay to quote Jean and Christophe phonetically (as transcribed by Rick Reilly): "Jean was peezed. He sayz to me, 'Why don't you make me hit wedge?' I theenk that he and I, we want too much show." Imagine someone printing verbatim the illiterate, profanity-filled patois of the typical NFL or NBA locker room. You have to imagine it because, fortunately, you don't have to read it. But there's a double standard regarding the French, who don't seem to mind anyway.

"That's an interesting point," said Garrity. "I'm not usually given to ethnic jokes; in fact I can't remember ever doing one before. You couldn't do it with other cultures or nationalities. But I think our comfort level insulting the French comes from the fact that Americans think a French accent is classy, continental, and suave. Given their history, I don't know how the English feel about them, but we really like Maurice Chevalier, Jacques Cousteau, Brigitte Bardot. . . . I think it was clear that we were all charmed by Van de Velde."

Meanwhile, Jean had not lost yet. With a decent pitch and his usual one-putt, he could still come out on top. The crowd hushed . . .

. . . and Van de Velde dumped his fifth shot into the bunker. Another burst of incredulous noise that sounded like a blend of shouted oohs and aahs. Again total strangers exchanged bug-eyed, open-mouthed, can-you-believe-this looks. Jesus! A play-off! With Leonard and Lawrie—and Van de Velde, if he could get up and down from the sand, something that didn't seem likely given the previous few minutes.

"Just error after error, mentally," said Rosburg, which was true.

"He has to be somewhat humiliated," said Strange, which was not.

The forgotten man, Craig Parry, had hit his second shot into the same right-side bunker as Jean. The other ball lay farther from the flag, but Parry splashed out first. Right into the hole. Another wave of delirium swept the place as Parry walked calmly to the hole to retrieve his ball. Those who believed in the Myth of the Inevitable Birdie said that if Parry had not missed a little putt on the previous hole, he'd also be in the play-off. But golf isn't like that. It's a chain, not a series of discrete events. Every shot affects the next one or the one after that; possibly Parry needed a double bogey on seventeen to achieve the perfect balance of tension and what-the-hell relaxation on eighteen. Furthermore, the folly of assigning such import to a single stroke is clear from a look at the Aussie's back nine, which included a triple bogey, the double on seventeen, a bogey on a par hole, the thirteenth, and a par on a birdie hole, the fourteenth. And two birdies.

Now Van de Velde had the stage to himself. More than the course, more than the big clock on the hotel, he'd unified the now-cozy-feeling gathering of twenty thousand or so. We'd all been through so much together.

His bunker shot from fifteen yards skidded up to eight feet. All the world had given up on the battered golfer by this point, but Van de Velde never quit. He stroked the putt, and the ball rolled perfectly, squarely, in. One fist pump, a scream to the right—"Yes!"—then a toss of his ball to the fans on the left. The encircling thousands stood as one and cheered and shouted. A three-way play-off loomed, four holes of stroke play. The combatants would be the local lad, the new favorite, who'd bounced his ball over the burn on eighteen; the well-liked American who'd rolled it into the hazard; and the now more-mysterious-than-ever Frenchman, who went over, back, in, out, over, in (sand), on, and, finally, in.

The winning score of 290, six over par, was the highest in the Open since 1947—Fred Daly at Hoylake, the year Sam Snead did not return to defend. If Leonard won, he'd equal the record he shared for largest final-round deficit made up, five. Lawrie had been *ten* back at the start of the day. If he won, he'd not only double the Open comeback record, he'd beat Jack Burke Jr.'s all-time most-shots-made-up-on-the-last-day mark, which was eight, in the fourth round of the 1956 Masters. If Van de Velde won, he'd be the first Frenchman to win the Open since 1907. If Lawrie won, he'd be the first home-based and home-bred Scot to win since Willie Auchterlonie in 1893. If Leonard won, he'd be the fifth consecutive champion golfer from the United States.

Carr watched the Tartan Army rush toward the fifteenth tee to cheer on Lawrie in a giddy, school's-out atmosphere. He held his hands out to feel the rain and happily returned to his corner in the riotous hotel bar. Not everyone felt so good about the extra innings, however. Someone claimed that Jean had sobbed once into his hands in the scorer's trailer under the grandstand. Leonard should have been thrilled with his unexpected reprieve, but he emanated none of his usual aura when stalking first prize. The engraver had started to chisel the first four-name champion in Open history on the Jug but had been interrupted by the bizarre finish. The play-off also inconvenienced a lot of people who'd already been on their feet or on a microphone for a long time. Or both: "The last thing I wanted was to stand out in the rain for another hour and a half," Rosburg said.

But the crazy finish invigorated the writers. "Three times out of five I sit down to write a tournament story, I say to myself, 'How do I make this a story anyone will care about a week from now?' " said Garrity. "I knew that wouldn't be a problem this time."

Like Hogan in 1953, Van de Velde disappeared for a few minutes. He had to go to the bathroom and did not want to talk to anyone while he did, a natural impulse under any circumstances, so he retreated to his first-floor, £167-a-night hotel room. He did not pause to stare at himself in the mirror or to laugh or cry or give himself a talking-to. He just answered the nature call and put on a light gray sweater. During this interlude, Lawrie, then Leonard, marched to the carts waiting to drive them out to fifteen. The Scot sat in the third buggy in the six-vehicle caravan, Leonard in the fourth. They did not wait for the representative from France. The carts rolled through the half-pipe tunnel of gorse bushes and dunes bordering the seashell service road.

Umbrellas up, Lawrie and Leonard waited on the fifteenth tee. The rain fell a bit harder; long minutes dripped by. When his cart finally dropped him off, Van de Velde walked on the tee with a smile and congratulatory handshakes for his opponents. "Good evening!" he said heartily to the referee, which drew a laugh. When the official began to explain the ground rules, he interrupted with "Do I have to play eighteen?" More laughs. The players drew for teeing order: Jean, Paul, Justin. Just under thirty minutes had passed since the last putt of regulation.

"The half hour was too much or not enough," Jean said months later. "If I sign [the scorecard] and go, okay. There was time to think but not to answer. *Avec votre fesse entre deux chaises.*"

Huh?

"You have your bum between two chairs. I wasn't *there* when the play-off started. It started to rain a lot, and I'd been on the golf course a long time, especially on eighteen. Then to be the first to play . . . I would have loved to see them pull their drives first, and to gather myself."

The fifteenth at Carnoustie was not a place to get comfortable. Statistically the second-hardest hole on the course that day (the twelfth was the toughest; the eighteenth, third hardest) the 472-yard hole offends the golfer's sense of right and reason. Too long, too narrow, and worst of all, curving to the left but cambered to bounce balls right.

Van de Velde felt unsettled but still hit his driver, though not very well. His hands remembered a dead-right shot here earlier; this one flew straight left and disappeared into a gorse bush. Lawrie went next, also with a driver. His equally unheroic effort also veered left, into the wet hay a few yards from the first ball. Now Justin, the betting favorite in the Carnoustie hotel bar, took two easy practice swings. Even the Lawrie partisans admitted that a win by Leonard would be most just. Van de Velde had blown it, forget him. Lawrie hadn't hit a shot all day, even his last one, that he or anyone else thought might be to win. Ten back, where's the pressure? But the best grinder in golf winning on the most difficult course in the world would tie up the loose ends. No question that his résumé best suited entrance into the pantheon of Carnoustie champions. Justin chose a three-wood, such a wise club with the other two in trouble. With his arms-extended setup, he resembled a tripod.

"Unbelievable," said Rosburg, as the ball landed. "Absolutely unbelievable." Mr. Steady had pulled it into the hay, too. Fearing that his first ball might be lost, Van de Velde hit from the tee again. And when his provisional ball also scattered fans on the *rive gauche,* the play-off for the Open was off to a thoroughly ugly start.

Van de Velde found his ball in the fragrant and unplayable recesses of a gorse bush. He had three options, all of which cost a stroke penalty: he could drop two club lengths from where he found his ball—not the way to go, since that wouldn't get him out of the gorse; he could return to the tee and start over; or he could drop back as far as he wished, while keeping the spot where his drive had stopped on a line between himself and the hole. He chose the last option. It took a long time. The air cooled, the rain fell, and Leonard and Lawrie waited.

Counting the delay caused by his playing partner David Frost on the second hole, the pre-play-off interlude, and now this one, Leonard had been thrown off schedule all day. Each of the combatants eventually found the surface in four shots. Jean missed from fifteen; Justin made from five; Paul tapped in from a foot. And the partisans jumped up and punched the air, bellowing like the Aberdeen lad had holed a snake. "It was just a circus," Lawrie said later. "Everyone was inside the ropes and everyone was shouting my name." After one play-off hole:

LEONARD:	+1
LAWRIE:	+1
VAN DE VELDE:	+2

The ugly pageant continued on sixteen, with two tee shots in the bunkers and one in the rough. Van de Velde's second from the pit on the left thirty-five yards from the hole sailed over the flagstick and stopped ten feet away, a superlative shot. Leonard, with a good lie in the bent grass, fluffed it, and his ball did not even reach the green. From the bunker on the right, Lawrie hit an excellent shot to five feet. Jean missed, and Leonard pitched up for another one-putt bogey. In the hotel bar, twenty Scottish fists pounded tabletops when Paul lipped out his little putt. After two play-off holes:

LEONARD:	+2
LAWRIE:	+2
VAN DE VELDE:	+3

Paul and Jean hit solid, uneventful long-iron shots into the fairway on seventeen, but Justin's ball drifted left toward the burn. No one at the scene had the cheek to wish it onward into the ditch, but in the bar, the beered-up Scottish lobby frantically waved at the TV monitors like Carlton Fisk gesturing at his fly ball in the sixth game of the 1975 World Series. Justin's drive stayed dry despite the pantomimes, though in a nasty downhill lie. His shot onto the front of the green was his best of the play-off, perhaps his best of the day.

Lawrie hit next, from 225, then Van de Velde, from two steps closer. Both four-iron shots landed short of the green and skipped up spectacularly close. A hundred people jumped up and down together in the hotel mosh pit. They settled down enough to gasp when Justin's putt from fifty feet died one inch from the hole, and to applaud when Jean rolled in his putt for birdie from fifteen feet. If Paul failed to hole from ten feet, the three would be tied with one play-off hole remaining. But he made it dead in the center. Perhaps from hours of overstimulation or from being out in the rain too long, the spectators around the eighteenth green began to do the Wave.

With one hole to play:

LAWRIE:	+1
LEONARD:	+2
VAN DE VELDE:	+2

Lawrie proved his mettle with his next swing, a full-blooded driver to the center of the elusive eighteenth fairway. And Van de Velde proved what had been apparent for a couple of hours, that his driver had abandoned him. Again his hands, if not his head, recalled his shot *à droit* that began his already infamous 7 on the seventy-second hole. This one was the overcompensated opposite, a little steered hook into the rough, a spot from which he couldn't hope to clear the burn in two. Leonard hit third, down the middle.

After Jean's layup, Justin paused to consider his options, his blue sweater heavy and glistening with rainwater. His straits were dire: one back, one to play, and the leader's ball lying well a few yards ahead. But if he could get on the green first, who knew what might happen? He chose a three-iron to traverse the 225 yards—not enough. The ball landed squarely in the Barry Burn.

Now, with all the reason in the world to lay up, Lawrie did not lay up. Though it looked certain he could win with a bogey, and though he'd seen his fellow competitors ruin their chances by hitting thrice into this ditch, and though he himself had relied on dumb luck to bounce over the thing hours before, he shot for the green. *Allez*, Paul. Something had clicked: measuring his yardage before Justin hit, he'd discovered he had the perfect-length shot for his new favorite club, the four-iron, the club he'd used to birdie seventeen twice today.

His powerful swing was a lovely thing and the resultant shot was even lovelier. The ball cleared the burn by a couple of yards, skirted the bunker, and rolled up to a yard from the hole.

A few moments later Paul Lawrie stroked his birdie putt in and extended two fists high above his head.

GROWN MEN WEPT. Strangers hugged. Nationalism burst like a scent in the air, and most of the crowd began to sing:

O flower of Scotland
When will we see your like again
That fought and died for
Your wee bit hill and glen

The presentation of the Claret Jug took place on the eighteenth green. A Cecil B. DeMille scene: a table, a silver trophy, and a long, straight row of dignitaries stood at the front of the green, in coats and ties, if you please, not golf clothing. Wet but exhilarated thousands surrounded the green, in the grandstands, in front of the hotel, and down the first fairway. The new champion stood at the back of the green, looking dazed, surrounded by grinning friends. John Philp was introduced, and he stepped forward out of the line and smiled and waved to loud applause. Two hours later he'd be asleep in a chair in his living room while the telly played Open highlights. Leonard looked somber. Van de Velde blew kisses to the crowd. The world will little note nor long remember Lawrie's remarks, but the emotion in his ovation will be hard to forget.

Derek Carr and his pal Bob Thomson jogged through the giddy crowd toward the Media Centre. Thomson composed a postcard greeting aloud for his wife: "I just came to Carnoustie and a wee boy from Aberdeen came down and was the first Scot to win in *sixty-eight years*. He took his *bollocks* in his hand on the final hole. Many beverages were consumed. Love, Bob."

A reporter got Mrs. Lawrie on the phone. What will you do for dinner tonight? he asked. "He'll have to get a chippie," she said. "My hands are still shaking and I won't be able to cook."

Carr and Thomson got past the Media Centre guard by carrying borrowed notebooks and forcing businesslike looks onto their faces. They sat near the back of the already jammed interview room. Justin appeared first, heartbroken, but composed. "As bad as I feel, he feels worse," Leonard said, the day's one hundredth incorrect public utterance regarding Van de Velde's mood. "I figured the worst he could make on eighteen was five, so I had to try to make three. If I had one shot to hit again, it would be the tee shot on eighteen. I'd have hit the driver instead of a three-wood."

Someone asked about the play-off. "I don't know how to describe it," Leonard said. "To wait there that long was . . . very strange. We were all pretty embarrassed [with the first two holes]. It was chaos out there."

Someone posed a meandering interrogatory that never quite reached question status. "Would you just ask a question?" Leonard said. "Thanks."

Leonard left the little table with a microphone on it and Van de Velde took his place. He looked at the hundreds of sympathetic faces. "Don't be so sad," he said. "We're gonna go over everything except eighteen, okay? . . . I made a lot of friends today, because a Scotland man won." Despite his jokes, his smile, and his generally lighthearted attitude, Van de Velde did not immediately lift the atmosphere of gloom in the room. While the writers admired his brave attitude, they suspected he didn't understand the gravity of the situation. They felt worse for him than he did for himself.

"On eighteen, I drive down the right—really down the right—and the ball is lying great, fantastic. I have 185, 189 to carry the water. Do you hit wedge when the ball is lying so good?

"I go well, okay, I'm gonna try for the [third] shot. The only thing I could try was to go forward. But the club went underneath the ball.

"Three-quarters of the ball was lying above the water. That's why I took my shoes off. But then I could see the ball sinking [as if saying], 'Hey, you silly man, not for you today.'

"I was very humble. I kept my composure and kept my head. It wasn't something absolutely mad I was trying to do, it just turned into a nightmare."

Someone wanted to know how he would deal with this nightmare. "I read the newspaper this morning, and so many bad things are happening to other people," Jean said. "Next time I'll hit a wedge and you all will forgive me."

Forgive him? *Other people?* We heard, we listened, we watched, but still we couldn't quite grasp this outward focus. The Hogan model of golf course comportment demanded a form of concentration that made the world go away, and almost every big pro played the Hogan way. But Van de Velde presented a totally unfamiliar point of view. His perspective was both delightfully trivial and Olympian. He actually cared about entertainment value, and for his entertainment and ours he would rather be sorry than safe. His loss did not crush him, because he perceived the flyspeck importance of games and gamesmen. The champions analyzing the play on TV kept saying that poor Jean probably wanted to bury himself in that bunker, that he needed a hug, that he was embarrassed, humiliated, mortified. They said this while poor Jean smiled and blew kisses.

"At the end of the day, it's a game," Van de Velde said succinctly three weeks after the Open. "Okay, it's not a friendly game, but it's still a game. You know, that's the part you have to understand and remember. So I played [that two-iron] because to me it was in the spirit of how I see the game and how I like to play it."

The jaded press applauded Van de Velde as he left the tent at Carnoustie, a rare salute. The new champion took his place in the bright lights at the table on the platform. "I played lovely in the play-off," Paul Lawrie said. "To birdie the last two holes is obviously a fairy story."

AT NINE ON Sunday night the pubs were joyously full and the winner was telling the press how he did it. Meanwhile, a thin young man sat alone on a bench in the golfers' changing room with his head in his hands. White cargo pants, a circumferential hat line etched through his transparent hair and into his pink scalp, a white golf shirt with a Disney logo on the right sleeve. A locker gaped open in front of him; to his right stood a big black golf bag.

For two minutes you share the silence. Finally you ask what he would do differently if he had another chance.

Christophe lifted his head at this, a half smile on his face. "Hit ze ball harder," he said. Then he dropped his head again and continued to study the carpet between his feet.

Postscript

———

Van de Velde fired caddie **Christophe Angiolin** after the U.S. PGA Championship in August 1999. According to people close to the situation, Christophe seemed to have become overfond of media attention. After entertaining a practice tee audience with a golf-ball-bouncing Tiger Woods imitation, he forgot to stock the boss's golf bag with snacks and water, and he made numerous yardage errors that week.

Jack Burke, Jr., watched on TV as Paul Lawrie broke his record for the greatest comeback in a major. "I think Van de Velde is the unluckiest man in the history of the world," Burke said. "But those Europeans play golf with a club in one hand and the flag in the other. Playing for Mother Earth is always a mistake."

Three weeks after the Open, the rough at **Carnoustie** shriveled up and died. What didn't dry out to nothing was mowed down to four inches. "That's what people didn't understand, and what the media overplayed," said John Philp. "Our rough was not particularly high at all—never above two feet tall. It was its strength and density, the sap in the leaf, that made it quite difficult." A freak of nature—a wet mild spring and a dry hot summer—made the rough so infuriatingly robust. Usually the high grass in Scotland has died back by Open time. "I can't believe the course will ever be that tough again," Philp said.

While the worst of the rough disappeared, the fairways were kept narrow because visitors wanted at least that much of the Open experience. But the course lost at least two of its teeth. Philp's crews filled a fairway bunker on the left on the fifth, and to the links superintendent's great regret the new Hogan Bunker on the sixth. "They just forget about the forefathers, or the architect's design concepts," said Philp indignantly. "The committee only listens to the loudest voices and the poorest golfers."

A final wee change to the links took place on what Philp calls "Van de Velde country." At the end of 1999, Philp designed and built some hollows and mounds in front of the burn in front of the green on eighteen, and on the ground around the members' tee on seventeen areas that, Philp thought, were "flat and mundane."

Flush with optimism and money after the 1999 Open, the Angus County Council began discussing the construction of a world-class teaching facility—they used to be called driving ranges—and a hospitality center close to Carnoustie links.

Derek Carr, aka Wally Bampot IV, has set up a "client meeting" with Elkington at the Masters in 2000.

"One of the most difficult aspects of client management is finding someone people can relate to," observed Van de Velde's agent, **Jamie Cunningham** of Professional Sports Partnership. "Not that he's had any clever media training, but Jean's personality and straight answers make a wonderful starting point." He'll be getting started with Cleveland Golf, which will replace Cobra as the supplier of his golf clubs. Cleveland is owned by Rossignol, a French company that also manufactures snow skis, "so that's a nice fit." He'll also endorse Never Compromise putters and serve as a spokesman for French golf, and has launched his own Web site, AllezJean.com. Wine and golf balls are among the items purveyed.

A couple of days before the Open, Van de Velde asked Cunningham to start the paperwork for the U. S. PGA Tour qualifying tournament. But with winnings in the Open counted as "official money" for the first time, his runner-up $305,250 got him his card.

Clark Dennis lost his card. Only the top 125 money winners retain their playing privileges on the PGA Tour; Dennis finished 162nd, with $180,843. Deduct taxes, caddie fees, meals, and travel expenses, and you have . . . not much. In the three-stage tournament to requalify for the Tour, he lost in a play-off to reach the finals. Fed-up and tired, he pronounced himself sick of golf. But in November, the tournament director talked him into playing the Mexican Open; in a fitting end to a lousy year, he got the *turista* and had to drop out after three rounds.

Armed with a new forty-seven-inch driver, he plans to be back in Scotland to again try to qualify for the 2000 Open.

Steve Elkington finished thirty-fifth on the U.S. Tour money list with $1,086,376, the third-best money-winning year of his career. Two other notable events: he severed ties with *über*-agency International Management Group; and construction began on a golf course he designed and will co-own in The Woodlands, north of Houston. "It's a great piece of ground," he said. "It'll be a little Royal Melbourney, a bit Pine Valleyish. Not your run-of-the-mill slap-and-giggle."

After first saying he might purchase a Ferrari with his Open winnings, **Paul Lawrie** bought a Boxster instead, a silver streak of a Porsche just like Andrew Magee's. The house he bought in Aberdeen further stretched his first-place check for £350,000 ($577,500), but money won't be a problem for the Lawries for a while.

While appearance and endorsement income rises like the tide for the first-time winner of a major tournament, the less-tangible rewards of recognition are not automatic. Two weeks after the Open, Blackie Sherrod of *The Dallas Morning News* wrote in his Sunday ellipsis column, "Quick now, who won the British Open?" Given Van de Velde's mesmerizing loss and Lawrie's pre-Open obscurity, a fair question.

At the PGA Championship in August, a writer asked Lawrie if he sensed that "you're not getting the credit for having won the British Open and there's more focus on Van de Velde for having lost it?"

The Open champ waffled. "I did what I had to do," he said in caveat-filled reply. "I mean, okay, he should have won. . . . But I felt as though I won it. I didn't feel as though he— Well, he obviously threw it away. But I played nice in the play-off. So I have no problem with it at all."

While browsing in the pro shop during a rain-delayed practice round [in August], at the World Series of Golf at Firestone Country Club in Akron, ten-year-old James Wilson noticed the Open champion looking at the rain jackets. The boy cleared his throat and approached the man: "Mr. Lawrie, I just want to say that four-iron you hit was the best golf shot I've ever seen," said James. And Lawrie lit up like a Christmas tree. He hugged the boy's shoulders, gave him a signed golf ball, and chatted him up for five minutes.

Lawrie played in every match and performed well in the European team's narrow defeat in the Ryder Cup.

"What happened at the Open was disappointing, but it's not something that spoils my year," said **Justin Leonard**. "I don't think there was a huge lesson learned other than you have to give yourself every opportunity to win. I think I made the right decisions."

He explained two of the key decisions. First, his burn-bound shot to the green on the last hole of regulation: "I knew it was something with a low probability of success. The lie was not that great. If I put down ten balls, I might get two over. But I had to try."

On the first hole of the play-off, Leonard watched as first Van de Velde, then Lawrie, hit pull-hooks into the wet hay and gorse left of the fifteenth fairway. Did he consider hitting a one-iron at that point? (Instead, he hit a three-wood, which followed his opponents' shots into trouble.) "No," Leonard said. "Fifteen was playing into the wind. If I'd hit a solid one-iron, I'd have to hit another one to reach the green. And if I mis-hit it, I couldn't get there in two." Better than anyone, he knew the likelihood of an off-center strike.

"I really didn't have my best game on Sunday," he recalled. "I'd hit it much better the previous three days. . . . I was getting the club back too far. I've shortened my swing since then."

After it was over, Leonard spoke with Davis Love III, who has a deserved reputation for wisdom. "I feel like I lost twice today," Justin said. "At least you gave yourself a chance," replied Love, and Leonard took some comfort from that.

In September, Leonard holed a forty-five-foot putt that effectively won the Ryder Cup for the United States side. But the next month brought despair to blunt the ecstasy. The death of Payne Stewart and five others in a private jet crash on October 25 affected Leonard deeply. He and Stewart had become good friends in recent years and frequently ate dinner and played practice rounds together.

Partly for his disposition but mostly for his tireless and effective charity work, **Andrew Magee** won the first annual Payne Stewart Award. Golf tournaments he helps run in Dallas and in Phoenix have contributed $1.5 million to various charities. The award comes with $100,000 donated by the Southern Company for Magee to distribute as he sees fit. Fifty thousand dollars will go to the John Croyle Ranch in Alabama, $25,000 will buy dental equipment for one of his Dallas charities, and the Santa Claus Foundation in Phoenix gets the other $25,000.

Magee won $911,565 officially in 1999, forty-second on the PGA

Tour list. He decided that was enough. He took November and December off to work on his charities and play with his kids, passing on the easy money available to top players in the end-of-the-year "silly season."

He compared Van de Velde's fantastic finish to "the French at the Argonne Forest in World War I."

Writer **James Mossop** of the London *Sunday Telegraph* formed a light-hearted group called the Nevertheless Golf Society. Van De Velde volunteered to serve as president, with two conditions: anyone laying up short of water would be immediately expelled; and he would order the postround wine, and the others would pay for it.

Sales of the **Never Compromise** putter continued to go "through the roof," according to sales manager Scott Wallach. "People know it wasn't the putter that made Van de Velde lose," he said.

In December 1999, Van de Velde, a camera crew, and several Never Compromise executives returned to Carnoustie to film the golfer playing the eighteenth again—this time, with just a putter. After John Philp's men de-iced the green, Van de Velde had another go. He played the hole in 9 the first time, but got as low as a 6 in a subsequent take.

To those who think professional golf has become as easy as tennis without a net, Links Superintendent **John Philp** became a hero. "I've received quite a few letters from Americans apologizing for the whingeing of the competitors," Philp said. "The Open was certainly not just a putting contest. The penalties fit the crime. Not the truth that the average fan felt short-changed."

Other reasonable people disagreed vehemently. *Golfweek*'s John Hawkins, for example, referred to Philp in print as "the Mad Agronomist." "Instead of ending the century on a joyous note," wrote Hawkins, "the Royal and Ancient inexplicably cast itself as the Ruthless and Arrogant, turning one of the world's most demanding courses into a 7,400-yard pinball machine and allowing the Unabomber of greenskeepers to man the flippers."

But journalistic reaction to the unforgettable week mattered little to Barbara Philp as she watched her father's introduction during the final ceremony on the eighteenth green. "I was standing soaked to the bone and freezing cold and surrounded by strangers and starving hungry, but I've hardly been happier," she recalled. "I was so proud of him and happy for him, that he'd finally seen the result of what he'd worked for. . . . If I could make him half as proud of me as his dad was of him . . ."

Not only his daughter was proud of Philp's accomplishment and style. In November, a letter arrived from number 10 Downing Street, from British prime minister Tony Blair, stating that the superintendent would be knighted. John will become Sir John at an investiture ceremony at Buckingham Palace in early 2000.

"It's an honor for a team effort," Philp said. "And a bit of a vindication."

Shortly after the Open, **Hugh Campbell** of **The Royal and Ancient Golf Club of St. Andrews** spoke with writer Dermot Gilleece of *The Irish Times*. "The course remains a really difficult test of golf, but I was amazed at how defensively some of the best competitors played it," said the chairman of the Championship Committee. "The thinking had to be done on the tee and the best players didn't work out how to play the course."

Campbell had no regrets that the 159th-ranked player in the world won, nosing out the 152nd-ranked Van de Velde (and Leonard, then ranked twelfth): "Paul Lawrie knew about Carnoustie and that must have been a help, while the one guy who handled the rough best was Van de Velde. Each time he went in, he just knocked it out sideways." Well, not every time . . .

"Plans by the Royal and Ancient to bring the British Open back to Carnoustie," wrote Gilleece, "indicate a confidence that their championship is bigger than the concerted sniping of some disenchanted Americans." The Open would return to Carnoustie, Campbell said, "towards the end of the next decade."

"This Open has been a tremendous success," said Campbell. "We coped comfortably with thirty-five thousand people a day, and the week had triumph, tragedy, romance, anger, drama, farce, pathos, and controversy. [They] follow the Open around."

Yvonne Robb had to pay a modest fine for breach of the peace, but removing most of her clothes and giving Tiger Woods a kiss on the eighteenth green at Carnoustie may prove to be a good career move. The American tabloid TV show *Extra* taped a segment with her in January 2000, and she's been accepted to drama school. Meanwhile, she continues to dance exotically at Private Eyes in Aberdeen.

Zane Scotland played well in amateur tournaments after the Open, including a fourth in the English Under-18 Boys and a top thirty in the European Amateur. If his game continues to progress at a rapid rate, he plans to turn pro in two years, at the ripe old age of nineteen. "The Open was a big stepping-stone for me," Scotland says. "It put my name on the map."

The biggest change he's noticed since becoming one of the youngest-ever qualifiers at the Open? "I've got a lot more friends. Everyone's trying to give me advice and tell me what to do."

Curtis Strange asked a go-between to apologize to Van de Velde for calling his actions "stupid" on TV. "Tell him I called it the way I saw it and that I'll speak with him about it in person." No problem, said Jean. "I completely understand," he said. "I think people are very emotional. You feel like it's almost you out there. And then I do something almost out of any thought."

Commenting on letters to editors that held that "it just wasn't

Jean's time to win," Strange said, "Bull*shit*. It *was* his time to win and he screwed up."

"Usually, he makes more stupid mistakes on the golf course," said **Brigitte Van de Velde** of her husband's famous two-iron. "[That] was the only mistake he made all week. He went for every shot, maybe too much, but he had to play that way to have a chance."

What most surprised **Jean Van de Velde** in the aftermath of the 1999 Open? The attention, of course. "It's not like I'm new on the tour," he said. "I've been here ten years. But it's like a lot of [the media] have just discovered me. That's normal, I've never been in the spotlight. In August and September, wow. It's pleasant, but sometimes I need to say 'Sorry, I need to get organized.' "

His clubs did not arrive with him at the U.S. PGA Championship at Medinah, Illinois, in August, so with an unexpected day off, he asked tournament volunteer Lynn Marinelli about the sites to see in Chicago. "Just don't go near the river," she said, sensing he could take the joke. He could; he threw his head back and laughed. He continued to provide a model for sportsmanship and mental health, and it was no act. "You've talked a lot about the positives that have come out of the experience at the British Open," someone asked at his PGA news conference. "Is there still heartache, though? Has it been difficult at times, even well past the event?" No, Van de Velde said, he just isn't wired that way. "Not that I tend to forget things very quickly, but that's it. You don't live in the past. . . . I do think about it sometimes, but not in a bad way. . . . I give one hundred percent and I walked out of there with my head and my chin pretty straight."

He sat on the bench for all but one match at the Ryder Cup in Boston in September, and he didn't like it. "No, [European team captain Mark James] hasn't explained himself to me yet," Jean said. "To me, he made a mistake. But he said he would do the same thing again."

Van de Velde lost his lone match, and the Europeans lost the Cup by half a point.

As the autumn leaves fell in St. Martin, Van de Velde shrugged once more. The next day he would fly to Japan for two weeks, then on to Australia. "My name is not on the trophy, but a lot of good things come from it. It took a lot of bad luck for me to lose," he said. "That's just the way it goes. Worse things happen, as we see every day. As we see this week.

"When I think about it now, I'm a little nostalgic. It's not like I burn emotionally . . . but I'm having a little trouble getting up for these tournaments. I left more over there than I expected."

Acknowledgments

F OR AN AUTHOR, parceling out thanks and credit is like a round of golf at Carnoustie: you know you're going to go wrong somewhere. But without the help of Clark Dennis, Steve Elkington, Andrew Magee, John Philp, Zane Scotland, and Jean Van de Velde, this book wouldn't be what it is. Perhaps it wouldn't even *be*.

Jim Donovan, Bill Earley, Peter Gethers, Bruce Selcraig, John Strawn, and Shauna Toh also deserve special thanks for, respectively, agenting, advising, editing, researching, encouraging, and editing some more.

Bob Blyth of Carnoustie; Barbara Philp, also a Carnoustieite; Brian Siplo of Pepperell, Massachusetts; and Don M. Wilson III of New York City dug through the dusty library stacks for this book, and I'm very grateful.

The inimitable Derek Carr bought the last round.

No further attempts will be made to rank the contributions. But thank you to:

Scotland: Emma Cardosi, Kay Davidson, Rhod McEwan, Richard Montgomery, Robert Morrison, Elliot Rowan, Martin Roy, Earle Smith, Louisa Winton

England: Peter Bown, Jamie Cunningham, Peter Crabtree, Nigel Gracey, Dave Griffiths, Mike Harris, James Mossop, Peter Oosterhuis, Terry Stacey

Australia: Mike Clayton, Alex Mercer, Jack Newton

France: Thierry Stotts

United States: Chip Atkeisson, Bobby Cole, Alistair Cooke, Mike Cassell, Judith Curr, Vickie L. Dryden, Josey Edwards, Michael D'Antonio, John Derr, John Garrity, David and Michele Glenn, Gaylen Groce, Gary and Judy Hewson, Mac Hunter, Mike Long, Pat Madden, Glen Mahler, Byron Nelson, Barbara Ordway, Mike Purkey, Bob Rosburg, Thomas F. Rosenthal, Bob Sampson, Geoff Shackelford, Tom Skidmore, Frank Stranahan, Curtis Strange, Dan Strimple, Jan Strimple, Ben Wright

Families:

Daisy and Eben Dennis, Vicki Vargas Dennis

Lisa DiStefano Elkington

John, Jonathon, Mary Margaret, and Matthew Magee; Susan Magee

Helen, David, and Barbara Philp

Clay, John, and Cheryl Sampson

Bernie and Ann Scotland

Appendix

		Playoff				
PLAYER	COUNTRY	HOLE				PLAYOFF TOTAL
		1	2	3	4	
Lawrie, Paul	SCO	5	4	3	3	E
Leonard, Justin	USA	5	4	4	5	+3
Van de Velde, Jean	FRA	6	4	3	5	+3

PLAYER	COUNTRY	ROUND TOTALS				TOTAL STROKES
		1	2	3	4	
Lawrie, Paul	SCO	73	74	76	67	290
Leonard, Justin	USA	73	74	71	72	290
Van de Velde, Jean	FRA	75	68	70	77	290
Cabrera, Angel	ARG	75	69	77	70	291
Parry, Craig	AUS	76	75	67	73	291
Norman, Greg	AUS	76	70	75	72	293
Frost, David	RSA	80	69	71	74	294
Love III, Davis	USA	74	74	77	69	294
Woods, Tiger	USA	74	72	74	74	294
Dunlap, Scott	USA	72	77	76	70	295
Furyk, Jim	USA	78	71	76	70	295
Goosen, Retief	RSA	76	75	73	71	295

PLAYER	COUNTRY	ROUND TOTALS				TOTAL STROKES
		1	2	3	4	
Parnevik, Jesper	SWE	74	71	78	72	295
Sutton, Hal	USA	73	78	72	72	295
Montgomerie, Colin	SCO	74	76	72	74	296
Verplank, Scott	USA	80	74	73	69	296
Yoneyama, Tsuyoshi	JPN	77	74	73	72	296
Coltart, Andrew	SCO	74	74	72	77	297
Langer, Bernhard	GER	72	77	73	75	297
Nobilo, Frank	NZ	76	76	70	75	297
Rocca, Costantino	ITA	81	69	74	73	297
Sjoland, Patrik	SWE	74	72	77	74	297
Westwood, Lee	ENG	76	75	74	72	297
Els, Ernie	RSA	74	76	76	72	298
Martin, Miguel Angel	SPA	74	76	72	76	298
O'Malley, Peter	AUS	76	75	74	73	298
Watts, Brian	USA	74	73	77	74	298
Woosnam, Ian	WAL	76	74	74	74	298
Harrington, Padraig	IRE	77	74	74	74	299
Bjorn, Thomas	DEN	79	73	75	73	300
Clarke, Darren	N IRE	76	75	76	73	300
Fulke, Pierre	SWE	75	75	77	73	300
Herron, Tim	USA	81	70	74	75	300
Maggert, Jeff	USA	75	77	75	73	300
Mattiace, Len	USA	73	74	75	78	300
Stewart, Payne	USA	79	73	74	74	300

PAST BRITISH OPEN CHAMPIONSHIP WINNERS

The Belt

YEAR	WINNER	COURSE	SCORE
1860	Willie Park, Sr.	Prestwick	174
1861	Tom Morris, Sr.	Prestwick	163
1862	Tom Morris, Sr.	Prestwick	163
1863	Willie Park, Sr.	Prestwick	168
1864	Tom Morris, Sr.	Prestwick	167
1865	Andrew Strath	Prestwick	162
1866	Willie Park, Sr.	Prestwick	169
1867	Tom Morris, Sr.	Prestwick	170
1868	Tom Morris, Jr.	Prestwick	157
1869	Tom Morris, Jr.	Prestwick	154
1870	Tom Morris, Jr.	Prestwick	149
1871	[No Championship]		

The Cup

YEAR	WINNER	COURSE	SCORE
1872	Tom Morris, Jr.	Prestwick	166
1873	Tom Kidd	St. Andrews	179
1874	Mungo Park	Musselburgh	159

YEAR	WINNER	COURSE	SCORE
1875	Willie Park, Sr.	Prestwick	166
1876	Bob Martin	St. Andrews	176
1877	Jamie Anderson	Musselburgh	160
1878	Jamie Anderson	Prestwick	157
1879	Jamie Anderson	St. Andrews	169
1880	Bob Ferguson	Musselburgh	162
1881	Bob Ferguson	Prestwick	170
1882	Bob Ferguson	St. Andrews	171
1883	Willie Fernie	Musselburgh	159
1884	Jack Simpson	Prestwick	160
1885	Bob Martin	St. Andrews	171
1886	David Brown	Musselburgh	157
1887	Willie Park, Jr.	Prestwick	161
1888	Jack Burns	St. Andrews	171
1889	Willie Park, Jr.	Musselburgh	155
1890	John Ball (A)	Prestwick	164
1891	Hugh Kirkaldy	St. Andrews	166

[72 holes played in succeeding years]

YEAR	WINNER	COURSE	SCORE
1892	Harold Hilton (A)	Muirfield	305
1893	Willie Auchterlonie	Prestwick	322
1894	J. H. Taylor	Sandwich	326
1895	J. H. Taylor	St. Andrews	322
1896	Harry Vardon	Muirfield	316
1897	Harold Hilton (A)	Hoylake	314
1898	Harry Vardon	Prestwick	307
1899	Harry Vardon	Sandwich	310
1900	J. H. Taylor	St. Andrews	309
1901	James Braid	Muirfield	309
1902	Alex Herd	Hoylake	307
1903	Harry Vardon	Prestwick	300
1904	Jack White	Sandwich	296

YEAR	WINNER	COURSE	SCORE
1905	James Braid	St. Andrews	318
1906	James Braid	Muirfield	300
1907	Arnaud Massy	Hoylake	312
1908	James Braid	Prestwick	291
1909	J. H. Taylor	Deal	295
1910	James Braid	St. Andrews	299
1911	Harry Vardon	Sandwich	303
1912	Ted Ray	Muirfield	295
1913	J. H. Taylor	Hoylake	304
1914	Harry Vardon	Prestwick	306
1915–19	[No Championship]		
1920	George Duncan	Deal	303
1921	Jock Hutchison	St. Andrews	296
1922	Walter Hagen	Sandwich	300
1923	Arthur Havers	Troon	295
1924	Walter Hagen	Hoylake	301
1925	Jim Barnes	Prestwick	300
1926	Bobby Jones (A)	R. Lytham	291
1927	Bobby Jones (A)	St. Andrews	285
1928	Walter Hagen	Sandwich	292
1929	Walter Hagen	Muirfield	292
1930	Bobby Jones (A)	Hoylake	291
1931	Tommy Armour	Carnoustie	296
1932	Gene Sarazen	Prince's	283
1933	Densmore Shute	St. Andrews	292
1934	Henry Cotton	Sandwich	283
1935	Alf Perry	Muirfield	283
1936	Alf Padgham	Hoylake	287
1937	Henry Cotton	Carnoustie	290
1938	Reg Whitcombe	Sandwich	295
1939	Richard Burton	St. Andrews	290

YEAR	WINNER	COURSE	SCORE
1940–45	[No Championship]		
1946	Sam Snead	St. Andrews	290
1947	Fred Daly	Hoylake	293
1948	Henry Cotton	Muirfield	284
1949	Bobby Locke	Sandwich	283
1950	Bobby Locke	Troon	279
1951	Max Faulkner	R. Portrush	285
1952	Bobby Locke	R. Lytham	287
1953	Ben Hogan	Carnoustie	282
1954	Peter Thomson	R. Birkdale	283
1955	Peter Thomson	St. Andrews	281
1956	Peter Thomson	Hoylake	286
1957	Bobby Locke	St. Andrews	279
1958	Peter Thomson	R. Lytham	278
1959	Gary Player	Muirfield	284
1960	Kel Nagle	St. Andrews	278
1961	Arnold Palmer	R. Birkdale	284
1962	Arnold Palmer	Troon	276
1963	Bob Charles	R. Lytham	277
1964	Tony Lema	St. Andrews	279
1965	Peter Thomson	R. Birkdale	285
1966	Jack Nicklaus	Muirfield	282
1967	Roberto de Vicenzo	Hoylake	278
1968	Gary Player	Carnoustie	289
1969	Tony Jacklin	R. Lytham	280
1970	Jack Nicklaus	St. Andrews	283
1971	Lee Trevino	R. Birkdale	278
1972	Lee Trevino	Muirfield	278
1973	Tom Weiskopf	Troon	276
1974	Gary Player	R. Lytham	282
1975	Tom Watson	Carnoustie	279

YEAR	WINNER	COURSE	SCORE
1976	Johnny Miller	R. Birkdale	279
1977	Tom Watson	Turnberry	268
1978	Jack Nicklaus	St. Andrews	281
1979	Seve Ballesteros	R. Lytham	283
1980	Tom Watson	Muirfield	271
1981	Bill Rogers	Sandwich	276
1982	Tom Watson	R. Troon	284
1983	Tom Watson	R. Birkdale	275
1984	Seve Ballesteros	St. Andrews	276
1985	Sandy Lyle	Sandwich	282
1986	Greg Norman	Turnberry	280
1987	Nick Faldo	Muirfield	279
1988	Seve Ballesteros	R. Lytham	273
1989	Mark Calcavecchia	R. Troon	275
1990	Nick Faldo	St. Andrews	270
1991	Ian Baker-Finch	R. Birkdale	272
1992	Nick Faldo	Muirfield	272
1993	Greg Norman	Sandwich	267
1994	Nick Price	Turnberry	268
1995	John Daly	St. Andrews	282
1996	Tom Lehman	R. Lytham	271
1997	Justin Leonard	R. Troon	272
1998	Mark O'Meara	R. Birkdale	280
1999	Paul Lawrie	Carnoustie	290

Bibliography

Cocquet, Alain R. *Le Golf des origines à nos jours*. Paris: Editions Hervas, 1988.

Colville, George M. *Five Open Champions and the Musselburgh Golf Story*. Musselburgh, Scotland: Colville Books, 1980.

Cotton, Henry. *This Game of Golf*. London and Watford: Country Life, Ltd., 1948.

Darwin, Bernard, et al. *A History of Golf in Britain*. London: Cassell, 1952.

Fehrenbach, T. R. *Lone Star: A History of Texas and the Texans*. New York: Macmillan, 1968.

Ferguson, Niall. *The Pity of War*. New York: Basic Books, 1999.

Fraser, Antonia. *Mary, Queen of Scots*. New York: Delacorte Press, 1969.

Furber, F. R., ed. *A Course for Heroes*. Sandwich, Kent: Royal St. George's Golf Club, 1996.

Georgiady, Pete. "The Great Golf Cargo of the Lucania." *Golfiana* magazine, vol. 6, no. 1, 1994.

Gramont, Sanche de. *The French: Portrait of a People*. New York: G. P. Putnam's Sons, 1969.

Hackney, Stewart. *Carnoustie Links: Courses and Players*. Dundee, Scotland: Ravensby Publications, 1988.

Hanley, Clifford. *The Scots*. New York: Times Books, 1980.

Haultain, Arnold. *The Mystery of Golf*. First publication: 1908. Republication: N.p.: Ailsa, Inc., 1986.

Hobbs, Michael. *Great Opens: Historic British and American Championships, 1913–1975*. South Brunswick, N.J.: A. S. Barnes, 1976.

Howell, Audrey. *Harry Vardon: The Revealing Story of a Championship Golfer*. London: Stanley Paul, 1991.

Johnston, Alastair J., and James F. Johnston. *The Chronicles of Golf, 1457–1857*. Cleveland: privately published, 1993.

Mair, Norman. *Muirfield, Home of the Honourable Company*. Edinburgh and London: Mainstream Publishing, 1994.

Mitchell, Peter. *The Complete Golfer Peter Thomson: A Biography*. Port Melbourne, Australia: Lothian Publishing Company, 1991.

Nelson, Byron. *How I Played the Game*. Dallas: Taylor Publishing, 1993.

Player, Gary, with Michael McDonnell. *To Be the Best: Reflections of a Champion*. London: Sidgwick and Jackson, 1991.

———, with Floyd Thatcher. *Gary Player: World Golfer*. Waco: Word Books, 1974.

Preble, John. *The Lion in the North: A Personal View of Scotland's History*. London: Secker and Warburg, 1971.

Rabinowitz, Howard N., and MacDonald Smith. "The Golf Great Who Couldn't Win a Major." *Golfiana* magazine, vol. 6, no. 2, 1994.

Sarazen, Gene, with Herbert Warren Wind. *Thirty Years of Championship Golf*. New York: Prentice Hall, 1950.

Smail, David Cameron. *Prestwick Golf Club: Birthplace of the Open*. Privately published, 1989.

Snead, Sam, with Fran Pirozzolo. *The Game I Love: Wisdom, Insight, and Instruction from Golf's Greatest Player*. New York: Ballantine Books, 1997.

Tuchman, Barbara. *The Guns of August*. New York: Macmillan, 1962.

Tulloch, W. W. *The Life of Tom Morris with Glimpses of St. Andrews and Its Golfing Celebrities*. London: T. Werner Laurie, 1908.

von Nida, Norman. *Golf Is My Business*. London: Muller, 1956.

Ward-Thomas, Pat. *The Royal and Ancient*. Edinburgh: Scottish Academic Press, 1980.

Index
